CONTEMPORARY
FRENCH POLITICAL THOUGHT

Contemporary
French Political Thought

ROY PIERCE

1966
OXFORD UNIVERSITY PRESS
LONDON AND NEW YORK

FOR WIN

Preface

SINCE the end of World War II, there has been a lively and important discussion going on in France about fundamental problems of politics. This book analyses the political ideas of the six people whom I believe to be the principal contributors to that discussion.

The discussion naturally reflects France's particular circumstances and problems. The crises of the 1930s, the unsettled state of French political institutions, the occupation and the resistance, the sharp divisions among French political leaders, and the presence of a large Communist Party form the background of post-war French political discussion. But many of the questions which have been raised are not limited in their implications to the kind of situations out of which they may have emerged. Problems such as the extent to which men can control their political destiny, the kind of behaviour that is appropriate to the citizen, and how to make good or reasonable political choices are universal in their significance. For this reason, I have approached the ideas discussed in this book not as ingredients of French intellectual history but rather as contributions to the store of political ideas from which men select those on which they will live.

But if ideas once expressed no longer have a location, they do have a context at their origins, and for that reason I have included a first chapter which discusses the main political ideas prevailing in France as it entered the difficult years of the 1930s and 1940s, and a second chapter which offers a brief, collective biography of the six political thinkers set within the framework of a common pattern of historical events.

The principal analysis appears in the six chapters which treat each person's ideas separately, and where I also try to show cumulatively the relationships between sets of ideas, and in the final chapter, where I try to show what is common to the ideas of the six people, what is distinctive about them, and how they differ from the political ideas at large in France on the eve of the 1930s.

In quoting from the writings of these people, I have quoted the original French wherever I thought there was any risk of altering the exact meaning of the language through translation. Where I thought there was no such risk, I have quoted in English. All translations from the French are my own except where I have otherwise indicated in the footnotes.

It is a pleasure to acknowledge debts of gratitude which I have incurred in writing this book. I am grateful to the Horace H. Rackham School of Graduate Studies of the University of Michigan for assistance in the form of a grant from the Faculty Research Fund.

I am grateful to several publishers for permission to use previously published material. Part of Chapter 2 and much of Chapter 4 originally appeared in an article of mine and are here reprinted with permission from the *Political Science Quarterly*, Vol. 77, No. 4, December 1962, pp. 505–25. Part of Chapter 8 originally appeared in my article published in the *Journal of Politics* in February 1963, and is republished here with permission. The quotations from Jean-Paul Sartre's *Being and Nothingness*, Translated and with an Introduction by Hazel E. Barnes, New York, 1956 are used with the permission of the Philosophical Library.

I am grateful for the advice, assistance, and encouragement I have received from Mario Einaudi, John W. Chapman, Leslie W. Dunbar, and Arnold S. Kaufman, on one side of the Atlantic, and from Jacques Freymond, François Goguel, and Jean Touchard and his colleagues of the *Fondation Nationale des Sciences Politiques*, on the other.

None of these people, of course, bears any responsibility for the views I have expressed or for whatever errors appear in this book.

CONTENTS

CONTEMPORARY
FRENCH POLITICAL THOUGHT

I

French Political Thought
on the Eve of the Thirties

I Classifications of French Political Ideas

B ETWEEN the end of the First World War and the beginning of the Great Depression, the dominant currents of political thought in France were a special form of liberalism, expressed and typified by the writings of Alain; a special form of traditionalism, expressed and typified by the writings of Charles Maurras; and Marxism, expressed in the divergent and rival forms of communism and socialism.

To speak in terms of three main currents of French political thought during this particular period is not to deny the validity, from certain points of view or with reference to different periods, of those analyses of French political thought which find either more simplified or more complex patterns. The notion of 'the two Frances', for example, has substantial analytical utility and more than a little philosophical significance.[1] This view regards the Revolution of 1789 as the origin of two broad and conflicting traditions, those of the Red and the Black, the latter defined by its attachment to the Church and the institutions and principles of the Old Régime, the former defined by its identification with anti-clericalism, republicanism, and the aspirations of the revolutionary movement generally. This notion of two Frances, as its critics have pointed out, is inadequate to account for the rich variety of political ideas which has inspired political movements in France since 1789, and on this ground it cannot be accepted without qualification. It remains true, however, that at various times during the nineteenth century and even during the

[1] Paul Seippel, *Les Deux Frances et leurs origines historiques*, Lausanne and Paris, 1905.

twentieth, when Frenchmen were confronted with major choices, they divided in ways which are more adequately explained with reference to the dichotomy between the revolutionary tradition and historic loyalties to the principles of the Old Régime than by any other principle of analysis. The Dreyfus Affair, the Popular Front, and the Vichy régime were all events which caused Frenchmen to divide along lines that are intelligible primarily in the context of the existence of these two historic tendencies.

It might be argued also that if the schism between the two Frances was not the only dividing line of French political thought, it was, at least until the Russian Revolution, the most important dividing line with respect to the philosophic differences which produced it. The French Revolution was, after all, a political consequence of the Enlightenment, and the Enlightenment marked a decisive breach with the intellectual habits of the past. Compared with the conflict between the notions of tradition and progress, of clericalism and secularism, of faith and reason, the other conflicts of nineteenth-century and even of early twentieth-century France might appear to be of much reduced significance. Until 1917, it might have been possible to treat Marxism as simply one current of post-Revolutionary thought, more concerned with the economic organization of society and less concerned with its political organization than its liberal rival, but nevertheless at one with it on the fundamental notions of progress, secularism, and reason. I doubt whether this argument is valid, even for the period prior to the Russian Revolution, because liberalism's constant preoccupation with the problem of the control of political power compared with Marxism's disregard of this problem implies a difference in the two theories' sensitivity to moral questions which is at least as important as their agreement on certain values. Since the Russian Revolution, however, there has been a divergence between the communists, on the one hand, and both socialists and liberals, on the other, which is as important as the divergence between pre-Revolutionary and post-Revolutionary France. This divergence is over the application of reason. The establishment of a single-party dictatorship and severe limitations on freedom of criticism run directly counter to the requirements of the exercise of reason, and no group which supports such policies is a complete heir of the Enlightenment.

The notion of two Frances, therefore, has limited validity but is an inappropriate framework for the identification of political ideas during the decade from 1919 to 1929. The same may be said of the two main schemes of analysis which emphasize a multiplicity of French political currents, those suggested by David Thomson and Albert Thibaudet.

Thomson sees the Revolution of 1789 as the great source of modern French political ideas and as the essential point of reference by which they can be understood, but he believes that the legacy of the Revolution is not exhausted by only two currents of thought.[1] Thomson regards the uncompromising supporters of the characteristic features of the Old Régime as constituting a main force, which he calls anti-revolutionary, and he emphasizes the importance of the revolutionary forces, but he also takes into account those groups, which he calls the counter-revolutionary forces, which sought some kind of reconciliation between contending revolutionary and anti-revolutionary groups. Moreover, Thomson subdivides the revolutionary forces into that strand which was concerned primarily with political change and another strand which was concerned more with economic and social affairs and which gave rise to the socialist movement, and he subdivides the counter-revolutionary forces into three distinct groups, the Liberals, the Bonapartists, and the Liberal Catholics. Instead of finding two Frances, Thomson identifies three main forces consisting of six different groups.

Albert Thibaudet had earlier identified six 'spiritual families' in France, although his analysis does not spring from any unifying principle, as do both the two Frances notion and Thomson's categories, because of their common reference to the Revolution of 1789.[2] Thibaudet's groups include the Traditionalists, the Liberals, the Industrialists, the Social Christians, the Jacobins, and the Socialists, and he subdivides the Jacobin family into two branches: the Radicalism of the proconsular

[1] David Thomson, *Democracy in France; the Third Republic*, London, 1946, Chapter I.
[2] Albert Thibaudet, *Les Idées politiques de la France*, Paris, 1932.

variety which he related to Bonapartism and the Radicalism characteristic of provincial party committees. These categories coincide almost exactly with those established by Thomson. The main difference between the two sets is actually less the inclusion by Thibaudet alone of what he calls the Industrialists (who would today be called the technocrats) than the absence from Thibaudet's system of any internal principle, such as Thomson's contains, which would enable one to judge the relative importance of each group.

Both Thomson's and Thibaudet's classifications are useful to the student of French political thought, but just as the two Frances notion contains too little for the period between 1919 and 1929, these classifications contain too much. Bonapartism is a political current which is latent more often than it is active, and it was latent during those years. Liberal Catholicism (or the Social Christian movement) has been present in France since 1848, but it was never more than a marginal political force until the Second World War. What both Thomson and Thibaudet call Liberalism was never a strong force in France before World War II, and is not to be identified with the liberalism of Alain, which predominated during the decade under consideration, and which corresponds to Thomson's political strand of the revolutionary tradition and to Thibaudet's provincial committee Radicalism. Technocracy did not win many supporters until the nineteen thirties, and even then it remained a tiny current attached to the main stream of other political movements. Alain's liberalism, Maurrassian traditionalism, and the two warring versions of Marxism were by far the most powerful streams of French political thought between 1919 and 1939 compared with which the other movements represented only swirls and eddies.

II Alain's Liberalism

Alain's liberalism, which came to be known as 'la doctrine radicale'—the description of and justification for the behaviour of the Radical Socialists who played such a prominent role in the government of the French Third Republic—is not so much a systematic political theory as a series of reflections on the central theme of the corrupting influence of power. 'Power corrupts all those who exercise it', Alain wrote in 1910,[1] and this remained the guiding principle of his thought throughout the entire decade between 1919 and 1929 as well. But while Alain was constantly concerned with the permanent threat to the liberty of the citizens presented by the exercise of political power, he was not an anarchist. Political organization is essential to the maintenance of order, and without order there can be no liberty. How to maintain both order and liberty, how to avoid the twin evils of tyranny and anarchy (which only leads, in turn, to tyranny), are the problems towards which Alain's thought was directed. The solutions which he proposed are of three kinds, although they are closely related. One is to limit sharply the functions of the state; a second is to exercise constant control over the people who exercise power; and the third is to combine one's obedience to the laws with an underlying attitude of resistance.

Alain's political theory is perhaps the most classic example of those liberal theories which take an essentially negative view of the role of the state. His conception of the proper function of the political system was literally exhausted in the statement that 'the role of the political authorities is to ensure the fulfilment of contracts, and not to dictate the contracts'.[2] Alain was not only radically opposed to grand designs for pursuing social reform through political means, but he also was sceptical of the possibility of the government promoting any positive programme without doing more damage than there would be if the state remained inactive. 'Voter, do not ask for too much', he wrote in 1924. 'It may be that the State will be generous and beneficent in the future. In our time the State proves itself to be naturally injurious. . . . Let us not ask the State to enrich us; let us ask it first of all not to ruin us.'[3] The state must be closely confined within the limits of an essentially minimal police function, because if it is permitted or encouraged to extend its activities, the natural inclination of the people who hold power will be to abuse it at the expense of the liberty of the citizens.

Limiting the role of the state and counteracting the corrupting influence of power requires constant vigilance on the part of

---

[1] Alain, *Éléments d'une doctrine radicale*, Paris, 1933, p. 27.
[2] Ibid., p. 232.   [3] Ibid., pp. 253–4.

the citizens. Democracy, for Alain, meant exclusively the control of political power. The role of the elected deputy is to check and limit the action of the executive and the bureaucracy; the role of the voter is to pick and choose among candidates who best fulfil this controlling function. The whole democratic political process was viewed by Alain as constituting negation. It hardly occurred to him that the initiative for positive action might spring from the electorate, so convinced was he that these initiatives would come from ambitious governors. It is true that his perspective on the democratic system allows for the acceptance of government activities of which the deputies and their voters approve, but 'the first article' of Alain's hypothetical 'Charter of the Governed' was that one must 'moderate this ambition that all governors have to settle [*régler*] everything by laws'.[1]

The state's functions are narrowly circumscribed and the role of both the citizens and their elected representatives is essentially negative, but the state still does have a function and the citizens must be governed. Alain's method of reconciling these conditions was to urge that the citizens both obey and resist. 'Resistance and obedience, those are the two virtues of the citizen. By obedience he guarantees order; by resistance he guarantees liberty.'[2] The distinction between obedience and resistance was based on the more fundamental distinction which Alain made between the temporal and the spiritual orders. The temporal order is the domain of force, action, and the body. The spiritual order is the domain of the mind and spirit. By obedience, Alain meant simply carrying out the orders of the legitimate authorities. It is the duty of the citizens to obey the laws. By resistance, he meant constant application of the critical function; the maintenance of a permanently sceptical attitude towards all authority; the refusal to commit one's mind as well as one's body to the duty of obedience.

This theory, or rather this body of political prescriptions, has been widely criticized for its negativeness. It has been called the doctrine of 'the disgruntled citizen',[3] described as 'negative,

---

[1] Alain, op. cit., p. 232.   [2] Ibid., p. 281.
[3] Joseph Fontanet, 'Alain ou le citoyen grognard', *Terre Humaine*, 2 (July–August 1952), pp. 48–59.

desiccated, small-minded'[1] and held partially responsible for
the political and moral weakness of French democracy during
the later years of the Third Republic.[2] Some of these criticisms
rest more solidly on the cynical tone of Alain's homilies than on
the sceptical philosophy which underlies them. Moreover, it is
impossible to determine the extent to which Alain's writings
actually affected the attitudes of his fellow-citizens and the
extent to which they simply rationalized existing behavioural
patterns.[3] On balance, however, the logic of these criticisms is
sound. His doctrine has serious shortcomings and these were
magnified in their effects by the particular context in which
it was produced.

Alain's doctrine, like all liberal theories, makes a distinction
between the state and society. The state's role must be confined,
and social forces must be given free play within an atmosphere
of critical liberty. It is this free play of social forces which
actually determines what the laws will be and not the conscious
decisions of the legislators. The state, in other words, is a
reflection of society, in the sense that it ratifies the rules of
conduct that have already been decided upon by the 'good
sense' of the citizens acting with a critical spirit. '. . . Reforms,
social organization, new laws, all that is determined much more
by circumstances and the conditions of labour than by the will
of the voters.'[4] Up to a point, this view is consistent with the
theory of a much more positive liberal, Ernest Barker. Barker
writes that 'the action of the legislature is not creation, but

1 Gordon Wright, *France in Modern Times: 1760 to the Present*, Chicago, 1960,
p. 327.

2 Raymond Aron, 'Prestige et illusions du citoyen contre les pouvoirs', in
L'Homme contre les tyrans, Paris, 1946, p. 99.

3 In a poll taken in 1957 among persons born between 1927 and 1939, only one
per cent. of the respondents indicated that they thought Alain was the one author
who had 'particularly struck the mind of people of your age', although a French
sociologist, Michel Crozier, has found in his studies of the personnel of bureaucratic
organizations in France the propensity to obey authoritative decisions combined
with the propensity also to criticize them and to disassociate oneself from responsibility for them, a behavioural pattern remarkably faithful to Alain's prescription
to 'obey while resisting'. See Françoise Giroud, *La Nouvelle Vague, portraits de la
jeunesse*, Paris, 1958, and *L'Express*, 5 and 12 December 1957. Also see Michel
Crozier, *Petits Fonctionnaires au travail; compte rendu d'une enquête sociologique effectuée
dans une grande administration publique parisienne*, Paris, 1955, and 'Les Relations de
pouvoir dans un système d'organisation bureaucratique', *Sociologie du Travail*,
II (1960), pp. 61–75.

4 Alain, op. cit., p. 124.

declaration; and its essential function is to declare the implications of the idea and ideal of justice, or the right ordering of human relations in an organized society, and to declare them as they are generally felt by the members of that society and as they are expressed in the form of its common conviction'.[1] This analysis is essentially the same as Alain's view that 'the laws are made by common agreement and without any partisan spirit'. 'In short,' he adds, 'in the legislative sphere I do not see that the majority makes its pressure felt; it is, rather, unanimity, which requires public debates, continuous and impartial work, and complete liberty for every opinion and for every criticism.'[2] For Alain, as for Barker, the legislature simply expresses in law what has already been decided upon as proper by the whole community.

It is a weakness of this view, as expressed by both theorists, that the process by which the whole community makes its common will known to the legislature is not adequately explained. But Barker, who is by far the more rigorous of the two thinkers, at least includes a theory of political institutions within his overall framework. It is not relevant to this argument to examine Barker's institutional theory; it is enough simply to point out that he has one, and that because he does, he necessarily establishes some framework for the organization of community opinion and for the exercise of political leadership. Alain, however, pays almost no attention at all to institutions and his treatment of leadership—in so far as there is one—is within his familiar framework of suspicion and distrust rather than related to the problem of how social opinion becomes translated into legislative decisions. In fact, Alain is so indifferent to institutions that he sees no difference in the consequences for legislation of different forms of political system. 'An absolute king undoubtedly would have enacted the law on workmen's compensation [*accidents du travail*].'[3] But elsewhere, Alain makes complete freedom of criticism a condition for arriving at the unanimous decision of the community, which presumably determines whether or not the law on workmen's compensation will be adopted, and the suffrage— as opposed to absolute rule—is the symbol of this freedom.

[1] Ernest Barker, *Principles of Social and Political Theory*, Oxford, 1951, p. 176.
[2] Alain, op. cit., pp. 202–3.   [3] Ibid., p. 124.

The significance of Alain's neglect of the role of political leadership may be illustrated by comparing Alain's liberalism with the liberal doctrine which prevailed, at least until the nineteen thirties, in the United States.[1] Both liberal doctrines contain an *a priori* suspicion of the exercise of political power which is absent, by way of contrast, from all the main currents of English political thought. Neither the framers of the American constitution nor Alain shared anything like the English utilitarians' reliance on state power to achieve desired social goals or the Burkean veneration of political institutions, provided they be old, which conduces much more to confidence in the beneficence of governmental decisions than to suspicion of them. The United States' system of divided power, expressed in federalism, the separation of powers, and bicameralism, has its doctrinal counterpart in Alain's rejection of numerical majority rule and his approval of close and continuing parliamentary control over the executive.

Yet there is an important difference between the implications of these two liberalisms, outwardly so similar, which springs from the different contexts in which they appeared. When American liberal theory was being made explicit at the time of the drafting of the constitution, Americans were in the process of changing their institutions from a situation in which they contained inadequate provisions for leadership to one in which this leadership could be supplied, and their concern with controlling the exercise of power by establishing numerous checks and balances was a logical corollary to their efforts to build an institutional structure through which governmental authority could be more firmly exercised than it had been before. Alain's doctrine was implicit in the activities of French Republican leaders and the French citizenry even before Alain reached adulthood. It was first expressed in the processes by which the Republican leaders sapped the powers of the Presidency and put all incumbent and prospective Prime Ministers in a position of permanent subordination to the elected deputies. This French development was precisely the opposite of what had occurred in the United States a century

[1] For United States liberalism I rely essentially on Louis Hartz, *The Liberal Tradition in America*, New York, 1955.

earlier. While Americans had strengthened the provisions for political leadership, Frenchmen were weakening them. A liberal doctrine which casts suspicion on the exercise of political power is bound to have different consequences when it appears in a society where the suspect institutions are already weak than when it appears in a society where those institutions are strong. American liberalism operated against the abuse of power, but American institutions permitted power to be exercised; Alain's liberalism served to reinforce an existing institutional tendency towards governmental inaction.

The view that because governmental activity can be dangerous virtually no governmental activity should be undertaken can be acceptable only so long as society is free of significant conflicts or as it can furnish non-governmental institutions through which those conflicts which exist can be resolved. It may be said that until the First World War, France generally fulfilled those conditions. During the decade between 1919 and 1929 they were already breaking down, and by the nineteen thirties they no longer existed. A doctrine which urges governmental idleness until such time as social unanimity permits governmental activity to pass unnoticed, without prescribing the methods or sketching the institutions by which such unanimity can be brought about, is useless for a society where various social groups are competing for wealth, status, or power. It would be a serious mistake, however, to think that Alain's doctrine, or at least all the elements out of which it is constructed, have disappeared from French political thought. His student, Simone Weil, who was to surpass him in inventiveness and intellectual rigour, never fully escaped his pessimistic influence. Bertrand de Jouvenel has expressed in different form themes which resemble those of Alain. Raymond Aron criticizes the use which Alain made of the distinction between temporal and spiritual power, but he retains the importance of the distinction itself. At the same time, however, it may also be said that when, during the nineteen thirties and later, a reaction developed against the politics of the Third Republic, the efforts of political thinkers to produce a political theory appropriate to France's needs was in large part an effort to overcome the influence of Alain.

III Maurrassian Traditionalism

Alain's doctrine was a remarkably accurate statement of the attitudes and description of the behaviour of the majority of France's political class during the Third Republic. Ministers and deputies developed unwritten rules for political activity which reflected, and even caricatured, Alain's prescriptions for limiting the power of government.[1] The largely rural and small-town population which elected these deputies and ministers appeared satisfied with the results, and in this sense it may be said that Alain had a large body of followers throughout the nation, and particularly in the provinces of the Republic whose capital he thought should be Tours or Châteauroux.

The position of Charles Maurras and of the organization which he headed, the Action Française, was precisely the opposite, as the Maurrassian distinction between the *pays réel* and the *pays légal* clearly suggested.[2] Maurras' supporters were, for the most part, outside the boundaries of the French political system. Alain's followers were to be found in parliament and the Radical-Socialist provincial party committees, among the elementary-school teachers who were so active in promoting the cause of the Republic, and among France's numerous farmers and small businessmen. Maurras' supporters were less numerous, and they included principally those sections of the population against which Alain sought to put his readers on guard: the higher administrative echelons, the military (particularly the navy), the rich and powerful in the cities, the large landowners and titled in the provinces, the literati of the Paris salons, and the clergy who had not yet rallied to the Republic, much less to the Revolution. Virtually no one among the French political class was a Maurrassian, and the Action Française could never mobilize large numbers

[1] Alain, for example, wrote that 'the good deputy . . . is one who menaces, not one who strikes, one who makes the minister work, not one who votes him out of office'. Op. cit., p. 92. But work at what?

[2] There is a rich body of recent literature on Maurras and the Action Française, on which I have relied heavily. See Michael Curtis, *Three against the Third Republic: Sorel, Barrès, and Maurras*, Princeton, 1959; Samuel M. Osgood, *French Royalism under the Third and Fourth Republics*, The Hague, 1960; Edward R. Tannenbaum, *The Action Française: Die-Hard Reactionaries in Twentieth-Century France*, New York, 1962; and Eugen Weber, *Action Française, Royalism and Reaction in Twentieth-Century France*, Stanford, 1962.

of people. The socially and economically strategic position of Maurras' followers, however, compensated considerably for their lack of numbers. Their literary and journalistic influence in particular was great, with the result that Maurrassian notions were given wide circulation.

Maurrassian doctrine cannot be summarized in any simple statement. It was not an orderly body of thought, either in the sense of springing from a single, central principle or in the sense of consisting of a series of logically connected parts even in the absence of any unifying principle. To the extent that it did start from a fundamental base, that base was naturalism— the view that what is natural is right and should be emulated in human constructions[1]—but quite apart even from the question of whether nature is an adequate source of ethics, all the tenets of Maurrassian doctrine can hardly be drawn from nature. Nor was there any necessary connexion between its various elements. The doctrine was an unstable compound of diverse and separable elements, and its significance lies as much in the way in which it was propagated and in its interpretation of what it opposed as in its own positive content.

In part, Maurrassian doctrine can be called traditionalist. To this extent, it falls within one of the pure categories of each of the leading interpretations of the history of French political thought: the 'Black France' of the two Frances notion, the antirevolutionary force among David Thomson's categories, or the traditionalism of Albert Thibaudet's system of classification. It advocated a return to the characteristic institutions of the Old Régime: monarchy, an established social hierarchy, decentralization, and a prominent role for the Catholic religion in sustaining the order on which these other institutions would rest.

In addition to traditionalism, Maurras' doctrine embraced a particular form of nationalism. Maurras himself· did not conceive of nationalism apart from the traditionalist elements of his thought; rather he combined the two in what he called integral nationalism. This nationalism is actually 'integral' in two senses. On the one hand, it is integrated into traditionalism in that Maurras conceived of nationalist sentiments as

[1] See Charles Maurras, 'La Politique naturelle', in *Mes Idées politiques*, texte établi par Pierre Chardon, Paris, 1937.

capable of being fully expressed only within the framework of the traditional institutions whose revival he advocated. On the other hand, it is integral in the sense that it admits of no higher claims. The nation is the prior condition of every social and individual good, and any challenge to the nationalist sentiments upon which national unity rests, whether external or internal, must be fully resisted. It is useless, in this view, to oppose justice to national unity, for example, because national unity is the condition of justice; this was the essence of Maurras' position at the time of the Dreyfus case.

Lastly, but by no means least important with respect to the significance of the impact of Maurras' ideas on French society, there were the negative counterparts to the two positive themes of traditionalism and nationalism. These were hatred of the Republic and unrelenting hostility to what Maurras called 'the four confederated states: the Jews, the Protestants, the Masons, and the "metics" '.[1] These hatreds and hostilities were so prominent a feature of Maurras' thought that it is as reasonable to believe that he preached traditionalism and nationalism because of his hatreds as it is to believe that he nursed his hatreds because of his traditionalism and nationalism. And as might be expected, these negative themes played a larger role in the daily activities and unceasing polemics of the Action Française than did argument in favour of the positive themes. In fact, Maurras and the Action Française vented their hatreds with such vehemence, dogmatism, and vituperation that they were eventually repudiated by the very authorities whose co-operation was essential to the success of their cause.

The most important single ingredient of Maurras' traditionalism was his advocacy of monarchy. Yet both he and the other leaders of the Action Française were too obsessed with the rightness of their total position to maintain any personal allegiance to the pretenders to the French throne. They were uncompromising in their attitudes whenever conflicts between them and the pretenders occurred, and they explained the very existence of the conflicts in terms which could hardly contribute to raising the level of popular respect for and confidence in the pretenders themselves. The wonder is not so much that the Comte de Paris finally repudiated the Action

---

[1] Maurras, *Mes Idées politiques*, pp. 200–1.

Française in 1937; rather it is that he and the other Princes of France so long persisted in the view that it was to the interest of the monarchy to uphold the legitimacy of the Action Française as a spokesman for the monarchist cause.

Maurrassian traditionalism also held that Catholicism was an indispensable pillar of a proper political system. This was not, however, because of any sympathy on the part of Maurras for the spiritual content of Catholicism. Maurras was an unbeliever and his view of Catholicism was strictly instrumental. He regarded the Church's commitment to hierarchy and social order as essential to the kind of social and political organization he wanted to create. For many years the Church and the Action Française, like the Action Française and the French pretenders, lived in a kind of uneasy alliance. By the middle nineteen twenties, however, both the Church of France and the Holy See were coming to believe that the Action Française not only failed to carry any spiritual message but was also succeeding in undermining the Church's leadership of French Catholics. Even Pius X, who had condemned the Sillon and discouraged the activities of French liberal Catholics, grew concerned over the influence of the Action Française on French Catholics, although he did not promote a break with Maurras. The more liberal Pius XI, however, decided quickly that the true interests of French Catholicism did not coincide with those of the Action Française, and in January 1927 the group was formally condemned.

The combination of traditionalism and nationalism in Maurras' doctrine could not really be served by the bitterness and violence of his denunciations of the Republic, its supporters, Jews, and foreigners. For if Maurras' appeal to hatred suggests a comparison with the aggressive and hysterical nationalism of Nazi Germany, Maurras did not conceive of harnessing the nation's energies by totalitarian methods. His emphasis on decentralization, for example, implied a purely voluntary acceptance of the national community through and across provincial loyalties. His notion of authority implied personal respect for one's superiors in a freely accepted social hierarchy, with the monarch at the top, rather than the concentration of power in a central governmental system. He was as opposed as Alain was to centralized state power. Yet his appeals for national unity were built less on positive claims than on vituperation, and while people may sustain hatreds for long periods of time, hatred is hardly an adequate basis for enduring and unselfconscious social ties. Despite his organic view of society and the institutional recommendations he based on it, which included economic decentralization through a version of corporatism, as well as geographical decentralization based on historic regions, Maurras really had little understanding of the complex nature and delicacy of the ties which bind together a nation. The goal of national unity, conceived in fundamentally voluntary terms, could not be promoted by encouraging divisiveness and covering with invective and ridicule the political leaders who tried to find some common bases on which the country could be governed.

For all Maurras' claim that his doctrine was natural, it was little more than a statement of his political preferences. It is true that in its positive elements, Maurrassian doctrine was based on institutions which had existed in France earlier, but that gives the doctrine only an historical, and not a natural, origin. An historically-based doctrine has no inherent superiority simply because it is historically based. Even before its merits can be debated, it has to be shown that it is relevant to the conditions of the society at the time it is proposed. Maurras never succeeded in making that demonstration. It was a curious application of a nationalism which applies, 'rather than to the Land of one's Fathers, to the Fathers themselves, to their blood and to their works, to their moral and spiritual heritage, more than to their material one',[1] to overlook more than a century of history during which France's moral and spiritual heritage was created as much by the Republicans as by their enemies. In this respect, Maurras' doctrine was as much an abstraction, despite its historical basis, as any purely imaginative construction.

By a natural politics, Maurras meant simply the projection into political organization of the institution of the family, and he sought to demonstrate the value of such régimes by pointing to their longevity and prosperity in the past. It did not occur to him that the great issues of politics in his own time revolved, not around whether the state would be organized like

[1] Maurras, op. cit., p. 264.

a family, but around questions which implied whether or not free play would be given to the very institution of the family itself. In this respect, and despite the ferociousness with which it was propagated, Maurrassian doctrine amounted in the final analysis to an evasion of the problems of politics. By insisting dogmatically on a whole package of historically-oriented preferences, the doctrine could not cope with a situation in which a choice had to be made among other competing political claims. This weakness became operative at the time of the Vichy régime, and particularly after 1942, when French political leaders were confronted with a choice between collaboration and resistance.[1] Maurras' only answer was to deny the claims of both under the formula of 'France alone', the kind of France which did not exist. This was, of course, something that was still off in the future, as far as the years from 1919 to 1929 are concerned. But this was the kind of doctrine which Maurras and the Action Française were preaching during those years and which permeated influential levels of the French population. It was a set of institutional recommendations unrelated to the real forces at work in the contemporary world.

IV Marxism

One is tempted, in describing the role of Marxism in French political thought, to adopt categories of Marxism itself. Alain's liberalism was the expression of the instinctive prejudices and practices of the middle-class groups which dominated French political life during almost all of the Third Republic. Maurrassian traditionalism reflected the nostalgia of the social groups whose political influence had been declining since the French Revolution. The Marxian scheme of social analysis would identify Marxism as the doctrine of the third major social category, the industrial workers. This scheme, however, will not quite do. The history of Marxism as a political force, as opposed to its use as an instrument of social analysis, is closely connected with both the French working-class movement and

[1] But what was happening was not analysed until later. The classic analysis is by Stanley Hoffmann, 'Aspects du régime de Vichy', *Revue Française de Science Politique*, VI (January-March 1956), pp. 44–69. The fullest statement of the principles underlying this type of analysis is in Raymond Aron, *Espoir et peur du siècle; essais non partisans*, Paris, 1957, and will be treated below in Chapter 8.

French socialism, but neither of these two movements (which have, of course, been connected) has ever been dominated by a single doctrine. Nevertheless, they have both been profoundly affected by Marxism, and the influence of Marxism upon the leaders of both movements increased throughout the life of the Third Republic.

French socialism and the French working-class movement have an impressive heritage of indigenous socialist and syndicalist doctrines on which to draw. The 'utopian' socialists whom Marx both acknowledged and criticized were French, as were the two thinkers, Pierre Proudhon and Georges Sorel, who provided so much of the inspiration for and rationalization of French syndicalist behaviour. The result was that 'scientific' socialism has always met with considerable resistance in France, even among socialists, and that socialist efforts to harness the trade union movement for political purposes have similarly been resisted. Yet a combination of zeal and patient organizational efforts by Marxists, peculiar historical circumstances, and tangential sympathies between Marxism and the older ideologies of the French working-class movement all combined to facilitate the penetration of Marxism into France.[1]

Before the Paris Commune, Marxist ideas were not widely held in France. Marx had been in contact with French working-class leaders, of course, but only one member of the Paris Commune was a Marxist and most of its members probably had never even heard of Marx. Marx was to enlist the Commune in the cause of Marxism by describing it sympathetically, Engels was to refer to it later as the dictatorship of the proletariat, and French Marxists to this day celebrate its anniversary ritually, but the Paris Commune was a product of pre-Marxist French history. There are two senses, however, in which the Commune was important to Marxism. In the first place, its failure helped to discredit the older currents of French socialist and working-class thought, thereby creating

[1] For this section I have relied mainly on Samuel Bernstein, *The Beginnings of Marxian Socialism in France*, New York, 1933; Alexandre Zévaès, *De l'Introduction du marxisme en France*, Paris, 1947; the special number of *La Nef*, 7 (June-July 1950), entitled 'Le Socialisme français, victime du marxisme?'; John Plamenatz, *The Revolutionary Movement in France 1815–71*, London, 1952; Aaron Noland, *The Founding of the French Socialist Party (1893–1905)*, Cambridge, Mass., 1956; and, of course, Roger Soltau, *French Political Thought in the Nineteenth Century*, New Haven, 1931.

a crevice—although far from a void—into which Marxism could penetrate. In the second place, the Marxist emphasis on the class struggle could really bite deeply into the consciousness of French working-class leaders only after the Commune. The notion of a class struggle had been at large in France well before Marx; it was already adumbrated by Babeuf. But the history of the French working-class movement before 1871 is inextricably intertwined with that of the Republican movement in general. Before the Commune, working-class leaders and socialists were allied with middle-class and non-socialist Republicans in the effort to establish the Republic. It was not until the Commune failed—that is, until the Republic was established—that the French socialists could permit themselves the luxury of taking on new enemies. The failure of the Commune meant the success of the Republic. But it meant little else that might satisfy French socialists. The Republic was conservative, and once again, as in 1848, French working-class leaders began to wonder about the value of alliances with the middle classes, even the extreme Republicans among them. By the 1870s, therefore, the establishment of the Republic had removed the main ground for alliance between socialists and non-socialists, between the working class and the middle classes; and the repression of the Commune, combined with the conservatism of the Republic, encouraged the belief that class conflict was inevitable. The Marxists were not the only group which believed in class conflict, but the historical circumstances which made the notion of the class struggle plausible were also congenial to the growth of French Marxism.

Marxism has been taken to mean many things. As long as Marx was alive, he could put his personal seal of approval upon the orthodoxy. Later, after 1917, when there was an operating government run by men who called themselves Marxists and claimed to have made a successful Marxist revolution, there was also a centre of authority for the interpretation of Marxism. Between Marx's death in 1883 and the Bolshevik Revolution of 1917, however, there was no fount of Marxist orthodoxy and, consequently, various groups could and did conflict with one another over the true meaning of Marxism. As it is precisely during this period of interpretative freedom that Marxism took hold in France, it is not surprising that the content of Marxism itself should appear fluctuating and uncertain. Beginning in the late 1870s, however, and culminating in the foundation of a united Socialist Party in 1905, Marxist ideas increasingly displaced older French socialist and working-class doctrines. The very idea that a political party should be the principal instrument of the working class in its struggle against the bourgeoisie ran counter to the syndicalist tradition, which held that the unions were the workers' main agents. The adoption of a programme calling for the collectivization of the means of production both fixed a goal, which the revolutionary Blanquists had never held, and implied a centralized role for the state, which the Proudhonians had never envisaged. The willingness to envisage the use of violence in order to seize control of the state, while it was attractive to Blanquists, was not in the tradition of one of France's leading collectivists, Louis Blanc. And the notion of making the state the main target was also outside the syndicalist tradition which, in its suspicion of politicians, preferred to limit the efforts of its more trusted union representatives to fighting employers.

The unification of French socialists under largely Marxist principles in 1905 did not end conflicts among them, of course. In the main, these centred on whether or not the socialists should participate in or support governments in which the bourgeois parties were represented, an issue which usually pitted the adherents of an unrelenting view of the class struggle against those socialists who were primarily interested in achieving limited, but concrete, social reforms. The issue was first raised in 1899, when Millerand entered a ministry; it cropped up again during the 1920s; and it was eventually settled doctrinally for one group of Marxists, at least, by Léon Blum's ingenious if not completely convincing distinction between the conquest of power and participation in power, on the one hand, and the exercise of power, on the other. According to Blum, the conquest of power was impossible and participation in power undesirable. The exercise of power, however, was both possible and desirable, and it was this paper-thin argument which sustained doctrinally the formation by the Socialist Party of the Popular Front government of 1936 under the leadership of Léon Blum.

The most important schism among French Marxists occurred as a result of the Russian revolution. This created a centre of socialist power which, because of its successful achievement of a revolution, acquired an authority in the Marxist world which was to rend the French socialist movement only fifteen years after it had succeeded in becoming unified. In 1919, Lenin founded the Third International and presented the socialist parties of the world with a choice between modelling themselves on the Russian example or severing connexions with the world's only socialist state. At the Tours Congress of 1920, French socialism was once again divided, this time essentially between those who were prepared to accept the revolutionary intransigence of Lenin's party and those who were committed to the reformist pattern French socialism was acquiring.[1] To be sure, the division was not exclusively along these lines. Some revolutionary socialists remained attached to the reformist group because they objected to foreign domination of the French movement, and in the first few years relations between the newly-formed French Communist Party and the Third International or the Russian Communist Party were strained and marked by individual defections from the Communist group. But the division was essentially between revolutionary socialists and reformist socialists, between socialists who placed the conquest of power over democracy and those who placed democracy over the conquest of power, and this division remains to the present day.

The French Socialist Party and the French Communist Party both regarded themselves as authentic carriers of the Marxist tradition. They disagreed sharply over means, over the importance of democracy, over the implications to be drawn from acceptance of the notion of the class struggle. Yet they both adhered in the final analysis to what must be the fundamental assumption of socialism, whether Marxist or otherwise: that only a fundamental change in the structure of the property system can produce a good society. French communism was revolutionary and dictatorial; French socialism was gradualistic and democratic; but both movements

[1] See Gérard Walter, *Histoire du parti communiste français*, Paris, 1948.

The schism among the socialists also produced a schism in the union movement. See Édouard Dolléans, *Histoire du mouvement ouvrier*, Vol. II, 1871–1936, Paris, 1948, pp. 350–1.

shared the assumptions of Marx that the property system inevitably divides men into antagonistic classes, and that the abolition of private property in the means of production will produce social harmony. This simple approach to the problem of conflict in industrial society contained an appeal for the growing numbers of industrial workers which neither Alain's liberalism nor Maurras' traditionalism could possibly have. Alain's liberalism was relevant only to a nation of farmers and small businessmen. Maurras' traditionalism was also irrelevant to the inhabitants of industrial cities which had little potentiality for transformation into integrated communities based on eighteenth-century models of social organization. Both branches of the Marxist family attracted young and vigorous adherents who could see the obvious deficiencies of the competing liberal and traditionalist doctrines simply by observing the consequences of industrial development all around them.

The dominant currents of thought in France after World War I, then, were Alain's liberalism, Maurras' traditionalism, and Marxism, which was divided into a democratic reformist wing and a dictatorial revolutionary wing. The first two currents were increasingly anachronistic, in that they assumed the existence of a kind of society which was in the process of disappearing, although this process was slow enough to create the illusion that French society was stable. Marxism was better attuned to the social requirements of the times, and this no doubt accounts for its relative success. Both democratic socialism and revolutionary communism are viable modes of political organization, whatever one may think of their merits. But the success of democratic socialism depends upon either the existence of an industrial working class large enough to provide by itself a majority for a socialist party which emphasizes its class basis or abandonment by the socialist party of the Marxist view that society is divided between necessarily hostile social classes. Neither condition was fulfilled in France. The industrial working class has never constituted a majority of the French population, yet the French Socialist Party continually insisted, in the face of all evidence to the contrary, that it was a class party, a party of the proletariat. In circumstances of this kind, democratic socialism might continue to be an important political force, but it could never hope to achieve its ultimate goal of the conquest of power.

Similarly, the success of a revolutionary socialist party depended upon conditions which were hardly likely to be found in France. A party like the French Communist Party, closely linked to an international revolutionary movement directed by the government of the Soviet Union, was bound to meet resistance in the nation that invented nationalism as soon as, in its search for supporters, it reached groups of people at a level of living where they had more to lose than their chains. But even on the assumption that a revolutionary movement needs no more than a small minority of dedicated supporters, the possibility of the success of a revolutionary movement depends, among other things, on the resistance offered to it by democratic sentiment in the nation. Maurras' traditionalism did everything it could to sap the strength of this democratic sentiment, and as expressed in Alain's liberalism it was perhaps inglorious, but the historic record of the French revolutionary movement throughout the nineteenth century, in which middle-class republicans had always participated, left no doubt as to the intensity of their commitment. After each successive defeat, the Republicans emerged stronger than they had been before.[1]

Even if one discounts the strength of the democratic tradition in France, by 1924 there was evidence of what could happen to a revolutionary socialist movement when it frightens the rest of society by appearing to be on the point of seizing power. Italian fascism was the reply to revolutionary socialism of a society in which democratic ideals had not firmly taken hold, just as nazism was to be the similar reply in Germany a decade later. Even nineteenth-century France had indicated, in the repressions which followed the June Days of 1848 and the Commune of 1871, what the response to revolutionary violence by the working classes could be. But hope springs eternal in the revolutionary imagination of the Blanquist, and it waxed strong in the minds of Marxists whose doctrine convinced them that their success was assured.

The Marxist doctrine, however, whether in its reformist or revolutionary version, was far from unassailable. Marxism is notable more for its efforts to demonstrate that the triumph of the

[1] Plamenatz, op. cit., passim.

party of the proletariat is inevitable than to demonstrate that it is desirable. Marx was hardly more explicit than Blanqui about the kind of society which would follow upon a successful revolution, and the Marxists agreed on little more than that the economy should be collectivized through the transfer to state ownership of the means of production. How that transfer alone would put an end to conflicts in society depended, in Marx's argument, upon a sequence of definitions of terms and not upon accurate analysis of how a society operates. Even before the turn of the twentieth century, the Dreyfus case had demonstrated to French socialists that the problem of ensuring justice was more complicated than the Marxist categories assumed. No more than Alain's liberalism or Maurras' traditionalism did Marxism satisfy the needs of French society. When the rethinking of French political doctrines began in the nineteen thirties, Marxism came in for re-examination along with its older competitors.

Attacks on these three political doctrines occurred before 1929, due to conflicts between generations, personal rivalries, distaste for routine, and nostalgia for glory, but 1929 marks a major turning-point in contemporary French political thought. The Great Depression and the rise of foreign totalitarianisms forced Frenchmen to take a close look at the ideas on which they had been living. The period of intense political speculation which was opened in France at this time has not yet ceased. France and the world are no longer what they were when this period began, and the pressure of events has given answers to some of the questions that were raised at that time, but it would be a tragic mistake to think that either France or the world has found permanent answers to the most important of them. In fact, outside France the questions have hardly been raised at all. For if much of the political thinking of France since the nineteen thirties may seem jejune, much of it is relevant and some of it is central to the problems of politics everywhere. It is no doubt true that Frenchmen sometimes have an unfortunate way of treating as universal the problems of a small European hectagon. This may not be worse than not to argue fundamental problems of politics at all. 'Au moins ici', says one Frenchman who is a powerful critic of the former tendency, 'on discute.'

2

Biography of a Generation

I Six Political Thinkers

THE six thinkers whose political ideas are treated in this book are all members of the post-1929 generation. They were born within the span of a single decade: the oldest is Bertrand de Jouvenel, who was born in 1903; the youngest was Albert Camus, who was born in 1913. Simone Weil was born in 1909, and the other three—Raymond Aron, Emmanuel Mounier, and Jean-Paul Sartre—were born within four months of one another in 1905.

None of them was out of his teens by the end of World War I. The eldest of them, de Jouvenel, once dated his 'oldest political memory' as of 1 May 1919, while he was still a student at the Lycée Hoche at Versailles,[1] and he was the only one of the six to play any kind of public role during the 1920s. None of the six, however, had passed his thirtieth birthday by the time Hitler came to power in Germany. Their political ideas developed against the convulsive background of the Great Depression, the rise of foreign totalitarianisms, the severe political conflicts within France during the nineteen thirties, the Second World War, and, except in the case of Simone Weil, who died in 1943, the post-war years as well. In every case, even when, as for Sartre and Camus, they did not turn to political thought on any considerable scale until the Second World War, they had developed central notions which were to be characteristic of their thought before the end of the nineteen thirties.

Emmanuel Mounier died in 1950 of a third heart attack within six months, and after a life during which he had never permitted himself any indulgence and which was probably

[1] *L'Émancipation Nationale*, 14 November 1936, p. 3. Raymond Aron was also a student at the Lycée Hoche at the same time.

shortened by his imprisonment during the Vichy régime. Albert Camus, who was awarded the Nobel Prize for literature in 1957, died in a motor accident in 1960. The other three thinkers, Raymond Aron, Bertrand de Jouvenel, and Jean-Paul Sartre, continue to be productive writers, and the appearance of a new work by any of them is an event of importance.

II Two *Normaliens*

Identity of age and common intellectual interests made two of the six close acquaintances. Raymond Aron and Jean-Paul Sartre were classmates of the École Normale Supérieure's *promotion* of 1924, and Aron (and possibly also Sartre) knew Simone Weil, who was in the *promotion* of 1928. Aron ranked first for the *agrégation* in philosophy in 1928 (Emmanuel Mounier ranked second); Sartre ranked first for the *agrégation* in philosophy in 1929.

For the first few years after receiving the *agrégation*, Aron and Sartre followed in each other's footsteps. The two men performed their military service at about the same time. According to Simone de Beauvoir, Sartre entered the meteorological section at Saint-Cyr on the advice of Aron, who was an instructor in the subject there.[1] And it must have been a rare treat for the students of philosophy at the Lycée du Havre between 1931 and 1935, as either Sartre or Aron was teaching there during those years. Sartre taught at Le Havre from 1931 until 1933, while Aron, who had been at the University of Cologne in 1930–1, spent 1931–2 and 1932–3 at the Maison Académique at Berlin. During 1933–4, Aron taught philosophy at the Lycée du Havre, while Sartre succeeded Aron at the French Institute in Berlin. Sartre spent the year in Berlin on the advice of Aron, who 'convinced him that phenomenology responded exactly to his preoccupations . . .'.[2]

After the academic year 1933–4, the parallel ceases. Sartre returned from Berlin and spent one more year at the Lycée du Havre while Aron went to Paris in 1934, where he worked as Secrétaire du Centre de Documentation at the École Normale

---

[1] Simone de Beauvoir, *La Force de l'âge*, Paris, 1960, p. 33. Eng. tr. by Peter Green, *The Prime of Life*, Cleveland, 1962, London, 1963.

[2] Ibid., pp. 141–2.

Supérieure and taught at the École Normale at St. Cloud. He was preparing his dissertation for the doctorate, which he received in 1938, upon the presentation of the only dissertation of which I am aware which contains no footnotes.[1] After receiving the doctorate, Aron entered the university system as Maître de Conférences at the University of Toulouse. Sartre, on the other hand, remained in the secondary school system and worked for five years on his first novel, *La Nausée*, which was published by Gallimard in 1938.[2] Between his military service and the outbreak of World War II, Sartre also wrote several short stories,[3] and his psychological studies of the imagination,[4] the ego,[5] and the emotions,[6] and he began to write the first novel of the trilogy which appeared later under the general title *Les Chemins de la liberté*.[7]

As their professional paths began to diverge, so did the extent to which the two men concerned themselves with politics. While Sartre's interests led him to psychology and fiction, Aron's led him to sociology and the philosophy of history, and the difference in the political implications of the two sets of interests is evident. Aron was not, however, a political activist. During his student days he had been, like

[1] The dissertation was published as *Introduction à la philosophie de l'histoire, essai sur les limites de l'objectivité historique*, Paris, 1938. Eng. tr. by G. J. Irwin, *Introduction to the Philosophy of History*, N.Y., 1961. Aron's secondary dissertation (this one with footnotes) was *La Philosophie critique de l'histoire, essai sur une théorie allemande de l'histoire*, Paris, 1938.

There is a summary account of Aron's defence of his dissertation in *Revue de Métaphysique et de Morale*, 45 (July 1938), Supplément, pp. 28–30.

[2] De Beauvoir, op. cit., p. 292. *La Nausée* appeared in English translation by Lloyd Alexander as *Nausea*, Norfolk, Connecticut, 1949, and in London (J. Lehmann, 1949) as *The Diary of Antoine Roquentin*.

[3] Published in *Le Mur*, Paris, 1939. Eng. tr. by Lloyd Alexander, *The Wall, and Other Stories*, New York, 1948.

[4] *L'Imagination*, Paris, 1936. Eng. tr. by Forrest Williams, *Imagination, a Psychological Critique*, Ann Arbor, Michigan, 1962. *L'Imaginaire, psychologie phénoménologique de l'imagination*, Paris, 1940.

[5] 'La Transcendance de l'ego. Esquisse d'une description phénoménologique', *Recherches Philosophiques*, IV (1936–7), pp. 85–123. Eng. tr. by Forrest Williams and Robert Kirkpatrick, *The Transcendence of the Ego, an Existentialist Theory of Consciousness*, New York, 1957.

[6] *Esquisse d'une théorie des émotions*, Paris, 1939. Eng. tr., by Bernard Frechtman, *The Emotions, Outline of a Theory*, New York, 1948; by Philip Mairet, *Sketch for a Theory of the Emotions*, with a Preface by Mary Warnock, London, 1962.

[7] The first volume is entitled *L'Âge de raison*, Paris, 1945. Eng. tr. by Eric Sutton, *The Age of Reason*, New York, London, 1947. This book was finished in 1941. See de Beauvoir, op. cit., p. 497.

Sartre, *à gauche*, and for a brief period he was a member of the Socialist Party,[1] but that was the extent of his political activity. Some articles he wrote for *L'Europe* about Germany in 1932 suggest a socialist and even revolutionary orientation which contrasts sharply with his later writings.[2] By 1934, a careful concern with definition and sociological method is evident,[3] as well as the view that German sociology 'is indissolubly linked to the political problem . . .'.[4] In 1936, he published a book on German sociology which emphasizes the implications for sociology of different political and philosophical assumptions.[5] By 1937, he was demonstrating a mastery of Marxism unparalleled anywhere, as well as considerable scepticism about its application in the Soviet Union.[6] In the same year, he was grappling with the problem of how to found a critique of ideologies,[7] a subject to which he was to return after the war. In 1937 also, he published an article critical of the economic policy of the Popular Front government in a philosophical review which, as he put it later, 'effectively protected my ideas from any compromising dissemination'.[8] In 1938, his dissertation was published, and while it contains a number of themes which reappear in his later works, it should be noted in particular that it already states the foundations of Aron's own sociological method and his moral theory, to both of which he

1 Raymond Aron, *L'Algérie et la République*, Paris, 1958, p. 5. See also de Beauvoir, op. cit., p. 34.

2 See 'Nouvelles Perspectives allemandes', *Europe*, 28 (1932), pp. 295–305, and 'Après les élections', *Europe*, 30 (1932), pp. 625–30.

3 Raymond Aron, 'Note sur l'objet et les divisions de la sociologie et ses rapports avec la philosophie', *Annales Sociologiques*, Série A, fasc. 1 (1934), pp. 101–16; 'Note: Individus et groupes. Société et communauté', *Annales Sociologiques*, Série A, fasc. 1 (1934), pp. 150–60; 'Philosophie de l'histoire et sociologie', *Annales Sociologiques*, Série A, fasc. 1 (1934), pp. 191–200.

4 Raymond Aron, 'Sociologie systématique et sociologie de la culture', *Annales Sociologiques*, Série A, fasc. 1 (1934), p. 231.

5 *La Sociologie allemande contemporaine*, Paris, 1936. Eng. tr. by Mary and Thomas Bottomore, *German Sociology*, Glencoe, Illinois, 1957.

6 Raymond Aron, 'Les Rapports de la politique et de l'économie dans la doctrine marxiste', in *Inventaires II, L'Économique et la politique*, Introduction de C. Bouglé, Paris, 1937, pp. 16–47. Also see 'Note sur l'histoire des idées et l'idéologie', *Annales Sociologiques*, Série A, fasc. 2 (1936), pp. 129–38.

7 Raymond Aron, 'L'Idéologie', *Recherches Philosophiques* (Paris), VI (1937), pp. 65–84.

8 The article is 'Réflexions sur les problèmes économiques français', *Revue de Métaphysique et de Morale*, 44 (1937), pp. 793–822. The quotation is from *Le Grand Schisme*, Paris, 1948, p. 7.

has closely adhered ever since. In the same year, his later participation in political debates was, perhaps, foreshadowed by his posing the question whether 'the sociologist can understand his epoch without taking part in it'.[1] And in a paper read before the Société Française de Philosophie in the summer of 1939, but not published until after the war, Aron both further indicated that 'we professors are susceptible of playing a small role in this effort to save the values to which we are attached', and developed a number of ideas to which he was later to return, such as the analysis of the German and Italian dictatorships in terms of Pareto's élite theory, the denial that popular sovereignty is essential to democracy, and the effort to seek the institutional basis for the preservation of liberal values without resort either to 'the radical cynicism of some and the detached moralism of others . . .'.[2] These pre-war writings do not completely exhaust the elements of Aron's political thought, but they contain its central features, and indicate with remarkable accuracy the direction it was later to take under the impact of wartime and post-war circumstances.

Sartre, on the other hand, seems to have had only a desultory interest in politics during the nineteen thirties. According to his own account, he was 'apolitical, refractory towards any engagement', even though his heart was 'on the left'.[3] He early developed an antagonism towards the bourgeoisie and he hoped for a proletarian revolution, but he did so apparently more because of what it would destroy than of what it would create.[4] He thought he would not be comfortable at all in a socialist society, which he identified with a civilization of engineers, and he was not interested in Marxism.[5] He voted neither in 1932[6] nor in 1936, although he greeted the Popular Front victory with enthusiasm.[7] Simone de Beauvoir writes

[1] Raymond Aron, 'Note sur la sociologie de la culture', *Annales Sociologiques*, Série A, fasc. 3 (1938), p. 83.

[2] Raymond Aron, 'États démocratiques et états totalitaires', *Bulletin de la Société Française de Philosophie*, XL (1946), pp. 41–92. The quotations are from pp. 55 and 70; the latter does not appear in the paper but in the discussion following its presentation.

[3] From the foreword by Jean-Paul Sartre to Paul Nizan, *Aden Arabie*, Paris, 1960, p. 56. The foreword was reprinted in Jean-Paul Sartre, *Situations, IV*, Paris, 1964, pp. 130–88. Eng. tr. by Benita Eisler, *Situations*, N.Y., London, 1965.

[4] De Beauvoir, op. cit., p. 37.

[5] Ibid., pp. 37–38.   [6] Ibid., p. 116.   [7] Ibid., pp. 271–2.

that he was vaguely tempted to join the Communist Party during the early thirties but that he decided he could not reconcile it with his personal activities.[1] He regarded the United States as the epitome of a detestable capitalism but he was fascinated by its dynamism, while he could generate no enthusiasm for the Soviet Union, whose undertakings he admired.[2] He had created an 'esthetic of opposition'[3] which required a constant opponent; basically, he liked the existing order, so he could 'throw those bombs at it: my words'.[4]

During the nineteen thirties, therefore, Sartre showed little real interest in politics and none in political speculation. But just as Aron was already carving out the areas of interest which he was to develop, expand, and probe more deeply later on, Sartre was also acquiring certain basic notions which he was later to apply in a political context. He forged the concept of 'bad faith' during 1932 or 1933,[5] and between 1934 and 1935 he developed his conviction of the complete emptiness of the unconscious,[6] both of which are fundamental to his view of liberty. And if we take Simone de Beauvoir's account as a guide, Sartre and Aron already displayed during the late nineteen twenties and early thirties certain intellectual characteristics which they retain to this day. Sartre rejected science and the analytical method, while Aron was displaying his capacity for critical analysis. Sartre thought in terms of both individual and cosmic syntheses, while Aron sought to place Sartre in dilemmas and present him with categorical choices. Sartre's penchant, according to Simone de Beauvoir, was towards invention rather than logic.[7] On the whole, this interpretation of the orientation he displayed early is sustained by his works of later years.

III   Three Forms of Engagement

Aron and Sartre developed certain interests and concepts during the nineteen thirties which they were later to apply to political problems, but they remained outside the world of

---

[1] De Beauvoir, op. cit., pp. 140; 143–4.   [2] Ibid., pp. 146–7.

[3] Simone de Beauvoir, *La Force des choses*, Paris, 1963, p. 15. Eng. tr. by Richard Howard, *Force of Circumstance*, N.Y., London, 1965.

[4] Foreword to Nizan, op. cit., p. 24.

[5] De Beauvoir, *La Force de l'âge*, p. 134.

[6] Ibid., p. 216.   [7] Ibid., p. 35.

political activity during those years. The activists of the nineteen thirties were Simone Weil, Emmanuel Mounier, and
Bertrand de Jouvenel. Those years were notable in France for
the extent to which the desire for political change and social
improvement on the part of young people produced a proliferation of new groups and ideologies, and no selection of only three
people could possibly be representative of the broad spectrum
of intellectual ferment which took place.[1] Simone Weil, in
particular, is outstanding for the extent to which she remained
independent of some of the characteristic thought of the period.
At the same time, Mounier, de Jouvenel, and even Weil are
symbolic figures. All of them, in their separate ways, became
engaged in the struggles of the times. Simone Weil's commitment took the form of a personal identification with the
proletariat. Mounier's was to respond to that 'divine economy'
which 'makes every Frenchman the founder of a review'.[2]
De Jouvenel's was to seek a party which would provide an
effective answer to France's political problems.

Throughout her entire brief life, Simone Weil displayed an
extreme asceticism, compassion for the suffering of others,
and an overriding tendency to identify herself with the poor and
downtrodden.[3] Like Aron and Sartre, she was a graduate of the

[1] On the new French groups and ideologies during the nineteen thirties, see the
following works: Pierre Andreu, 'Les Idées politiques de la jeunesse intellectuelle
de 1927 à la guerre', *Revue des Travaux de l'Académie des Sciences Morales et Politiques et
Comptes Rendus des ses Séances*, 110e Année, 4e Série, Année 1957 (2e semestre),
Séance du 8 juillet 1957, pp. 17–35. Jean Touchard, 'L'Esprit des années 1930: une
tentative de renouvellement de la pensée politique française', in Colloques, Cahiers
de Civilisation, *Tendances politiques dans la vie française depuis 1789*, Paris, 1960, pp.
89–120. Stanley Hoffmann, 'Paradoxes of the French Political Community', in
Stanley Hoffmann, et al., *In Search of France*, Cambridge, 1963, pp. 21–32.

[2] Letter of 1 April 1941 to Jéromine Martinaggi, in *Mounier et sa génération, lettres,
carnets et inédits*, Paris, 1956, p. 70.

[3] During the last months of her life, Simone Weil did not eat adequately and
during her last days, which were spent in an English sanatorium, she apparently
refused to eat at all, saying that she could not eat while Frenchmen were starving in
France. Her death certificate stated 'Cardiac failure due to myocardial degenera-
tion of the heart muscles due to starvation and pulmonary tuberculosis. The
deceased did kill and slay herself by refusing to eat whilst the balance of her mind
was disturbed.' An inquest was held a few days after her death and it was reported
that 'the Coroner recorded a verdict of suicide while the balance of the mind was
disturbed'. Her principal biographer, Jacques Cabaud, writes that 'this refusal to
eat, this impossibility to nourish herself adequately, this almost clinical anorexia,
had a physiological basis which was not apparent at this time, but which was
revealed later. Totally unaware of the morbid origin of her revulsion to food,

École Normale Supérieure (of the *promotion* of 1928), where she apparently displayed a combination of grim intellectual qualities and revolutionary sentiments which resulted in her being dubbed 'the categorical imperative in skirts' and the 'Red Virgin'.[1] She received the *agrégation* in philosophy in 1931, and she taught at the Lycées of Le Puy (1931–2), Auxerre (1932–3), Roanne (1933–4), and Bourges (1935–6). Apart from her teaching, she spent most of her time during those years in the company of miners and factory workers, engaged in union activities of a revolutionary syndicalist kind, and wrote on problems of social and political organization. During part of 1934 and most of 1935, she worked in factories in the Paris area, an experience which was literally agonizing for her and which she recorded in her 'Journal d'usine' and in other writings published together as *La Condition ouvrière* by Gallimard in 1951. Between 1935 and 1938, which included a brief and disillusioning period spent with the Republican forces in Spain, she underwent a spiritual conversion, the culmination of which she dated at Easter of 1938.[2] She had visited Germany in 1932 and, like Aron, wrote articles for publication in France about the political developments in that country.

The years during which Simone Weil underwent her spiritual conversion constitute a dividing line between two phases of her thought. Prior to 1935, she wrote almost exclusively on social and political affairs. After 1938, she wrote more on religion and the supernatural than she did on social and political organization. Her interest in society and politics remained strong, however, and some of her most important later writings are on these subjects. Simone Weil's later writings are all stamped with spirituality, but there is continuity

Simone believed herself to be motivated by reasons for not eating that were valid in her eyes. . . . To deprive herself of what was necessary had become a strict moral obligation. It seemed to her as though some divine law of compensation operated in favour of the unfortunate, and that the nourishment she refused did profit, in a mysterious way, that little child in France whose image haunted her.' Jacques Cabaud, *Simone Weil, A Fellowship in Love*, N.Y., 1964, pp. 336–7. He cites the death certificate on p. 348 and the press account of the inquest on p. 349. This book is an enlarged, English version of the same author's *L'Expérience vécue de Simone Weil*, Paris, 1957.

[1] Cabaud, *L'Expérience vécue de Simone Weil*, pp. 33–34.

[2] Simone Weil, *Attente de Dieu*, Paris, 1950, p. 75. Eng. tr. by Emma Craufurd, *Waiting for God*, New York, 1951; *Waiting on God*, London, 1951.

between these later works and her earlier works as well. While there is a turning-point in Simone Weil's thought, it is clear that she plunged early into the problems of politics, quickly acquired a synthetic grasp of both national and international affairs, and was moved always by a spirit of impending disaster. In this respect, she resembles Mounier, but Mounier' view of the tragedy of his times was always illuminated with an optimism which seldom lightened the grim aspect of the brilliant young woman who, by the time she was thirty, had come closer than any of her compatriots to producing an original political theory and was already giving expression to the mysticism which was eventually to envelop her.

Emmanuel Mounier was born and raised at Grenoble, where he attended the University between 1924 and 1927, and studied under the direction of a Professor of Philosophy, Jacques Chevalier, who was later to become Minister of Information under the Vichy Government. In the fall of 1927 he went to Paris, where he received the *agrégation* in 1928, worked closely for several years with a Lazarist priest, Father Pouget, and participated regularly in a discussion group that had been organized by Jacques Maritain. In collaboration with Georges Izard and Marcel Péguy, he wrote a book on *La Pensée de Charles Péguy*, which was published in 1931; he taught philosophy for a year at the Lycée de Saint-Omer (1931–2) as well as at the Collège Sainte-Marie de Neuilly, a private school, and he sought for some time after receiving the *agrégation* to arrive at an agreement about a subject for a doctoral dissertation with the professors at the Sorbonne. By the end of 1929, however, Mounier had virtually reached a decision not to embark on the teaching career to which the course of studies he was undertaking would normally lead him. Deeply convinced that the times in which he lived represented a profound crisis of civilization, depressed at the extent to which he believed that Christianity was implicated in the social evils which characterized that crisis, persuaded that there were no adequate means of expression for the young generation, Mounier began to think of establishing a new review.[1] In this desire, Mounier was no different from many of his contemporaries, for the early thirties were marked by a proliferation of reviews and ephemeral

[1] See the letter cited on p. 30, note 2.

journals in which young people expressed both their discontents and their aspirations for a better society. But Mounier's experience was to be exceptional in that *Esprit*, the review of which he was the principal founder and which he directed until his death, was the only new review of the nineteen thirties to survive the Second World War.

Bertrand de Jouvenel's early experiences with politics were of a different order from those of either Simone Weil or Emmanuel Mounier.[1] The son of Henry de Jouvenel, a diplomat, member of Parliament, and newspaper editor, Bertrand de Jouvenel was introduced to the political world early in life. He joined the Radical-Socialist Party, in which he was associated with the 'young Turks',[2] ran unsuccessfully for Parliament in 1928 (although under age) against a conservative candidate, and wrote a book on the crisis of American capitalism after a visit to the United States in the early thirties. By 1934 he was disillusioned with the Radical-Socialist Party and opposed to the French parliamentary system. He resigned from the party that year and launched a short-lived weekly called *La Lutte des Jeunes*, which reflected his hope to achieve the social ideals of both the traditional French left and French right without, however, accepting the left's parliamentary system or the right's capitalist system.[3]

After the episode of *La Lutte des Jeunes*, de Jouvenel became a foreign correspondent, travelled widely, and interviewed such leading figures as Mussolini and Hitler. His political preoccupations of 1934 remained, however, and in 1936 he joined forces with the Parti Populaire Français, which was formed by Jacques Doriot, a former communist. De Jouvenel's enthusiasm for the P.P.F. and its leader was tragically misplaced. Doriot

---

[1] De Jouvenel was the only one of the six thinkers discussed in this book who did not specialize in philosophy at the university. His university studies were in mathematics and biology, as well as in law. I am grateful to M. de Jouvenel for providing me with this information.

[2] De Jouvenel has commented on this phase of his experiences in *Arts*, No. 565, 25 April–1 May 1956, p. 7. This article, on 'Les Jeunes Radicaux', forms one of a series of articles of 'Une Grande Enquête de Gilbert Ganne sur les mouvements intellectuels d'avant-guerre, "Qu'as-tu fait de ta jeunesse?" ', *Arts*, Nos. 560–76, 21–27 March through 11–17 July 1956.

[3] See *La Lutte des Jeunes*, I (25 February 1934), for his letter of resignation from the Radical Socialist Party. For an interview of the time, see Philippe Boegner, 'L'Heure des ligues? VII. Les Nouveaux-nés', in *Marianne*, 18 April 1934, p. 9.

offered only a demagogic anti-communism, and he eventually
became a nazi collaborator during the occupation. De Jouvenel
left the P.P.F. at the time of the Munich Pact, which the P.P.F.
supported but which he opposed.

Most of de Jouvenel's pre-war writings do not resemble the
main books he was to write during and after World War II.
Their subjects are more topical than are those of his later
works,[1] and some of his newspaper articles display a curious
mixture of syndicalist doctrine and authoritarianism.[2] There
is a readiness to recommend vast schemes of social reorganization of which he was later to become suspicious.[3] He placed
Mussolini and Hitler in the category of 'restorers of social
order' and raised the question of whether an accommodation
with them by the Church and 'the humanists' was necessary
and possible.[4] At the same time, however, *Le Réveil de l'Europe*,
which was published in 1938 and which de Jouvenel indicated

---

[1] Bertrand de Jouvenel, *L'Économie dirigée*, Paris, 1928; *Vers les états-unis d'Europe*,
Paris, 1930; *La Crise du capitalisme américain*, Paris, 1933.

[2] 'Non, les ouvriers français n'ont pas renoncé aux grands et beaux espoirs du
XIXe siècle. Ils affirment leur capacité politique. Ils sauront se conduire eux-
mêmes selon le rêve proudhonien. Ils ne se laisseront pas prussianiser.

'Le syndicalisme français, détourné de sa voie par Marx et Guesde, reprend son
essor.' *L'Émancipation Nationale*, 15 April 1938, p. 5.

He wrote of Spain before the civil war: 'Il suffisait de faire régner le patriotisme,
le sentiment d'une juste subordination de chacun à la chose commune; il suffisait
d'imposer de petits sacrifices régulièrement consentis; il suffisait d'imposer silence
aux braillards et de faire reculer l'insolence des intérets particuliers. Il suffisait de
gouverner.' Ibid., 7 January 1938, p. 8.

[3] 'Transformer des faubourgs en forêts, des pâtes d'immeubles en jardins, fonder
des cités nouvelles avec leurs vastes maisons communes et leurs terrains de jeux,
entourés d'un réseau de petites demeures familiales, changer en un mot la figure
de la France, tel est le seul moyen de transformer la condition de la classe ouvrière
au delà de ses espérances.' Bertrand de Jouvenel, *Le Réveil de l'Europe*, Paris, 1938,
p. 219.

[4] 'Partout les régimes autoritaires ont offert de conclure et ont conclu des
concordats. Ils se sont montrés déçus lorsque les autorités ecclésiastiques n'ont pas
marqué la coupure psychologique entre l'ancien ordre de choses et la tentative de
restauration, lorsqu'elles n'ont pas stimulé vigoureusement les esprits, et entraîné
les coeurs aux tâches nouvelles. Il y a eu alors des conflits où les autorités civiles ont
apporté souvent de la maladresse et de la colère. Il y eut alors, dans le camp du
spirituel, des révoltes contre la collaboration ébauchée, des rappels éloquents de la
primauté du spirituel. Cette primauté effectivement, n'était pas en cause. La
seule question qui se posait était celle-ci: Y a-t-il, dans certaines conjonctures
historiques, des redressements nécessaires, comportant parfois des brutalités
fâcheuses, et l'Église est-elle dans son rôle en faisant comprendre la nécessité de
l'oeuvre, ce qui ne l'empêche pas d'intervenir pour adoucir certains procédés?'
Ibid., p. 282.

he had been working on between October 1933 and August 1937,[1] is clearly the product of an important formative period in the development of his political thought. Some of the ideas which he expresses in later works can be traced back to themes which appear in this pre-war work: a low opinion of democracy, concern with the historic growth of the power of the state, emphasis on the need for some form of moral unity in society, rejection of utilitarianism, a severely critical view of the Enlightenment, and a cyclical view of the historic development of political forms.

IV A Quiet Voice from a Distant Shore

For all the differences in the experiences during the nineteen thirties of Aron, Sartre, Weil, Mounier, and de Jouvenel, they had in common direct experience with the political forces that were agitating Europe. Sartre may have been fundamentally apolitical, and Aron may have been an analyst rather than a participant, but they had both lived in Germany during the final surge of nazism before its conquest of power and they lived in Paris, where they could hardly escape the swells of the political turbulence of the period. Albert Camus' engagement in the political world was real—more real than the lyricism of some of his early writings might suggest—but his link with Europe was indirect. He was inescapably tied to Europe, but at the same time he was sufficiently remote from it during his youth to acquire a detachment that is one of the characteristics of his thought. Camus has been criticized for the inadequacy of 'the temple of a new Mediterranean sun-cult' he is alleged to have built,[2] and while the criticism is unjust it does have foundation. It may be, however, that Camus' preference for the Mediterranean over the north is less important for whatever virtues the southern shores may have than for its reflection of Camus' capacity to stand back from Europe, even when he was deeply immersed in its history, and view it through the eyes of a stranger.

Camus was educated in the public schools, the Lycée, and the University of Algiers. He received the Diplôme d'Études

[1] De Jouvenel, *Le Réveil de l'Europe*, p. 13.
[2] Herbert Luethy, 'The French Intellectuals', in George B. de Huszar, Ed., *The Intellectuals, A Controversial Portrait*, Glencoe, Illinois, 1960, p. 448.

Supérieures in philosophy in 1936, but the tuberculosis which he had acquired in 1930 disqualified him from pursuing his studies further. Like Mounier, Camus decided early not to follow a teaching career and devoted himself instead to the theatre and journalism, professions which he was always to enjoy, and like Simone Weil, whose own writings he was to admire greatly and make available to the public, his activities were constantly inspired by compassion for the poor and a zealous pursuit of justice.

Camus joined the Communist Party in 1934, and while accounts differ as to whether he left it during 1935 or 1937, the reason for his separation from the party, regardless of when it occurred, seems to be that he took a pro-Moslem position against the position of the Communist Party.[1] He was one of the organizers in Algiers of the Amsterdam-Pleyel Committee, an organization founded by two pro-communist writers, Henri Barbusse and Romain Rolland, which was the French section of the Comité Mondial pour la Lutte contre la Guerre et le Fascisme. Along with some friends, he organized the Maison de la Culture at Algiers, which appears to have quickly come under the control of the Communist Party and which sponsored lectures by anti-fascist writers.[2] In 1936, he founded the Théâtre du Travail, whose purpose was to make the drama available to the common people and whose participants were mainly sympathetic to left-wing political movements. In 1937 the Théâtre du Travail was dissolved, possibly in connexion with a breach between Camus and the Communists, and by October of that year Camus organized its successor, the Théâtre de l'Équipe, which seems to have been without political connexions and inspired exclusively by love for the drama.

Camus appears to have earned his living during 1936 and 1937 as an actor with the Radio Algiers company which toured Algerian cities and villages, and at various times as a salesman of automobile accessories, an employee for a ship-brokerage firm, and an employee at the prefecture. In 1938, however, he

---

[1] This and other biographical data appear in Albert Camus, *Théâtre, récits, nouvelles*, Préface par Jean Grenier, textes établis et annotés par Roger Quilliot, Bibliothèque de la Pléiade, Paris, 1962, p. xxix.
[2] Ibid., pp. xix and 1689.

began a career in journalism. From the fall of 1938 until September 1939, he worked for *Alger-Républicain*, which had been formed to support the Popular Front. In September 1939, he became the editor of *Le Soir Républicain*, an evening paper of similar outlook, and when, after a long struggle between Camus and the wartime censorship,[1] the paper was closed by the authorities in 1940, Camus left Algiers for Paris.

Camus published only two books before 1940: volumes of essays and stories which often revolve around the themes of nature and the body.[2] They are of little importance with respect to his political ideas, except in so far as they reflect an aspect of Camus' outlook which he never abandoned: a belief in the importance of beauty and happiness. Camus' most important political writings did not appear until after World War II. His newspaper articles during the thirties, however, are important documents of the development of his political ideas. His trial reporting displays an acute sense of justice and the desire to employ his professional talent in the pursuit of justice.[3] His approach to broad political or social questions is characterized by the effort to get at the truth through an examination of facts and without regard to preconceived notions.[4] And the main theme of his most important work in

[1] It got to the point where the censors struck out passages from Hugo, Voltaire, Pascal, Huxley, and even Jean Giraudoux, who was the High Commissioner for Information. See *Le Soir Républicain*, 27 November 1939.

The original masthead of the paper read simply *Le Soir Républicain*. Beginning on 16 November 1939, these words were added: Quotidien d'Information et de Critique au Service de la Vraie Paix. Beginning with the issue of 18 November 1939, the last six words were censored. On 22 December 1939, these words were added: Contre Toutes les Dictatures. Beginning with the issue of 28 December 1939, these words too were censored.

[2] *L'Envers et l'endroit*, Algiers, 1936, republished in Paris, 1958; *Noces*, Algiers, 1938, republished in Paris, 1947.

[3] As in his reporting of the trial for murder of Sheik El-Okbi, who was acquitted (*Alger-Républicain*, 23–29 June 1939); of the trial for fraud of Michel Hodent, who was acquitted (*Alger-Républicain*, 10 January, 4 February, 22 February, and throughout March 1939); of the penalties inflicted on striking municipal workers (*Alger-Républicain*, 7 and 28 December 1939); and of the unjust and disproportionately severe sentence inflicted on a group of workers accused of burning farm property during a strike (*Alger-Républicain*, 26, 27, 28 and 31 July 1939). There is a convenient summary of the Hodent case in Philip Thody, *Albert Camus 1913–1960*, New York, 1961, pp. 9–10.

[4] As in the series of articles 'Misère de la Kabylie', which appeared in *Alger-Républicain*, 5–15 June 1939, and most of which were reprinted in Albert Camus *Actuelles III, Chronique algérienne 1939–1958*, Paris, 1958.

political theory, *L'Homme révolté*, which was not published until
1951, appeared in his review of Ignazio Silone's *Bread and Wine*
in the spring of 1939: 'The militant who is too quickly convinced is to the true revolutionary what the bigot is to the
mystic. For the greatness of a faith is measured by its doubts.'[1]
The philosophy of doubt and moderation which Camus expressed only after years of thought about both Europe's history
and his own personal experience was already foreshadowed by
these lines written in Algiers before World War II.

V   War and Occupation

The Second World War naturally disrupted the lives of
everyone. Each of the men, with the exception of Camus, who
volunteered for military service but was rejected because of his
ill health, served with the French forces while France was at
war. Aron was in the air force, Mounier (who was exempt from
military service because he had lost the sight of one eye at the
age of thirteen) entered the Services Auxiliaires of the army,
Sartre was with the artillery, and de Jouvenel was in the
infantry. For each of them, the war was to be a determining
experience, either in confirming them in their prior preoccupation with political problems or in turning them towards
them in a way which they had not followed before.

Simone Weil was in Paris when the Second World War
broke out, and in the spring of 1940 she was trying to persuade
the military to set up a special corps of nurses to provide first-
aid treatment in the front lines. The armistice interrupted this
effort, which she later pursued unsuccessfully in a correspondence with Maurice Schumann, who was with the Gaullist
resistance group in London. She left Paris for southern France
in June 1940, spent most of the next two years at Marseille,
and made several efforts to go to London. Concerned about
her parents, who were of Jewish descent, who wanted to
escape Vichy's anti-Semitic laws, but who did not want to
part from her, she went with them to New York in 1942. In
France, she had participated in the distribution of the clandestine resistance publication, *Les Cahiers de Témoignage Chrétien*,
and by July of 1942 she was in contact with Maurice Schumann,

[1] *Alger-Républicain*, 23 May 1939, p. 2.

whom she had known as a student, seeking a mission—in her words, 'preferably dangerous'—in Metropolitan France.[1] She succeeded in getting to London in November 1942, but neither her plan for a special nursing corps nor her request for a mission in France was approved. She wrote reports for the Free French organization, however, a task which seems to have inspired the book-length *L'Enracinement*, which must surely have come as a surprise to resistance officials considering ways and means of renovating post-war France. She had tuberculosis, she did not eat adequately, and in April 1943 she went into hospital. In August she died, with most of her writings unpublished.

After the armistice, Raymond Aron went to London, where he became an editor of *La France Libre*, a resistance publication directed by André Labarthe. This publication was started in the fall of 1940. It was published in London and reprinted in Algiers and Cairo. It was reported to have a circulation of almost 40,000 and that a clandestine edition circulated in France.[2] Some of Aron's articles for *La France Libre* were reprinted in separate volumes in France after the war.[3] These articles are not, however, to be placed in the category simply of wartime propaganda on behalf of the resistance. They naturally bear the mark of the circumstances under which they were originally written, but they are scholarly political analyses of totalitarianism, democracy, war, and the possibilities of reform in post-war France. And one can find clear lines of continuity between his pre-war writings and what he was to write later, after the war. In particular, Aron had definitely settled on his central instrument of political analysis: the idea that 'one chooses always, in history, between wholes' and that 'the worst form of utopian thought is reduced to a misunder-

[1] The biographical data so far referred to in this paragraph rest on Simone Weil's letters to Maurice Schumann, in Simone Weil, *Écrits de Londres et dernières lettres*, Paris, 1957, pp. 185–215.

[2] *La France Libre*. Edition Anthologique pour la France, No. 1. Apportée par la R.A.F. (n.l.n.d. but London after January 1944). The only other number of *La France Libre* in the Bibliothèque Nationale in Paris is Vol. I, No. 1 (November 1941) of the Édition pour la France. These publications are tiny: the first measures $10 \cdot 5 \times 13 \cdot 5$ cm. and the second $9 \times 12 \cdot 5$ cm., probably in order to facilitate their delivery from the air.

[3] Raymond Aron, *De l'Armistice à l'insurrection nationale*, Paris, 1945; *L'Âge des empires et l'avenir de la France*, Paris, 1945; *L'Homme contre les tyrans*, New York, 1944, and Paris, 1945.

standing of the solidarity between good points and bad
points or of the incompatibility between equally precious
values'.[1]

Mounier was captured shortly before the armistice, released,
and then demobilized in July 1940. He went with his wife to
Grenoble and then to Lyon, where they lived in poverty until
July 1941, when his income, mainly from teaching and lecturing, became adequate to permit him to rent an apartment.[2]
Mounier's attitude toward the Vichy régime was equivocal for
a short period following the fall of France. He had been a critic
of the social and political systems of the Third Republic for
so long that he seemed to think momentarily that it might be
possible to achieve his goals by working within the Vichy
régime.[3] He quickly altered this view, however, and he had
continual difficulty with the censors while he produced the ten
issues of *Esprit* which appeared between November 1940 and
August 1941, when the publication was banned. Mounier
opposed collaboration with the Germans, and he exploited his
position in a Vichy youth group and his opportunities to
lecture at schools and assemblies organized by the Vichy
régime to convey an anti-totalitarian message.

After *Esprit* was banned, Mounier organized a centre for
clandestine studies, which he later claimed was 'the first
federated organ of the resistance in the southern zone'.[4]
Lyon was a centre of resistance, and Mounier was able quickly
to make contact with the people who were in the process of
founding the famous group, Combat, and Mounier wrote that
his own study group was formed with the agreement of Henri
Frenay, André Philip, and François de Menthon, all leaders of
Combat.[5] Little is known about the activities of Mounier's
group, except for its preparation in 1941 of a Declaration of
Rights which was published in *Esprit* after the liberation.[6]
It is not known either how closely Mounier worked with

[1] *L'Âge des empires et l'avenir de la France*, p. 15.
[2] The main sources of biographical information about Emmanuel Mounier are
the special issue of *Esprit*, 18 (December 1950), and *Mounier et sa génération*.
[3] See Mounier's 'Entretiens X', in *Mounier et sa génération*, p. 260.
[4] 'Faut-il refaire la Déclaration des Droits?', in *Les Certitudes difficiles*, Paris, 1951,
p. 165.
[5] Letter of February 1945 to Jéromine Martinaggi, in *Mounier et sa génération*,
p. 316.
[6] See the article cited in Note 4.

Combat. Vichy, however, regarded Mounier as the intellectual leader of the movement, and he was arrested in January 1942, along with several leaders of Combat. He spent most of that year in prison, and he succeeded in securing his own and the other prisoners' temporary release by going on a hunger strike. At the trial, the prosecution was unable to prove that Mounier participated in the Combat movement and he was released.[1] Mounier then moved to Dieulefit, in the Drôme, where he kept in contact with his friends by holding two congresses of the *Esprit* group[2] and where he continued to study and write. Mounier also contributed to two other resistance journals, *La France Intérieure* and *Les Cahiers Politiques*, which was the organ of the Comité Général d'Études, the main resistance organization for planning the future of post-war France.[3]

When Camus arrived in Paris in 1940, he went to work for *Paris-Soir*, although not as a writer. He finished his novel *L'Étranger*, and when the Germans invaded France in the spring, Camus moved to Clermont with the staff of *Paris-Soir*. In the fall he moved to Lyon, and in January 1941 he left France for Oran, where he finished *Le Mythe de Sisyphe* and worked on *La Peste*.[4]

Some time in 1941, Camus returned to France. He later wrote that he made his decision to join the resistance when, in Lyon, he read of the execution of Gabriel Péri, a French Communist deputy, in December 1941.[5] Probably he entered the Combat group at Lyon through Pascal Pia, who had been the editor of *Alger-Républicain* and who had gotten Camus his job with *Paris-Soir*. Pia was one of the leading resistance journalists. He was for a while editor of *Le Progrès de Lyon*, which was an important resistance newspaper, and in February 1943 he became editor-in-chief of *Combat*.[6] Sometime after late March 1944 Pia made Camus his second-in-command at *Combat* and, according to Claude Bourdet (who was one of the top leaders of the entire Combat group),[7] from that time on the

[1] For the Combat trial and Mounier's experience in prison, see *Esprit*, 18 (December 1950), pp. 721–75; 1032–8; and *Mounier et sa génération*, pp. 316–58.

[2] *Esprit*, 18 (December 1950), p. 1045.

[3] Henri Michel, *Les Courants de pensée de la résistance*, Paris, 1962, pp. 796–7.

[4] Camus, *Théâtre, récits, nouvelles*, p. xxxii.   [5] Ibid.

[6] Marie Granet and Henri Michel, *Combat, histoire d'un mouvement de résistance de juillet 1940 à juillet 1943*, Paris, 1957, p. 140.

[7] Ibid., pp. 132–3.

paper was all Camus'.[1] By the time *Combat* appeared openly late in August 1944, Camus had become its editor-in-chief.

In 1943, Camus had moved to Paris, where he worked as a reader for the Gallimard publishing house. In addition to his work for *Combat*, Camus also contributed to other clandestine journals, including the *Revue Libre* and the *Cahiers de Libération*.[2] These resistance writings were published either anonymously or under the pseudonym Louis Neuville, so their readers did not know at the time that they were the work of the same man who was acquiring a reputation as the author of *L'Étranger*, which was published in 1942, and *Le Mythe de Sisyphe*, which was published in 1943.

Of all the six thinkers, Jean-Paul Sartre appears to have been the most decisively affected by the experience of the war, at least with respect to his acquisition of a political consciousness. One day, perhaps, Sartre will produce a full account of his own development during these years, but, for the time being, the fullest account of his experience appears in Simone de Beauvoir's *La Force de l'âge*.[3]

Sartre was mobilized in September 1939 and taken prisoner in 1940. He escaped from the German prison camp where he was held and returned to Paris about March 1941. He took up a teaching position at the Lycée Pasteur in Paris, and then taught at the Lycée Condorcet from 1942 until 1944. His play, *Les Mouches*, was produced in 1943, and his main philosophical work, *L'Être et le néant*, was published in the same year. In 1944 he retired from teaching to devote himself entirely to writing.

When Sartre returned to Paris in 1941 he was interested in joining the resistance. Simone de Beauvoir says that he organized a group called 'Socialisme et Liberté' with the object of

[1] Claude Bourdet, 'Camus ou les mains propres', *France-Observateur*, 7 January 1960, p. 18.

[2] It was in these clandestine journals that Camus' first and second 'Letters to a German Friend' first appeared. Albert Camus, *Resistance, Rebellion, and Death*, translated from the French and with an Introduction by Justin O'Brien, New York, 1961, p. 3, n. 1.

[3] Sartre discusses his childhood in *Les Mots*, Paris, 1964, and says that more autobiography will appear (p. 210). Eng. tr. by Bernard Frechtman, *The Words*, N.Y., 1964.

Simone de Beauvoir tells us that Sartre intended to produce his own account of his life and that he kept notebooks at least while he was in the army, but his letters to her during June 1940 were lost. *La Force de l'âge*, pp. 10, 431, 448, and 452, n. 1.

planning for France's future on a basis which would reconcile the two words of the group's name.[1] His efforts to integrate 'Socialisme et Liberté' into a larger group failed. Various people whom he consulted during the summer of 1941 discouraged him, and the French Communists were suspicious of him and refused to have anything to do with him at that time.[2] By 1943, however, the Communists invited Sartre to join the Comité National des Écrivains and to contribute to the clandestine publication *Les Lettres Françaises*.[3] Simone de Beauvoir also indicates that Sartre belonged to what she designates only by the initials C.N.Th.[4] He was well acquainted with Camus after 1943 and, according to Simone de Beauvoir, had links through Camus with Combat.[5]

With respect to his intellectual development, the period during which Sartre was a prisoner was apparently of decisive importance. In an interview published in 1951, Sartre said that he discovered the true nature of liberty while he was in the prison camp, and that it was at that time that he decided to become a 'militant democratic writer'.[6] Simone de Beauvoir actually reports 'a serious change' in Sartre earlier; he had decided that he would engage in politics after the war in February 1940, after he was mobilized but before he was captured.[7] She too, however, remarks upon a major change in Sartre's outlook after he returned to Paris from the prison camp. She says that she was 'disoriented' by 'the severity of

[1] Sartre's group is evidently not to be confused with the clandestine publication *Socialisme et Liberté*, an organ of the French Socialist Party from December 1941 until January 1943. Michel, op. cit., pp. 809–10.

[2] Simone de Beauvoir, op. cit., pp. 504–15.

[3] Ibid., p. 550. Sartre contributed four articles to the clandestine *Les Lettres Françaises*: 'Drieu la Rochelle ou la haine de soi', No. VI, April 1943, pp. 3–4; 'La Littérature cette liberté', No. XV, April 1944, p. 8; 'Un Film pour l'après-guerre,' No. XV, April 1944, pp. 3–4; and 'L'Espoir fait homme,' No. XVIII, July 1944, p. 2. See *Les Lettres Françaises Clandestines*, Rééditées en fac-similé, Paris, 1947.
Both communists and non-communists belonged to the Comité National des Écrivains and contributed to the clandestine *Les Lettres Françaises*.

[4] Simone de Beauvoir, op. cit., pp. 581–2. The initials no doubt refer to the committee which ran the Front National du Théâtre. This was an organization parallel to the Comité National des Écrivains. It published *La Scène Française*.

[5] Ibid., p. 604.

[6] Philip Thody, *Jean-Paul Sartre: A Literary and Political Study*, New York, 1960, pp. 40–41.

[7] Simone de Beauvoir, op. cit., pp. 442–4.

his moralism'. Until his prison-camp experience, she writes, Sartre had 'imperiously affirmed his ideas, his dislikes, his preferences . . . but he never expressed them in the form of universal maxims; the abstract notion of duty repulsed him'. Simone de Beauvoir had 'expected to find him again given over to convictions, rages, projects, but not blazing with principles'.[1] This development in Sartre's thinking is important because two of the fundamental characteristics of Sartre's political thought are the ambiguity of his use of the word liberty and the impossibility of deriving any general principles of behaviour from its basic assumptions. If Sartre has not yet clarified these issues, it is not because he has not directly confronted situations which suggest the importance of doing so.

After being demobilized, Bertrand de Jouvenel returned to the Corrèze, the seat of his family home. Between July and November 1940, he wrote *Après la Défaite*, in which he set forth his interpretation of French weaknesses and errors between the wars as compared with German vitality and sense of purpose, and this work was published in Paris in 1941, as well as published in German translation in Berlin in the same year.[2] Earlier, he had written the first volume of a history of Europe after the First World War, and he completed the second volume, which brought his account to 1932, in 1941.[3] The central theme of these three books is the incapacity of French political leadership in particular and of democratic political leadership generally between the wars: 'The drama of post-war Europe is that the political democracies did not produce the personnel capable of international collaboration and bridled the leaders with the control of classes naturally ignorant of everything beyond their frontiers.'[4] The link between these works and both *Le Réveil de l'Europe* of 1938 and books which he was to write later lies in the notions that aristocratic-based régimes are structurally better suited than is democracy to providing good political leadership, and that a nation can be strong only if its people are united by a common pattern of beliefs.

---

[1] Simone de Beauvoir, op. cit., p. 493.

[2] Bertrand de Jouvenel, *Nach der Niederlage*, Berlin, 1941.

[3] *D'Une Guerre à l'autre*, Vol. I, *De Versailles à Locarno*, Paris, 1940; Vol. II, *La Décomposition de l'Europe libérale*, Paris, 1941.

[4] Ibid., Vol. II, p. 440.

De Jouvenel taught a course on the world economy of the twentieth century at the École Supérieure d'Organisation Professionnelle in 1941-2, in which he emphasized the need for government-stimulated investment in the capital goods industries if France was to become a great power again, and his lectures were published in 1944.[1] Before the book appeared, however, de Jouvenel was pursued by the Germans, and he crossed the border into Switzerland in September 1943. His family home was plundered by the Germans, who suspected it of being an underground centre,[2] and sources close to him indicate that he was involved in the resistance.[3] De Jouvenel himself refers to a time in the Corrèze in 1943 when he plied with questions about England a young man who was parachuted to instruct the maquis of the canton of La Roche-Canilhac in guerrilla warfare and weaponry.[4] In Switzerland, he worked as a journalist and published his book *Du Pouvoir*,[5] which has evident links with *Le Réveil de l'Europe* but which will be treated below as part of the body of de Jouvenel's post-war political thought.

VI After the War

The post-World War II period was to see the five men pursue a variety of careers, but none of them abandoned the political preoccupations they had all either developed or acquired since the nineteen thirties. Mounier again took up the direction of *Esprit*, which reappeared in December 1944, six months before the other French reviews. Camus continued to edit *Combat* throughout 1944 and 1945, but he abandoned the editorship for several months during 1946 and retired from it completely in 1947. His only subsequent return to journalism was his collaboration with *L'Express* between June 1955 and February 1956, when that paper was actively promoting the political

---

[1] Bertrand de Jouvenel, *L'Économie mondiale au XXe siècle*, Paris, 1944.

[2] Rudolph Binion, *Defeated Leaders, The Political Fate of Caillaux, Jouvenel, and Tardieu*, New York, 1960, p. 403.

[3] See the publisher's preface to Bertrand de Jouvenel, *Raisons de craindre, raisons d'espérer, Quelle Europe?*, Paris, 1947.

[4] Bertrand de Jouvenel, *Problems of Socialist England*, London, 1949, p. ix.

[5] The full title is *Du Pouvoir, histoire naturelle de sa croissance*, Geneva, 1945 and 1947.

cause of Pierre Mendès-France. Apart from these journalistic activities, Camus devoted himself professionally to the writing of plays, novels, and essays.

In the fall of 1945, Sartre founded the review *Les Temps Modernes*, which he continues to direct, and, like Camus, devoted himself not only to fiction and the drama, but also to political writings. Aron contributed a few articles to the first numbers of *Les Temps Modernes*, and for a brief period he was one of its editors, but he contributed to it for the last time in June 1946.[1] He was a member of the staff of *Combat* during 1946 and 1947, and then became a regular columnist for *Le Figaro*, a position he continues to hold. Aron became a professor at the École Nationale d'Administration and at the Institut d'Études Politiques, both of which were established after the war, and in 1955 he was named Professor of Sociology at the University of Paris. For several years he was a member of the National Council of the political party founded by Charles de Gaulle in 1947, the Rassemblement du Peuple Français, but since the demise of the R.P.F. he has had no partisan political affiliation and remains an independent political analyst and critic. De Jouvenel seems to have continued to work as a journalist in Switzerland for a while after the war. He visited England in 1946 where he gathered the data for his book on *Problems of Socialist England* and he also visited the United States shortly thereafter to gather material for a book on the Marshall Plan.[2] Since then he has engaged in political and economic research, taught and lectured at various English and American universities, and served on several French official councils.

French political thought since World War II has been dominated by the works not only of the five men who survived the war but also of Simone Weil, who died in the midst of it, because by far the greater part of her writings were published posthumously in a series of volumes that began appearing after the war and continued to appear through 1960. Mounier, perhaps, was a man whose thought belongs to the nineteen thirties as much as to the post-war years, but only in the sense

---

[1] For Simone de Beauvoir's comments on Aron's collaboration with *Les Temps Modernes*, see *La Force des choses*, pp. 59–60, 108.

[2] *L'Amérique en Europe. Le Plan Marshall et la coopération intercontinentale*, Paris, 1948.

that he developed and began to give continuing expression to his central ideas early, for he was a vigorous, thoughtful, and prolific writer throughout the post-war years until his death in 1950. De Jouvenel's influence has spread from France both because of the translation of his main post-war works into English and because of his periodic lecturing or teaching in England and the United States.

The international prominence of Aron, Camus, and Sartre is, of course, great. In this connexion, it would be an error to place too much emphasis on the polemics in which they were, on occasion, involved. In the early nineteen fifties, after the publication of Camus' *The Rebel*, there was a public dispute between Camus and Sartre which attracted much attention,[1] although Camus was to say to an interviewer that he believed 'that our writers' quarrels do not have the importance that you say, except on the Left Bank, and in our personal friendships'.[2] Aron also took Sartre to task, along with other writers whose thought is impregnated with Marxism, first in articles[3] and later in his book *The Opium of the Intellectuals*.[4] The background of these debates was the Cold War and the existence in France of a large Communist Party, and much of the content of the debates revolved around the validity of Marxism. The disputes were more than simply polemics, however, and the significance of the ideas which formed the ultimate foundations of the arguments of the participants cannot be exhausted in terms only of their relation to Marxism. Aron and Camus, in particular, are powerful political thinkers in their separate ways, and the implications of their thought range far. Sartre is not a thinker of the same type, and probably not of the same order, but many of the problems with which he grapples are worthy of consideration even when his conclusions are unconvincing.

[1] The main arguments employed appear in Albert Camus, 'Lettre au Directeur des *Temps Modernes*', *Les Temps Modernes*, 8 (August 1952), pp. 317–33, and in Jean-Paul Sartre, 'Réponse à Albert Camus', ibid., pp. 334–53.

[2] Albert Camus, 'Entretien sur la révolte', in *Actuelles II: Chroniques 1948–1953*, Paris, 1953, p. 54.

[3] Reprinted in Raymond Aron, *Polémiques*, Paris, 1955, pp. 17–58. These are criticisms of the views expressed by Sartre in his three articles entitled 'Les Communistes et la paix', which appeared in *Les Temps Modernes*, 8 (July 1952), pp. 1–50; 8 (October–November 1952), pp. 695–763; and 9 (April 1954), pp. 1731–1819.

[4] *L'Opium des intellectuels*, Paris, 1955. Eng. tr. by Terence Kilmartin, N.Y., 1957.

Political thought is very much alive in France, because Simone Weil, Emmanuel Mounier, and Albert Camus took it seriously while they lived, and because Raymond Aron, Bertrand de Jouvenel, and Jean-Paul Sartre continue to take it seriously.

3

Emmanuel Mounier: Tragic Optimist

I *Esprit* and Personalism

OF the many new reviews which appeared in France during the 1930s, mainly to give expression to the fears and hopes of the young generation of the period, only one survived into the post-World War II period and continues to appear regularly. This review is *Esprit*, and its success was due largely to the talent, dedication, and energy of Emmanuel Mounier, who was one of its founders in 1932 and who directed the review until his death in 1950. Like most of the new groups which formed at about the same time, the *Esprit* group brought together people with a variety of perspectives on the crisis which disturbed them and impelled them to action, but over the years Mounier forged a political doctrine, which was to be called 'personalism', and which provided the touchstone for the initiatives and analyses of *Esprit* as long as Mounier lived.

It is questionable whether personalism is, as Mounier believed, a philosophy, although it is, as he claimed, more than an attitude and less than a system. It would be more correct to call it a set of attitudes to which Mounier continually referred and to which, on the whole, he adhered with uncommon consistency. These attitudes do not form a coherent logical structure so much as they constitute a reaction against the society in which Mounier lived, his aspirations towards a better society, and his awareness of the dilemmas of moving from the one to the other. At the same time, however, they were inspired by and superimposed upon a deep conviction of the proper relation between religion and politics which merits Mounier a unique place in the history of French Catholic political thinkers. For Mounier's ambition was no less than to sever religion from politics and at the same time infuse society with the spirit of Christianity. He faced squarely the problem of locating Christianity in the profane world of industrialization, and he did so with rigorous honesty, on terms which might not persuade but which would not offend the unbeliever.

Mounier did not build a political theory in the classical sense, nor did he attempt to do so. He regarded personalism as a philosophy which could guide men in making political choices, but he did not regard it as 'an automatic distributor of solutions and instructions, an obstruction to research, an assurance against disquiet, trial, and risk'.[1] Essentially, Mounier was a moralist: he believed that all political choices must be anchored in moral values and he did his best to elucidate them, but he knew that the specific application of values to concrete cases cannot be derived from any philosophical system, and he explicitly held that they could not be derived from his own. This was not only because, as he claimed, personalism contained unforeseeableness as a structural principle, but also because Mounier's entire political perspective, apart from those certainties he enjoyed because of his confident grasp of theology, on the one hand, and his uncontrolled prejudices, on the other, was based on contrasts and dilemmas. Critics have spoken of him as a philosopher of 'ambivalence' and of 'tension'.[2] The nature of these dilemmas will be amply displayed in this chapter. For the moment it may be enough to say that in an environment filled by men hot with certainties, there is an honourable role for men who realize that the search for truth would be meaningless if there were no possibility of error.

---

[1] Emmanuel Mounier, *Le Personnalisme*, Paris, 1950, p. 6. Eng. tr. by Philip Mairet, *Personalism*, London, 1952.

[2] Pierre-Aimé Touchard, 'Dernier Dialogue', in *Esprit*, 18 (December 1950), p. 781; Paul Fraisse, 'Sa Puissance d'accueil', ibid., pp. 792–4; Francis Jeanson, 'Une Pensée combattante', ibid., p. 856; Jean Lacroix, 'Emmanuel Mounier', in *Le Monde*, 23 March 1960, p. 8; Stanley Hoffmann, in a review of Reinhold Niebuhr, *Reinhold Niebuhr on Politics*, in *Revue Française de Science Politique*, XII (June 1962), p. 462.

Mounier's doctrinal assurance in matters of faith is noted by Henri Marrou, 'Un Homme dans l'Église', in *Esprit*, loc. cit., p. 889.

II The 'Established Disorder': Capitalism, the Bourgeoisie,
and Democracy

Mounier was a critic both of the characteristic institutions of his country and of the intellectual source from which they had emerged. Capitalism, the bourgeoisie, and parliamentary democracy were all manifestations of what he scornfully referred to as *le désordre établi*, but this in turn was only the decadent phase of a civilization in complete crisis. For Mounier believed that he was living at the end of an era which had begun with the Renaissance and had carried with it constructive values which had become corrupted and mean in the course of their development. The liberation of human initiatives which the Renaissance had brought about from the constraints of an over-burdensome social order and an excessively crystallized spiritual order was, in Mounier's view, a significant advance over the Middle Ages. It produced heroic values and it was economically constructive, but it gave way, particularly in France but elsewhere as well, to an exaggerated individualism which is destructive of the community, to a cult less of production than of money, to an ethic of comfort, and to an abstract rationalism which not only vitiated the constructive use of reason but also destroyed from the first what possibilities the Revolution of 1789 offered of building a political system which would simultaneously recognize the rights of the person and the legitimate claims of the community. Like virtually every dissident of the thirties, Mounier was anti-capitalistic, anti-parliamentary, and anti-bourgeois, but there was almost always in his criticism sufficient originality to protect him from being absorbed by the other critical currents of the time. In his attack on the individualism of 1789 he was at one with the Action Française, for example, but he could not wholly accept their pre-industrial nostalgia. His attack on rationalism was not dependent upon any ecclesiastical surrogate; rather it illuminated an aspect of the French liberal tradition which is not often understood. And his attack on democracy was an attack on existing practices and not upon the ideal, which he continued to support. Mounier's criticism of democracy was in part a criticism of the consequences of following Alain. His Christian convictions prevented him from adopting the Soviet version of Marxism. And while his views coincided in more than one respect with those of the Action Française, he was not a reactionary and could not build his vision of the future upon images of the past. At the start of his public career he called for a new renaissance and not a restoration.[1]

Of the three elements of the established disorder—capitalism, parliamentary democracy, and the bourgeoisie—capitalism was, in Mounier's view, fundamental. He thought that it was possible to imagine worse régimes than the one which existed in France during the nineteen thirties,[2] but the hostility to capitalism which was generated in him under the impact of the depression remained with him throughout his life, and was sustained by his equally deep conviction that European capitalism was in its death throes.[3]

Mounier objected to capitalism on both moral and technical grounds. The latter objections he voiced primarily during the nineteen thirties, while the capitalist world suffered from the effects of the Great Depression. Technological unemployment, overproduction, excessive concentration of ownership were among the symptoms of technical failure which Mounier cited. More fundamental, in his view, and more consistently and continuously expressed, was his objection to capitalism on moral grounds. The liberal optimism on which the whole capitalist system rested was, in Mounier's view, false. Left to themselves, free economic agents do not produce harmony; the strong oppress the weak. But even this objection was subordinate to Mounier's conviction that capitalism reversed entirely the proper order of values. Men are put at the service of the economy rather than the economy at the service of men; the economy and labour are at the service of money rather than money at the service of the economy and of labour; the profit motive drives out or warps all properly human values: 'love of work and its raw material, the sense of social service and of the human community, the poetic sense of the world, private life, inner life, and religion'.[4]

---

[1] See 'Refaire la Renaissance', in *Révolution personnaliste et communautaire*, Paris, 1935.

[2] 'Tentation du Communisme', ibid., pp. 141–2.

[3] *Le Personnalisme*, p. 119.

[4] 'Anticapitalisme', *Révolution personnaliste et communautaire*, pp. 193–4.

Unlike many of his contemporaries, such as the leaders of the *Ordre Nouveau* group with whom the *Esprit* group was at first closely associated, Mounier did not enlarge his hostility to capitalism into a general condemnation of industrial society. Although he referred early to the 'frightful rise' of the machine,[1] sometimes surrendered to a form of pastoral nostalgia,[2] and wrote in 1940 that he felt personally much closer to the peasant than to the city-dweller,[3] he could write as early as 1934 that for all its vices, modern industrial society represented progress and that 'it would be insane to want to return to the handicraft system under the pretext of returning to personal and "concrete" property'.[4] He was not afraid of the machine; he was perhaps more optimistic about the possibility of overcoming technological unemployment than the facts since his death actually warrant; and he could even see valuable aesthetic qualities in the architecture and design appropriate to the machine age.[5] He was tempted by the vision that abundance would liberate man from work, although he was not sure whether industrial rationalization would promote 'true' leisure or simply laziness.[6] But this concern about the indefinite future did not divert him from an appreciation of the benefits of industrial society: 'the spiritual genius of a people prospers only on a vigorous body: in this at least the bank notes speak the truth, commerce and industry support thought, the arts, and

[1] Letter of 16 January 1932 to Robert Garric, transcribed in 'Entretiens V', in *Mounier et sa génération*, p. 81.

[2] 'Autrefois, il y avait un peuple. Il sentait le passage des heures, l'odeur de la terre et des paysages, le frôlement multiple des âmes. Il n'avait pas le sou. Eh bien, il regardait les hommes, son métier, les événements qui venaient—pas les faits-divers, non, les événements, les *siens* et ceux des *autres*. Il ne savait pas toutes les nouvelles du monde, il ne quittait pas,—ni ses jambes, ni sa tête,—les abords de sa ville (ou de son village), il était aussi un monde de petits: petit par la fortune, petit par le coin de terre et de science qui le portait. Mais il communiait à une âme: l'âme du peuple, et par delà, le plus souvent, l'âme de sa religion. . . .' 'Argent et vie privée', in *Révolution personnaliste et communautaire*, pp. 155–6.

[3] Letter to Jacques Lefrancq, in *Mounier et sa génération*, p. 249.

[4] 'Note sur la propriété', *Révolution personnaliste et communautaire*, pp. 216–17.

[5] 'La Machine en accusation', in *La Petite Peur du XXe siècle*, Neuchâtel and Paris, n.d., but 1948, pp. 41–93. This remarkable essay is among the finest discussions of the problems and implications of industrial society which I have ever seen.

[6] 'Note sur le travail', *Révolution personnaliste et communautaire*, p. 204. Also see 'Lignes d'avenir', ibid., pp. 381–2.

the youthful heart. . . .'[1] When his fellow Frenchmen were for the first time accepting industrial society, he did not seek to divert them but rather to remind them of the risks of uniformity such a course would entail. There was in his warning some of the old habit of identifying Henry Ford with Joseph Stalin which had so seriously distorted French political thought during the nineteen thirties, but Mounier came to place less emphasis on fear of French corruption than on confidence in European judgement. In a comparison of the 'magnificently imbecilic countries' with the 'two or three absent-minded' ones, that suggests Camus' confidence in Mediterranean moderation, Mounier wrote that the latter should not be prevented from building bathrooms and model cities, so long as they build them with detachment.[2] Mounier could always see more than one side to every question, and it is not surprising that the disciple of Péguy sometimes spoke like Comte.

There was more to Mounier's approach to industrialization than simply his understanding of its material value and his impatience with the 'sort of Mediterranean anarchy and egoistic carelessness which cries out "Hitlerism" when the traffic cop takes out his book of tickets, or "robot" when it is suggested that we mitigate the overburdensome work of the housewife'.[3] With the keen intuitive sense he had for grasping the underlying significance and potentialities of certain social phenomena, even as he could wholly misunderstand the meaning of others (like purchasing on credit), Mounier was among the first of his generation to understand the implications of industrialization for the generalized application of reason in human affairs.

Mounier's attitude towards rationalism was ambiguous. On the one hand, he criticized the Voltairean rationalism which has so clearly stamped the French liberal tradition. He recognized, along with André Siegfried, that 'for a Frenchman, the Republic means first and foremost the progress of enlightenment', that in the countries with a Catholic tradition liberalism meant the liberation of reason more than it did the social democracy characteristic of the Anglo-Saxon and Nordic

---

[1] 'Lettre à quelques amis européens', *Carnets de route*, Vol. II, *Les Certitudes difficiles*, Paris, 1951, p. 328.

[2] Ibid., p. 325.

[3] 'Feu la Chrétienté', in *Carnets de route*, Vol. I, *Feu la Chrétienté*, Paris, 1950, pp. 270–1.

countries.[1] Mounier undervalued the ultimate significance of this rationalist tradition, and he did so because the self-conscious rationalism of the Enlightenment is vulnerable to caricature. One winces at the simplistic quotations which Mounier is able to extract from the more naïve political discourse of France. He wrote scornfully of utilitarianism and of a universe hardened by the 'impersonal languages of science'.[2] On the other hand, he acknowledged the encouragement which industrial society can give to a broader application of reason.

The technological approach places a system of regulation between desire and satisfaction. It operates against uncontrolled desire. Ambition motivated by purely affective forces . . . can produce limitless delirium as Hitler demonstrated. Technocratic imperialism is regulated by the yardstick of efficiency: the technocrat least disposed to socialism will establish it if organization will profit from it, the least humanitarian technocrat will hesitate to start a war which will not pay. There is therefore in the machine a sort of reason which operates against its unreason.[3]

This view, however, never became a central theme of Mounier's thought. He could see the implications of industry for society, but when he made society the central focus of his thought he inclined towards focusing on persons rather than on institutions. He had no sociology, although he recognized the need for one,[4] and in this respect it is illustrative of his preoccupations that his most monumental work—much and perhaps most of which was written while he was in prison—is his *Traité du caractère*,[5] a comprehensive and systematic study of personality. It was probably an error, from the point of view of political theory, that Mounier turned his attention around 1934 to current events, and *Esprit* ended what Mounier called its 'doctrinaire period' to enter the 'period of engagement'.[6]

[1] 'Court Traité de la mythique de gauche', in *Les Certitudes difficiles*, pp. 110–12.

[2] Ibid., p. 129. [3] 'La Machine en accusation', *La Petite Peur du XXe siècle*, p. 92.

[4] *Qu'est-ce que le Personnalisme?*, Paris, 1946, p. 57. Eng. tr. by Cynthia Rowland, *Be Not Afraid: A Denunciation of Despair*, N.Y., 1962.

[5] Originally published in Paris in 1946. Eng. tr. by Cynthia Rowland, *The Character of Man*, New York, London, 1956. References and additions which Mounier had noted for an enlarged and revised edition are included in the reprinting in Emmanuel Mounier, *Oeuvres*, Vol. II, *Traité du caractère*, Paris, 1961.

[6] Emmanuel Mounier, 'Les Cinq Étapes d'"Esprit"', *Dieu Vivant, Perspectives Religieuses et Philosophiques*, No. 16, 1950, pp. 42–44.

In Mounier's early writings there is evidence of a capacity for systematization of social facts[1] which the pressures of opting on the rapid succession of political choices which faced Frenchmen between 1934 and 1939 prevented him from developing.

If the machine could inspire a dream of reason, the organization of capitalism inspired base motives and resulted in economic failures. The worst of its products, in Mounier's view, were the inhuman types of people it created: the rich, the petty bourgeois, the proletarian.[2] The proletarian was inhuman because of his condition and was for Mounier an object of compassion and a partner in solidarity. The bourgeois, however, was the object of his scorn, and it is probably because he was moved by a passion bordering on hatred that his attitude toward the bourgeoisie displays an incoherence to be found nowhere else in Mounier's work.[3]

Mounier never approached the study of social classes in a scientific fashion; sometimes he spoke simply of exploiters and exploited,[4] sometimes he distinguished between the upper bourgeoisie and the petty bourgeoisie, as when he combined in common condemnation '*le grand bourgeois pétinist* who wants to make a deal with Hitler' and '*le petit employé* who does not want any disturbance in the vital impulse which moves him from his daily pinocle to his weekly movie'.[5] At other times he would distinguish between the bourgeoisie of heroic values

---

[1] Particularly in *Révolution personnaliste et communautaire*.

[2] 'Anticapitalisme', ibid., pp. 196–7.

[3] 'Chaque semaine, presque, ce compartiment de seconde où me contraignent les horaires de la Compagnie du Nord nourrit et amplifie en moi une haine sourde et tenace du monde bourgeois. . . . Encore la table d'hôte ici. Ils étaient quatre autour de moi: une femme d'industriel, péremptoire, d'une hargne froide; le jeune fils de patron racé, fin, intelligent, avec une brutalité et une sorte de vulgarité qui apparaît tout à coup lorsqu'il parle de "ces gens-là"; l'amie de la femme, insignifiante, qui pense avec ses bijoux, suit les autres; un cinquantaire à moustaches, type industriel d'avant-guerre, tenue modeste, régime, ne prend pas l'avion, semble avoir une grosse situation financière internationale. Voir toutes les pensées, tout l'appareil imaginatif des *ces gens-la* (ah! que cette fois l'impersonnel convient!) si servilement conformes aux dessins de Sennep et d'Avel Faivre. Ou est-ce Sennep et Faivre qui se les sont si bien assimilés? Pas un instant la pensée de chercher autre chose que grossièreté ou ambition dans tout ce peuple qui gronde à leur porte. . . .

'Une voix criait en moi: Salauds, salauds, salauds.' '*Carnets de Mounier*, Avril 1937. A bord du Général-Lépine', *Esprit*, 18 (December 1950), p. 1002.

[4] 'Des Pseudo-valeurs spirituelles fascistes', in *Révolution personnaliste et communautaire*, p. 134.

[5] 'Les Équivoques du pacifisme', in *Les Certitudes difficiles*, p. 380.

which at one time represented the creative and dominant forces of French life[1] and the petty bourgeoisie of his own era, which he saw as mean, calculating, selfish, fearful, and incapable of conceiving great enterprises or experiencing the simplest personal joys. For Mounier, the true bourgeois was the petty bourgeois.[2]

By conceiving the target of his wrath as the petty bourgeoisie, Mounier was able to criticize it from the vantage points of both aristocratic and working-class values. The upper bourgeoisie might have ground the faces of the poor, but at least it built industry, armies, and empires, which were not in themselves accomplishments in which Mounier personally took any pride but which at least did reflect ambitions worthy of admiration. But the petty bourgeois could be both an enemy of the poor and unworthy of his more enterprising ancestors. Mounier condemned him on both grounds simultaneously. Mounier probably acquired his view of the bourgeoisie from his reading of Péguy, and it was sustained as the Great Depression enhanced the protective and defensive reflexes of all economic groups. He acquired it early in life and never relinquished it; shortly before his death he reiterated his view and extended it to all Europe: 'The petty-bourgeois sickness is the cancer of all Western Europe . . . ,' he wrote.[3] And in the face of all evidence to the contrary, he never wavered in his conviction that the bourgeoisie was a declining force, eventually to be succeeded by newer and fresher social groups.

It was Mounier's belief that the bourgeoisie itself was aware of its weakness in the face of opposing social forces. Its sickness was only partly due to the avaricious, calculating habits fostered by the profit motive of capitalism; it was the result also of its fear of the groups challenging its supremacy. In Mounier's view, the bourgeoisie had lived in fear since 1848— in fear of socialism, of communism, and even of the democratic system which it had itself created. And what troubled Mounier most of all was his conviction that the most defensive and most reactionary element of the bourgeoisie claimed to be Catholic.

[1] Ibid., p. 374.
[2] 'Confession pour nous autres chrétiens', in *Révolution personnaliste et communautaire*, p. 355.
[3] 'Lettre à quelques amis européens', in *Les Certitudes difficiles*, p. 326.

This was, in his view, very difficult to explain logically. The bourgeoisie had originated and developed in opposition to Christian values; its metaphysic was essentially Voltairean. But eventually the bourgeois started going to Mass (albeit to a late one). He did so, however, not because he had been converted but because he was afraid. But Mounier did not regard Christianity as a religion for the timid; it was, in his view, a religion for the courageous. For the bourgeois to seek refuge in Christianity was hypocritical, therefore, in a dual sense. Both his motives for seeking to identify himself with Christianity and the values he wanted to defend were incompatible with the character and values of Christianity.[1]

Mounier's attitude towards democracy was based on a distinction between 'real' democracy, which was something yet to be achieved, and the liberal, parliamentary democracy of contemporary France, which he believed to be both 'strangled' by the 'reign of money' and falsified from the very start by a 'tainted ideology'.[2] In fact, Mounier's attack on democracy, like his hostility to the bourgeoisie, was mounted from several vantage points. But while it is logically possible to attack the bourgeoisie in the name of both aristocratic and working-class values, Mounier's criticisms of democracy were contradictory.

The tainted ideology underlying parliamentary democracy was, of course, the liberal individualism of 1789 which, while it had some merit, had in Mounier's view so corrupted the popular mind that fraternal relations among the members of the community had become impossible. Moreover, the same individualism which inspired the political system also inspired the capitalist economic system with the result that the political system had become captured by an oligarchy of the wealthy and transformed into 'a statism controlled by the big banks and big industry'.[3] Popular sovereignty was a snare and equality a mockery in a system in which power, press, education, culture, and even sometimes spiritual authorities were the monopoly of a caste. Corrupted by the pursuit of power, the political parties were all more or less impregnated with a totalitarian

---

[1] 'Confession pour nous autres chrétiens', in *Révolution Personnaliste et Communautaire*, pp. 336–7; 'Les Équivoques du pacifisme', in *Les Certitudes difficiles*, p. 374.

[2] 'Lettre ouverte sur la démocratie', in *Révolution personnaliste et communautaire*, p. 224.

[3] Ibid., p. 226.

aspiration to impose their views on the whole of society.[1] According to Mounier's analysis of contemporary European politics, the transformation of communism into the Stalinist dictatorship and what Mounier incorrectly regarded as 'Hitler's submission to the banks and to the Reichswehr' were not essentially different from 'the adventure by which anti-clerical republicans, Jacobins, social conservatives and opportunists took hold of the Republic of Courbet and of Péguy'.[2]

This assimilation of French democracy to totalitarianism under the control of occult capitalist powers was common fare for French social critics during the early nineteen thirties, when Mounier expressed these views. By 1938, however, while Mounier was no more indulgent towards democracy than he had been several years earlier, he shifted the basis of his attack. At this time, perhaps because of the disappointing experience of the Popular Front, Mounier no longer spoke of the state as a kind of instrument of tyranny in the hands of the capitalists; instead he attacked it for its weakness, and his criticism of French democracy becomes essentially a criticism of the practices prescribed by the liberal theory of Alain.

Mounier believed that fundamentally Alain was correct to be suspicious of power-holders, for he too believed that uncontrolled power becomes corrupted, but he doubted whether a definition of democracy as control—the 'doctrine of the distrustful peasant' or the practice of 'persecution by the persecuted'—reflected the proper attitude for citizens to take towards their government and towards one another.[3] He believed firmly that the citizens should not be defenceless before the state for he knew that there would always be tension between the claims of the state and the claims of spiritual freedom. But he also recognized that a nation can exhaust its substance and stifle its capacity for initiative if it is based on nothing but mutual distrust. Mounier was opposed to dictatorship in any form and he approved of the establishment of a balance of powers and influences. He never made clear,

[1] 'Pour une Technique des moyens spirituels', in *Révolution personnaliste et communautaire*, pp. 294–5.

[2] Ibid.

[3] 'Court Traité de la mythique de gauche', in *Les Certitudes difficiles*, pp. 104–10.

however, how this kind of balance could be prevented from producing the paralytic suspicion which he believed characterized French democracy. Although he was to make various institutional recommendations, Mounier actually had little confidence in the creative capacity of institutions. They could destroy vital initiatives, and they could at best provide a framework within which initiatives would flourish, but they could not create them.[1] At bottom, Mounier was less interested in reforming institutions than he was in reconstructing human attitudes. What was needed in France was 'a certain unanimity on fundamentals, limited to objective relationships, of course, but unquestioned and living. . . .'[2] Mounier realized, of course, that the French problem was precisely how to organize politically a society from which such agreement on fundamentals was absent. He was not a pure moralist, in that he recognized that exhortation would not bring about the results he desired unless structural changes were also introduced, but he was surely more a moralist than a builder of institutions.

Mounier's conception of democracy reflected a constant tension between his desire to free men from political concerns and his awareness that the only way to prevent an abusive concentration of power is to diffuse it, which implies enlargement of political participation. He certainly did not believe that the problem of political organization could be escaped by concentrating attention on economic or social organization. In a critical commentary on anarchism, Mounier indicated that the nineteenth-century positivists all more or less assumed that proper economic organization, based on scientific reason, would render government unnecessary or at least oppression impossible.[3] But this Newtonian image of personal relations did not satisfy his conception of a proper human society,[4] and he had no confidence, in any case, in any claim that a particular form of social or even political organization would

[1] *Manifeste au service du personnalisme*, Paris, 1936, pp. 78–79. Eng. tr. by St. John's Abbey, *A Personalist Manifesto*, N.Y., 1938; 'Pour une Technique des moyens spirituels', in *Révolution personnaliste et communautaire*, pp. 290–2.

[2] 'Court Traité de la mythique de gauche', in *Les Certitudes difficiles*, p. 109.

[3] 'Anarchie et personnalisme', in Emmanuel Mounier, *Oeuvres*, Vol. I, *1931–1939*, Paris, 1961, p. 681.

[4] 'Court Traité de la mythique de gauche', in *Les Certitudes difficiles*, p. 109.

automatically produce order and justice.[1] Yet he defined democracy as 'the system which rests on the responsibility and the functional organization of all the persons constituting the social community',[2] a definition which suggests either a sort of automatic harmony based on proper functional organization, in which case it would be similar to the system envisaged by the nineteenth-century positivists, or a constant process of discussion, negotiation, and compromise in which the citizenry at large would necessarily be deeply involved. But Mounier explicitly rejected a participatory notion of democracy. 'Democracy is not and must cease to be a system in which everyone pretends to competence in government.'[3] This view rested in part on a belief that government is a vocation appropriate for a limited number of people with the particular talent for it, just like any other specialized operation. More importantly, it also rested on Mounier's view that politics was not of as much importance for man's destiny as other activities. The political life is less important than simply living; the role of the citizen is less important than the role of the man. Excessive preoccupation with the political tends to make a religion of public affairs and conditions the public to an acceptance of totalitarianism. In Mounier's view, democracy had become a religion of which everyone wanted to be both a priest and a parishioner; the proper role of the citizen, on the contrary, is not to be a governor, it is to know how to be properly governed.[4]

At the same time, Mounier did not believe that the citizen's role should be merely that of a passive subject. The people must take positions on the broad ideological questions which affect the régime, they must protect themselves against abuses of power, and they must co-operate with one another in social organizations. The people should select and control their representatives, but they should leave the actual business of governing to specialists and avoid the dictatorship of the local

[1] 'Pour une Technique des moyens spirituels', in *Révolution personnaliste et communautaire*, pp. 290–2.

[2] 'Lettre ouverte sur la démocratie', in *Révolution personnaliste et communautaire*, p. 222.

[3] 'Pour une Technique des moyens spirituels', in *Révolution personnaliste et communautaire*, pp. 293–4.

[4] 'Lettre ouverte sur la démocratie', in *Révolution personnaliste et communautaire*, pp. 222–4; 'Pour une Technique des moyens spirituels', in *Révolution personnaliste et communautaire*, pp. 290–4.

café. It is difficult to reconcile this essentially electoral conception of democracy with the institutional recommendations
which Mounier sketched out at the same time. He conceived of
a régime which would be both organized on the basis of separate
functional hierarchies and decentralized on the federalist
principle.[1] His views on economic organization were based on
the notion of self-governing corporations.[2] He was always
aware that such a system could produce disintegrating particu-
larisms, and towards the end of his life he departed from this
initial Proudhonian inspiration and placed greater emphasis
on the need for governmental unity.[3] But the whole bent of his
analysis was towards bringing institutional forms into closer
contact with the people affected by them, at the same time as
he could not conceal his conviction that politics was, after all,
a secondary occupation.

There is in Mounier's approach to democracy a sort of
dialogue between Locke and Rousseau. On the one hand, there
is the representative principle which assumes a pattern of
vigorous group life that both sustains and limits the decision-
making process of the governors. On the other hand, there is
the nostalgia for an impossible small community and the recommendation of the federalist substitute. But while Mounier could
not accept Locke's majoritarianism,[4] neither could he accept
the notion of complete and constant absorption in the political
affairs of the community which is implied in the application
of Rousseau to the modern state, because he wanted to save the
larger share of man for private life. Mounier's institutional
recommendations were never wholly convincing, but his aim
was clear enough: to make it possible for variegated social forces
to transmit their impulses into politics without producing either
tyranny or anarchy. Perhaps this is why, in his last reference to
democracy, Mounier defined it as 'the *search* for a form of
government which is articulated on the spontaneity of the
masses, in order to assure the participation of the subjects in
the objective order of power'.[5]

---

[1] *Manifeste au service du personnalisme*, pp. 212–13.
[2] 'Anticapitalisme', in *Révolution personnaliste et communautaire*, pp. 198–200.
[3] *Qu'est-ce que le Personnalisme?*, p. 98.
[4] *Manifeste au service du personnalisme*, pp. 209–11; *Le Personnalisme*, p. 127.
[5] *Le Personnalisme*, p. 127. Italics added.

III   Religion and Politics

Mounier was troubled by the corruptive characteristics of what he called the 'established disorder'—capitalism, parliamentary democracy, and the reign of the petty bourgeois spirit—not only because they conflicted with his own moral principles, but also, and more importantly, because he regarded their existence as signifying the failure of Christianity, and particularly of Catholicism, to come directly to grips with the modern world. On the one hand, capitalism, liberal democracy, and the bourgeoisie had emerged and triumphed in conflict with the Christian spirit, yet Catholics were among the forces seeking to conserve them. On the other hand, the Catholic Church itself had lost direct contact with the modern world. What Mounier regarded as the great contemporary historical forces, 'American expansionism, Soviet communism, the Asiatic awakening', were all 'external to Christianity', while the Catholic Church remained linked to pre-modern civilization.

What are the sectors of its present power? In Europe: Ireland, Poland, Spain, Rhineland Germany, Austria, Hungary, Southern Italy; in France: Brittany, Alsace; outside of Europe: South America, Canada. This means, preponderantly, the old Hercynian bases of the patriarchal and feudal society where it was first implanted. The failure of Christians to provide leadership for urban and industrial civilization is inscribed there, geographically. This map is not the map of a triumph, it is the map of a sin.[1]

This solidarity of Christianity with declining social forces, this failure of the Catholic Church to assume the leadership of the urban and industrial world, this lag between modernization and Christianity were the profound sources of Mounier's concern. However, if Mounier was concerned he did not despair, because his perspective was the perspective of centuries

[1] 'L'Histoire chrétienne', in *Feu la Chrétienté*, pp. 120–1. See also *L'Affrontement chrétien*, Neuchâtel, 1945, p. 44: 'Christianity in our countries is rapidly becoming a religion of women, old people, and the petty bourgeoisie. It is about eliminated from the tough element of our modern populations: the working-class element.' Eng. tr. by Katherine Watson, *The Spoil of the Violent*, London, 1955, West Nyack, N.Y., 1962?

and his point of reference was a Church which is the world's
oldest continuing institution. Mounier did not implicate the
Church in the failure of Christianity to make adequate contact with the modern world. The Christian message rarely
arrives exactly at the right historical moment.[1] The Church
could, of course, make historical errors and such a hypothesis
may be entertained when it makes a decision; the Church is a
church of human beings, and subject to error.[2] Nor was the
failure the result of any necessary solidarity between Christianity and a given social order. There is no logical connexion
between any social or political system and Christianity, hence
the decline of pre-industrial society, with which Catholicism
has been so largely identified, does not mean the end of
Christianity; it means simply the end of one form of Christendom, which can be replaced by another. The failure was the
failure of Christians themselves to adapt the Christian method
to the exigencies of industrial civilization. Christians had failed
to incorporate the eternal Christian values in social structures
and personal habits adapted to the modern world.[3]

Mounier's approach to the problem of reconciling Christianity to industrial society is central to and characteristic of the
entire cast of his thought. He resolutely refused to identify the
cause of Christianity with any particular social or economic
system. He insisted that Christianity was not necessarily
connected with the established disorder of the present; it was not
connected with *any* particular social or political order. 'We
know very well that the Church is and can only be indifferent
to the democratic structure or to the authoritarian structure
of government, to the extent that they are only combinations
relative to place and time.'[4] No one can say 'whether a
socialist type of economic structure is more desirable for the
progress of the Kingdom of God than a market economy . . .'.[5]
'. . . Nothing is more ambiguous, fragile, and open to question
than political deductions drawn from Christian principles.'[6] No

---

[1] 'Feu la Chrétienté', in *Feu la Chrétienté*, pp. 257–8.
[2] 'Christianisme et communisme', in *Feu la Chrétienté*, p. 198; Letter of 9 October
1949, to André Dumas, in *Mounier et sa génération*, p. 408.
[3] 'L'Histoire chrétienne', in *Feu la Chrétienté*, p. 121.
[4] 'Court Traité du catholicisme ondoyant', in *Feu la Chrétienté*, p. 36.
[5] 'Feu la Chrétienté', in *Feu la Chrétienté*, p. 265.
[6] 'L'Agonie du christianisme ?', in *Feu la Chrétienté*, p. 23.

political movement, therefore, can claim identification with Christianity, whether it be of the left or the right, revolutionary or conservative.[1] Mounier disliked the label of 'Christian democrat' for this very reason: it suggested an invocation of Christian approval of purely practical political choices.[2]

To this extent, therefore, Mounier's purpose was to disassociate religion and politics. At the same time, however, he was convinced that it was essential for the Christian to play a political role. Christianity did not imply any political system or policy, but it did 'command a spirit in politics'.[3] It required a participation in politics in the sense that 'Christianity commands man to an active presence to everything temporal . . .'.[4] This is the duty of incarnation, the need for the Christian to be present in the world, to seek to suffuse the world with Christian values. There can be no withdrawal, resignation, or passivity on the part of the Christian.[5] The Christian cannot divide his life into two segments: one devoted to earthly problems, the other to those of heaven.[6] It is true that the spiritual and the temporal can never be identical, but Augustine's City of God is neither imaginary nor separate from the world of men; it is incorporated into the earthly city itself.[7] The absolute can never be achieved on earth, but the relativity of politics must be thought out against a backdrop of absolute principles.[8]

It is in connexion with his description of the perspective of the Christian that Mounier coined the expression 'tragic optimism'.[9] For despite his emphasis on 'engagement'—a word which he helped to popularize during the nineteen thirties, well before it became fashionable to speak of it in connexion with the *littérature engagée* of the existentialists

[1] Ibid., p. 14.
[2] 'Lettre à Monsieur le Secrétaire-général de la Police' of 19 June 1942 (written while in prison), in *Mounier et sa génération*, p. 339.
[3] 'Christianisme et communisme', in *Feu la Chrétienté*, p. 159.
[4] 'Feu la Chrétienté', in *Feu la Chrétienté*, p. 247.
[5] 'Confession pour nous autres chrétiens', in *Révolution personnaliste et communautaire*, p. 341.
[6] 'Christianisme et communisme', in *Feu la Chrétienté*, p. 142.
[7] 'Feu la Chrétienté', in *Feu la Chrétienté*, pp. 248–9.
[8] *Le Personnalisme*, pp. 17–18.
[9] 'Pour un Temps d'apocalypse', in *La Petite Peur du XXe siècle*, pp. 19–20, and 'Le Christianisme et la notion de progrès', ibid., p. 132.

following World War II—and despite his frequent references to
'revolution', he had a conception of political change quite
unlike that of most publicists who enter the political arena.
Mounier's mind was fashioned by history, and particularly by
religious history, rather than by the stuff of contemporary
politics, however much he was interested in the latter. He
thought of revolution, not primarily in terms of barricades, but
in terms of the action of Christian subversives in the Roman
Empire. And while he was convinced that the future lay with
socialism, he was less concerned with socialism than with the
new Christianity he hoped was arising and which he believed
could alone purge this socialism of its 'enormous potential for
tyranny'.[1] This was not to be the work of a day; on the contrary, Mounier's perspective was the perspective of centuries,
and he looked with equanimity on the possibility of some
dictatorial purgatory which would clear the terrain of its
encumbrances so that a new Christendom might be produced. '. . . The mould which covers the modern world has
taken such a hold that the collapse of its entire decrepit
structure is necessary before there can be new growth. Before
our Renaissance, it has been said, we need a new Middle
Ages.'[2]

There was in Mounier's 'tragic optimism' a similarity to
what Raymond Aron has labelled the 'catastrophic optimism'
of the Marxists. Just as orthodox Marxism looks on a crisis of
capitalism as essential to the triumph of socialism, so did
Mounier regard the total collapse of the civilization he was
convinced already was in crisis as the necessary prelude to
the establishment of the new civilization for which he so
ardently hoped. Unlike the Marxists, however, Mounier was
not sure what kind of purgatory the world would have to go
through before it could be revivified and improved. The image
which captured his imagination was that of the Rome of the
basse époque, decadent and under the attack of barbarians who
had little to recommend them but their vitality, but who could
be made the bearers of proper values. Many Christians of the
fifth century believed that Rome was the particular form of
civilization appropriate to Christianity, and that the barbar-

[1] 'Christianisme et communisme', in *Feu la Chrétienté*, p. 199.
[2] 'Refaire la Renaissance', in *Révolution personnaliste et communautaire*, p. 30.

ians were an absolute evil. But some Christians understood that the barbarians could be the instruments of a spiritual regeneration, and while rejecting the violence of their actions, refused nevertheless to tie the Church to the destiny of a dying civilization.[1] Mounier drew an analogy between that era and his own day, and on repeated occasions he referred to the new barbarians who might perform the work of levelling after which a new civilization could arise. Sometimes the barbarians appear to be the fascists,[2] sometimes the communists,[3] sometimes 'Babbitts bearing crosses, teeth, and hearts of gold';[4] sometimes they are 'perhaps distant, lost in the murmurs of the Orient, perhaps they are passing us in the streets'.[5]

This apocalyptic vision does not appear in Mounier's writings until World War II, and it is no doubt related to his momentary hesitation about the proper attitude to take towards the Vichy régime. But to the extent that he may have equated the nazis with the barbarians, he opposed the barbarians with all his resources. He would in all probability have done the same regardless of who the barbarians appeared to be, for despite his criticisms of bourgeois democracy, he seems in the last analysis to have preferred it to any other existing system. But if this be correct, we may ask why Mounier felt it necessary to place so much emphasis on his apocalyptic hypothesis. A prophet may hold that the final extirpation of the bourgeoisie can be accomplished only by fire and brimstone,[6] but the

---

[1] 'Entretiens XII', in *Mounier et sa génération*, pp. 297–8; 'Suite Française aux Cinq Étapes d'"Esprit" ', in *Dieu Vivant, Perspectives Religieuses et Philosophiques*, No. 16, 1950, pp. 51–52.

[2] 'C'est le césarisme constantinien qui a frayé les voies au christianisme, Napoléon à la Révolution. Pourquoi ne serait-ce pas le fascisme qui accoucherait l'Europe nouvelle?' 'Entretiens XII', 8 May 1941, in *Mounier et sa génération*, p. 300.

[3] As in the reference to the barbarians made after the defeat of Germany, in 'Les Cinq Étapes d' "Esprit" ', in *Dieu Vivant, Perspectives Religieuses et Philosophiques*, No. 16, 1950, pp. 51–52.

[4] 'Le Christianisme et la notion de progrès', in *La Petite Peur du XXe siècle*, p. 150.

[5] *L'Affrontement chrétien*, p. 47.

[6] 'Ne disions-nous pas, il y a quelques années, que nous ne sortirions de l'homme bourgeois, de l'Église bourgeoise, que par le fer et par le feu?' 'Entretiens XII', 8 May 1941, in *Mounier et sa génération*, p. 298.

The oscillation between prophetism and politics in Mounier's thought is pointed out by Jean Boulouis, ' "Les Certitudes difficiles" d'Emmanuel Mounier', *Revue Française de Science Politique*, II (April–June 1952), pp. 374–87.

citizen may ask why, if barbarians can be tamed, bourgeois society cannot also be cured of its ailments.

The question is all the more relevant in the light of Mounier's analysis of the manner and effectiveness of Christian behaviour in the past, because Mounier believed that the obligations of Christian engagement remained fundamentally the same, regardless of the kind of situation in which Christians found themselves. Just as his image of contemporary society was based on an analogy with Rome of the fifth century, so was his conception of the proper behaviour of the Christian modelled on that of those Roman Christians who refused to identify their faith with any particular set of temporal institutions. The Christians of Rome conformed to a way of life imposed by others; they did not try to conceive of new modes of life nor did they succumb to what would currently be called the obligation to be 'constructive'.[1] Their action was 'lateral, indirect, oblique'.[2] They did not withdraw from the life of their society, but neither did they seek directly to change it. They disturbed temporal institutions as little as possible, and then only by refusing to commit acts of idolatry.[3] Yet within three centuries they took possession of the Empire. Mounier seems to have believed that this kind of behaviour, which had successfully implanted and diffused Christianity, would also be adequate to transform some new society established by barbarians, but that it would not be adequate to transform the existing society, which he believed to be doomed. It is as though he had grafted on to his profound religious convictions the Marxist conception of the patterns of social change, and seen its confirmation in such various developments as the war, the first victories of fascism, the growth of American power, and the growth of Soviet power. Mounier's tragic optimism generally was the expression of his conviction of the capacity of Christianity not only to survive a succession of social and political orders, but also to affect them profoundly, and this view rested both on his faith and on a considerable body of historical evidence. But when he applied his tragic optimism to the contemporary world, he combined it with a premonition of impending disaster which may turn out to be correct but which surely was

---

[1] 'Feu la Chrétienté', in *Feu la Chrétienté*, p. 238.
[2] Ibid., p. 248.   [3] Ibid., pp. 238 and 248.

not proven. The very fluctuations and uncertainties of his specific diagnoses might have suggested to him how precarious the projection of contemporary events can be. In this sense, one may say of Mounier's application of his tragic optimism to his own time what Mounier said of those Christians whose historical pessimism his own tragic optimism was in part designed to oppose: it expressed only his own situation in the world.[1]

IV The Good Society

Mounier defined his vision of a good society in terms of personalism and community, which he contrasted with individualism and society. The notion of the individual was too superficial and abstract, and carried connotations too egoistic and isolated, to satisfy him. Similarly, the notion of society was too impersonal and mechanistic in its connotations to satisfy him. By personalism he meant to convey the idea of a wholly humanized individualism; by community he meant essentially a fraternal society. Most importantly, the notions of person and community depended upon each other, in Mounier's thinking, in a way which the individual and society did not. He seems to have thought that individuals could exist in societies on a purely unaffective basis, but that this was impossible with respect to the persons of a community. In Mounier's scheme, the person is partly defined in terms of his affective relation to other persons in the community, and Mounier held an organic notion of the community as a collective person, a kind of person constituted of persons.[2]

What prevented Mounier from reaching the totalitarian conclusion which must follow from such an organic view of society was his belief that only a perfect community had the right to be totalitarian, but that there could be no perfect community in this world.[3] He believed, however, that historical societies had temporarily approximated the ideal, and that certain social groups within the larger society temporarily

---

[1] 'Pour un Temps d'apocalypse', in *La Petite Peur du XXe siècle*, pp. 19–20.

[2] This paragraph is based on Chapters II to IV inclusive of *Révolution personnaliste et communautaire*. See also 'Relais et patrouilles', in *Feu la Chrétienté*, pp. 208–9.

[3] 'Révolution communautaire', in *Révolution personnaliste et communautaire*, pp. 102–5; 'Principes d'un rassemblement', ibid., pp. 113–15 and 123–4.

achieve the kind of communion which he postulated. Indeed, he believed that all men experience at one time or another this kind of relationship, in the form of love and friendship.[1] Mounier himself surely experienced it in the early meetings, for example, of the people who were to found and develop *Esprit*.[2] He does not seem to have questioned the extent to which his historical views might have been distorted by legend. History, as Simone Weil pointed out, is written by the survivors. But what are the conditions of approximating on a national scale to the bonds of affection that we know are possible in the forms of love and friendship?

Mounier knew that every social order is a function both of human motives and of concrete forms of economic and political organization. In his prescription for the economic organization of society, Mounier succumbed to the danger he was later to warn against in interpreting Papal condemnations: that of adopting the opposite of what is condemned.[3] 'A non-capitalist society,' he wrote in 1935, 'whatever its mechanisms, must start from principles diametrically opposed to those of the present economic system.'[4] This meant, for Mounier, a socialist form of economy, albeit a highly decentralized one, essentially corporate in its structure, and with vaguely defined provisions for the performance of central and co-ordinating functions.[5] In his early writings, Mounier sketched out schemes of social security and the principles which should govern the property system.[6] He conceived of a system which would distribute servile tasks among everyone and by which everyone would be helped also to pursue his 'personal vocation'.[7] He suggested the possibility of creating property in jobs or social functions as a way of preserving personal independence and erecting a

[1] 'Révolution communautaire', in *Révolution personnaliste et communautaire*, pp. 102–5.

[2] See Mounier's comments on the atmosphere of the Font-Romeu congress at which *Esprit* was founded in his 'Entretiens V' of 18 and 22 August 1932, in *Mounier et sa génération*, pp. 93–94.

[3] 'Feu la Chrétienté', in *Feu la Chrétienté*, pp. 262–3.

[4] 'Anticapitalisme', in *Révolution personnaliste et communautaire*, pp. 197–8.

[5] 'Révolution communautaire', in *Révolution personnaliste et communautaire*, pp. 111–12, and *Manifeste au service du personnalisme*, pp. 212–13.

[6] Particularly in *Révolution personnaliste et communautaire* and in *De la Propriété capitaliste à la propriété humaine*, Paris, 1936.

[7] 'Note sur le travail', in *Révolution personnaliste et communautaire*, pp. 206–7.

barrier against possible abuse of power by the state.[1] Politically, he was a Proudhonist in his early years, in that he urged
the decentralization of the political system; later he came to
believe that the Proudhonist formula was inadequate because
the forces of depersonalization were themselves organized on
such a grand scale that it would require similarly large-scale
organization to contain them.[2] But his early enthusiasm for
institutional invention gave way before the obligations of
engagement and Mounier's own personal bent for seeking to
conciliate opposites on a more abstract, philosophical level.
Mounier knew that a good society required good institutions,
but his heart was not so much in institutional study as it was in
seeking to change the nature of man. Even in his earlier days,
he was more specific about goals than he was about methods,
preferring to leave the latter to 'the engineers of human organization'.[3] After discussing the economic and social changes
which would be necessary for a good society, he added that
'all these measures suppose the parallel education of men; to
root out from their hearts, at the same time as the reign of
money from the social mechanism, their cupidities, violences,
pettiness, and the mediocrity to which they reduce all spiritual
life'.[4]

'Only socialization is capable, today as yesterday, of instilling
in a basically industrious people the habits of democracy,'
Mounier wrote in 1947, with reference to Germany.[5] But
neither democracy nor the socialization on which he thought
it depended sufficed, in his view, to create a good society.
Nor were a relatively high standard of living and the absence
of poverty adequate criteria of a social ideal. In 1950, Mounier
referred to the Swiss and Scandinavian 'oases' as 'hardly
enviable'.[6] The Scandinavian countries come as close as any,
in their political and social institutions, to satisfying the kinds of
requirements posed by Mounier, at least after he had moved
away from his early Proudhonian insistence on extreme
decentralization, but he was less than enthusiastic about the

[1] 'Lignes d'avenir', in *Révolution personnaliste et communautaire*, pp. 383–4.
[2] *Qu'est-ce que le Personnalisme?*, p. 98.
[3] *'Lignes d'avenir'*, in *Révolution personnaliste et communautaire*, p. 384.
[4] 'Anticapitalisme', in *Révolution personnaliste et communautaire*, p. 200.
[5] 'Pour une Politique allemande', in *Les Certitudes difficiles*, p. 360.
[6] 'Lettre à quelques amis européens', in *Les Certitudes difficiles*, p. 327.

quality of life which he found there. There was much he could
praise in Swedish life, of course, but this glimpse of a socialist
society convinced him that more than democracy, prosperity,
and peace were essential for the kind of life to which his
personalism aspired. The virtues which he found lacking from
this otherwise well-ordered society were 'suppleness' of life,
spiritual 'passion', and 'internal flame'.[1] Mounier's references
to 'flame' and 'passion' in this context are meant essentially as
individual, as the projection of a kind of spiritual energy. But
he came close to projecting similar values on the collective
level as well. Writing critically of the Popular Front, he said in
1938: 'Abundance, peace, leisure, pay increases, that is all
completely legitimate, but is it all that one can find to say to a
civilization which is dying? . . . Where is the revolutionary
appeal of great epochs to heroic accomplishments, to a universal
mission, to the asceticism of the militant?' Mounier did not
exclude happiness from his vision of the good life, but he
looked also for energy, devotion, and sacrifice.[2] Heroism,
risk, grandeur—these are what he demanded by way of
liberation from 'the bourgeois ideal of comfort and security'.[3]
To be sure, he wanted these heroic values to be inspired
constantly by generosity and love, 'that spiritual good which
unites all by leaving distinct those that it unites' and which is
'accomplished only by gift'.[4] But the question is not what
Mounier wanted so much as the implications of the appeal itself.
The appeal is so multi-faceted that it hardly bears analysis.
It reflects states of mind ranging from that of the romantic
revolutionary to that of the religious ascetic. It is less the
expression of an ethical attitude which might inspire varied
courses of action with a common purpose than an appeal to
varied discontents. Mounier was neither a demagogue nor a
fanatic, but the appeal to abstract collective passions has been
one of the curses of the twentieth century. His own motives
were pure enough, but this in no way alters the fact that he
heralded the decline of one civilization and the advent of
another with the sound of an uncertain trumpet.

[1] 'Du Bonheur', in *Les Certitudes difficiles*, p. 417.
[2] 'Court Traité de la mythique de gauche', in *Les Certitudes difficiles*, pp. 120–2.
[3] *Manifeste au service du personnalisme*, p. 218.
[4] *De la Propriété capitaliste à la propriété humaine*, pp. 40–41.

V   Revolution and Political Action

Like virtually every other French social critic of the nineteen thirties, Mounier employed the vocabulary of revolution, although he was convinced that he personally did not have the organizational talents appropriate to the revolutionary.[1] By revolution, he meant 'a reversal of course, a profound revision of values, a reorganization of structures and a renewal of élites'.[2] He did not advocate overthrowing the government in order to bring about these changes, but he calmly envisaged the violence which he believed would inevitably occur. '. . . The operation is fundamental, radical . . . it will not be accomplished without violent resistance which will lead to counter-violence.'[3] And yet this profoundly Christian man, for all his talk about not refusing an operation because it sheds blood,[4] about how one does not conduct politics with arch-angels,[5] about 'uprooting every social structure',[6] conceived of the basic motive force of structural changes as internal to the human heart.

It has been pointed out that Mounier regarded the social order as a function of the structure of human values and of concrete forms of social and economic organization. In this respect, his notion of revolution was consistent because he believed that it was essential to change both structures and attitudes. 'The human malady is dual; one cannot attack it on one front alone.'[7] A revolution would profoundly alter social structures, but it would be incomplete without 'the personal revolution of the revolutionaries'.[8] The personal revolution

[1] 'Entretiens VIII', of 5 June 1934, in *Mounier et sa génération*, p. 145.

[2] *Le Personnalisme*, p. 119. A few years earlier, he had defined revolution as follows: 'a whole set of transformations profound enough really to abolish the real evils of a society which has arrived at an impasse, rapid enough not to leave these expiring evils the time to poison a country by their decomposition, measured enough to allow time to mature what matures only with time'. 'Suite Française aux maladies infantiles des révolutions', in *Les Certitudes difficiles*, p. 151.

[3] Ibid., p. 152.

[4] 'Débat à haute voix,' in *Les Certitudes difficiles*, p. 204.

[5] Ibid., p. 208.

[6] 'Lettre ouverte sur la démocratie', in *Révolution personnaliste et communautaire*, p. 227.

[7] 'Révolution communautaire', in *Révolution personnaliste et communautaire*, pp. 94–95.

[8] Ibid.

which Mounier conceived of consisted in a sort of 'revolutionary bad conscience' which involved essentially the refusal to
participate in or to regard with complacency the evils of the
existing society.[1] The development of the proper consciousness
would permit the application of what Mounier called the
'technique of spiritual methods'. These involved organized
action to protect society from still worse ravages than those
which Mounier believed it already displayed, but essentially
they included forms of personal behaviour designed to avoid
participation by the person himself in the various forms of
evil which existed. Accordingly, Mounier recommended
setting examples in one's own personal life of the kind of
human relationships which he hoped the just society of the
future would support; continuous denunciation and criticism
of the evils of the existing society; and refusal to participate in
or profit personally from those social practices which characterize the *désordre établi*. By non-participation, Mounier meant
forms of action ranging from passive disobedience—mainly
strikes—to boycotts and sabotage, although his specification of
sabotage did not include anything more violent than organizing
'teams of whistlers for insolent spectacles'.[2] Most importantly,
however, Mounier urged a kind of engagement in the form of
deliberate abstention from the characteristic activities of the
social order. He recommended, always subject to the proviso
that imperative necessities could make dispensing with them
legitimate, actions deliberately designed to weaken the class
system, like travelling in third-class carriages; refusal to
speculate or even invest in perpetual, fixed interest securities;
refusal to accept income not earned by work; and turning over
to the community all income and property that could be
regarded as superfluous. He proposed, in other words, that the
individual person should live a life which would give him 'a
sense of poverty and simplicity and, correlatively, the virtue of
insecurity and improvidence, or, if you wish, the values of
adventure . . .'.[3]

Mounier preferred non-violence, but he also examined the
conditions under which violent means might be legitimate, and

[1] 'Pour une Technique des moyens spirituels', in *Révolution personnaliste et communautaire*, p. 269.
[2] Ibid., p. 308.   [3] Ibid., p. 309.

in every case this could only be after all non-violent means had been exhausted. He seems to have believed, however, that violence would inevitably accompany a revolution, even one to which the spiritual techniques would contribute, and he was continually troubled by the problem of how to limit the violence of a revolutionary movement. All political acts had to be judged by their admixture of purity and efficacity, according to Mounier,[1] and the revolution in which he was interested would have to be so controlled also.

Mounier was constantly preoccupied with the problem of how to keep revolution from the corruption inherent in violence. He did not solve the problem conveniently by some hopeful conviction that violence could be avoided. In particular, he was concerned about those moments of the revolutionary period when the vital changes which Mounier wanted to see take place in the structure of society would occur. These changes would be contracted into a short space of time and, consequently, would invite violence.[2] He seems to have regarded a sort of dictatorship of the proletariat as a necessary transitional stage. Accordingly, he was deeply concerned about the problem of means and ends. 'Yes, we must not conceal it,' he wrote in 1933, 'a dictatorship is indispensable to every revolution, especially a spiritual one, in order to neutralize and weaken the bad forces. . . . But this dictatorship can only be temporary and limited. . . . Our formula is: a material and controlled dictatorship to the fullest extent necessary, integral spiritual liberty.'[3] Later, in 1947, Mounier was no longer so ready to accept even a material dictatorship. It was all well and good for a generation to sacrifice its well-being to a future generation, 'but there has to be that assent to it without which there are only arbitrary method and sterile effects'.[4] Revolutions are brutal, but in the end they are right if they succeed in establishing greater justice.[5] But 'the end commands the style

---

[1] 'Réponse à Semprun', in *Les Certitudes difficiles*, p. 67.

[2] 'Suite française aux maladies infantiles des révolutions', in *Les Certitudes difficiles*, p. 140.

[3] 'Des Pseudo-valeurs spirituelles fascistes', in *Révolution personnaliste et communautaire*, p. 134.

[4] 'Christianisme et communisme', in *Feu la Chrétienté*, p. 138.

[5] 'Suite française aux maladies infantiles des révolutions', in *Les Certitudes difficiles*, p. 140.

of means, even the constraints, and the abuse of means heterogeneous to the end is very shortly the inevitable corruption of
the end pursued'.[1] To this problem, Mounier really had no
solution. He rejected dictatorship but he regarded it as necessary to every revolution. He aspired to something that he called
democracy, but he rejected 'formal' democracy, which he
thought would only 'dissolve the revolution'.[2] His fundamental
aim was to try to purify the men who would make the revolution. 'Our fundamental belief is that a revolution is an affair
of men, that its principal efficacity is the internal flame which is
communicated from man to man, when men offer themselves
gratuitously to one another . . .'.[3] This view contains the
revolutionary romanticism which cannot stand the test of
empirical investigation. And at the base of his appeal there
was also a dubious historical reference. The task, according to
Mounier, was to 're-invent democracy *in* the revolution, under
new forms, as Lenin tried to do . . .'.[4]

Mounier, then, saw in revolutionary change the only hope
for, indeed the inevitable outcome of, the society which he
believed to be decadent beyond recall. By revolution, he meant
both a change in social and political structure and a change in
the human heart. The change in social structure would be
essentially socialist. The change in political organization would
be the creation of a kind of democracy which would insure the
continuing responsibility of the political leaders to popular
wishes without requiring abnormal investments of time and
energy in political affairs by the citizens at large. The political
leadership would undergo a renewal, with a new set of 'popular'
élites replacing the bourgeois leadership. The change in the
human heart would produce a profound fraternity among men
and an intensity of mutual faith which would insure a kind of
continued exaltation even in the face of hardships. There
would be violence and demagogy[5] because any revolutionary
operation attracts its sadists and the passionately violent[6]

---

[1] 'Débat à haute voix', in *Les Certitudes difficiles*, p. 204.
[2] 'Christianisme et communisme', in *Feu la Chrétienté*, p. 138.
[3] 'Débat à haute voix', in *Les Certitudes difficiles*, p. 213.
[4] 'Christianisme et communisme', in *Feu la Chrétienté*, pp. 138–9.
[5] Letter of 17 February 1945 to Jean-Marie Delettrez, in *Mounier et sa génération*,
p. 390.
[6] 'Débat à haute voix', in *Les Certitudes difficiles*, p. 204.

and because of the egoism of the pre-revolutionary élites. 'The barbarism of revolutions is formed in and by the pre-revolutionary situation.'[1] But that barbarism would have to be controlled by force of the spirit, because of the intimate relationship of means and ends.

VI Marxism and Communism

In a speech which he gave in 1944, reviewing the evolution of *Esprit*, Mounier said that the fundamental problem of his movement remained what it had always been, 'to locate in spiritual elements the authentically revolutionary value that they have in face of the contemporary crisis' and 'to try to save the revolution from its inhuman temptations'. The emphasis, however, was now different from what it had been in the earlier days of *Esprit*. In 1932, the effort had been to make the spiritual revolutionary; in 1944 the necessity was to make the revolutionary spiritual.[2] The most revolutionary group in France, in aspiration if not always in behaviour, was the Communist Party and, throughout Mounier's thought, there is a constant dialogue with Marxism and communism.

Mounier seems to have read little or nothing of Marx at the time when he founded *Esprit*,[3] but by 1935 and 1936 he had certainly become familiar with Marxism, at least through secondary sources. The chronology here is important, because the middle 1930s are crucial for an understanding of the reception given to Marxism in France. It is now becoming normal to distinguish between Marx's early writings and his later ones, the dividing line being roughly 1848. The Marxism of the years since 1848 is generally called vulgar Marxism, and it is this Marxism which embraces the familiar theories of historical materialism, the class struggle, the state, surplus value, revolution, and the dictatorship of the proletariat. The early writings of Marx, on the other hand, include a philosophy

[1] 'Suite française aux maladies infantiles des révolutions', in *Les certitudes difficiles*, p. 135.
[2] 'Les Cinq Étapes d' "Esprit" ', *Dieu Vivant, Perspectives Religieuses et Philosophiques*, No. 16, 1950, pp. 49–51.
[3] 'Très bien de mettre le nez dans Marx. . . . Je m'y mettrai bien aussi un jour,' Mounier wrote to Georges Izard on 20 August 1933. See *Mounier et sa génération*, p. 130.

of which the central point is that man is alienated by his
economic condition, that the institutions of money and exchange separate him from the realities of his work, and that the
social fetishes which the organization of society creates prevent
men from giving free expression to their fullest potentialities.
The early writings of Marx do not display the economic
determinism which dominates the later writings; rather they
are a sort of clarion call for the liberation of the 'total' man who
is regarded as hedged in on all sides by the requirements of the
economy.[1]

Neither Marx nor Engels attributed much importance to
these early writings, and they made no effort to have them
published during their lifetimes. They were first published
only in the nineteen twenties and early nineteen thirties by
the Russians, and the first French translations began to appear
shortly afterwards. The new information these early writings
shed on the development of Marx's thought naturally reopened
the question of what Marxism actually was, and it began to be
suggested that in fact Marx was the harbinger of a new kind of
'humanism' which did not require adoption of the cut and
dried formulae of the prevailing Marxist orthodoxy.

Mounier, like other dissidents of the nineteen thirties, seized
upon these early writings and was always careful to take them
into account when he discussed Marxism. As early as 1935
he was emphasizing the Marxist dualism: there is 'a Marxism
that is a totalitarian philosophy which makes every spiritual
activity a reflection of economic circumstances . . .'. But
Marxism is also a remarkable method of investigation and 'a
group of intuitions about the condition of man, some of which
are similar to the most profound views of Pascal and of Christianity'.[2] By 1936, Mounier was speaking of 'the new Marxist
humanism, born about 1935', which is neither 'a fatalism nor
an absolute determinism', nor 'a philosophy of total upheaval',
nor an extension of 'bourgeois rationalism'.[3] By 1940, he was
saying that 'one even finds in the Marxist theory of alienation

---

[1] One of the clearest accounts of the distinction between 'vulgar' and 'philosophical' Marxism is Raymond Aron's 'Les Rapports de la politique et de
l'économie dans la doctrine marxiste', in *Inventaires II, L'Économique et la politique*,
Introduction de C. Bouglé, Paris, 1937, pp. 16–47.

[2] 'Tentation du communisme', in *Révolution personnaliste et communautaire*, p. 140.

[3] *Manifeste au service du personnalisme*, pp. 45–46.

one of the first forms of contemporary criticism of "objectiviza-
tion", of the transformation of man into a thing by certain
modes of life, and particularly by *matérialisation*, by money . . .
by the living world of merchandise and exchange'.[1] But Marx
did not follow the implications of this argument; rather 'Marx
froze his first criticism in a new materialism, less confining than
the one he opposed, but just as oppressive ultimately for the
real man'.[2] A year before his death, Mounier still saw Marxism
suspended between two conceptions of history: one in which
man moves freely in his efforts to overcome his alienation; the
other, in which 'history appears as a system and as an inevitability, and for better or for worse adds to the secular chain of
alienations an alienation still more cruel because it raises hope
of the end of alienation'.[3]

Such an ambivalent philosophy as Marxism was an almost
natural pole of attraction for Mounier, whose instinctive
approach to almost every problem was dialectical, in the sense
that he thought in terms of opposites. Mounier's own early
conception of ascetic virtue would tend in any case to sympathy
for a form of primitive communism. In 1934 he was mulling
over the phrase of an acquaintance: 'to integrate communism
and catholicism'. The formula was 'gross' and 'false in whatever
way one took it', but it was also 'perhaps on such a crude
formula that we will *precisely* recognize our men'.[4] It would not
be adequate to say that Mounier was attracted to Marxism
because Marxism is a revolutionary doctrine and Mounier was
a revolutionary, at least in spirit. There was more to his
affinity for Marxism than that. He approached it with
lucidity, and he was well aware of the risks which he ran as
a Catholic by flirting with Marxism. During one period in the
middle 1930s, in particular, he lived daily with anxiety in the
expectation that *Esprit* would be condemned by the Vatican.[5]
But he was convinced of the rightness of his position and of its

---

[1] 'Responsabilités de la pensée chrétienne', in *Feu la Chrétienté*, p. 93.

[2] Ibid., p. 94.

[3] 'L'Histoire chrétienne', in *Feu la Chrétienté*, p. 112.

[4] 'Entretiens VIII' of 28 June and 6 July 1934, in *Mounier et sa génération*, p. 147.

[5] 'Des nouvelles de Rome par une source très sûre. La condamnation d'*Esprit*
est donnée comme une chose à peu près décidée et imminente.' 'Entretiens IX',
30 May 1936, in *Mounier et sa génération*, p. 176. On 6 September 1933 he had
written to Paulette Leclercq, whom he was later to marry, that he believed 'more
and more that one day we will be condemned by the Church'. Ibid., p. 133.

perfect compatibility with the exigencies of Christianity, and he prepared a private report on *Esprit*'s origins, characteristics, general position, accomplishments, and potentialities for the use of Church authorities.[1] Mounier believed himself to be an anti-Marxist 'without any ambiguity whatsoever'.[2] He insisted in 1933 'that a philosophy of the Person is diametrically opposed to the communist philosophies' and that 'identical social structures cannot emerge from two radically opposed philosophies'.[3] He believed that *Esprit* was firmly anti-communist in that it was the only major review read by the 'most lively fraction of the cultured public' which was not under communist direction.[4] Yet there was truth as well as error in the communist doctrine, and Mounier's unshakeable attachment to the truth as he saw it led him to assign credit to Marxism for purveying those truths which he believed it contained. At the same time, of course, it contained errors, and fundamental ones, so that it could not be wholly adopted. This perspective on truth and error led Mounier to perform a kind of perpetual balancing act between the pros and cons of Marxism which could rightly be labelled inconstancy if it were not so clearly a reflection of his methodological ambivalence.

Sometimes Mounier tried to distinguish between Marxisms, between Marxism and communism, and between communism and Russian communism,[5] although in general his analyses were not precise in this regard. But regardless of the focus of his analysis, the same ambivalence resulted. His fundamental argument was that communism contained 'an admixture of radical errors and partially just and generous views' and that the error could only be destroyed 'by the virulence of the truth'. But 'the truth which is most likely to dislodge an error is precisely that portion of the truth which is captive of the error. It is through it that the error lives, propagates itself, and wins

[1] 'Extraits du rapport privé sur "Esprit" à l'usage de Mgr. Courbe et de l'Archevêque de Paris', in *Mounier et sa génération*, pp. 179–89.

[2] Letter of 24 October 1936, to Jacques Chevalier, in *Mounier et sa génération*, p. 192.

[3] Letter of 6 September 1933 to Georges Izard, in *Mounier et sa génération*, p. 132.

[4] 'Extraits du rapport privé sur "Esprit" à l'usage de Mgr. Courbe et de l'Archevêque de Paris', in *Mounier et sa génération*, p. 188.

[5] *Manifeste au service du personnalisme*, pp. 42–43.

hearts. It is by recapturing this breath of truth from the error which imprisons it, by giving it an avenue of escape and some vivifying air, that we will deprive the error of its capacity to lead astray.'[1] For Mounier this meant, in part, recognizing the social evils against which communism fought rather than indirectly strengthening communism through a denial of the realities to which it was opposed, and providing an alternate force to which Christian social critics could adhere.[2] In part, this meant abstaining from a general position of anti-communism, for the familiar reasons that the Communist Party (in France) has the confidence of the immense majority and most dynamic elements of the working class, that there can be no revolution in an industrial society without the support of the working class, and that 'every arrow directed at the [Communist] party wounds in its very flesh *l'espoir des désespérés* . . .'.[3] Sometimes his argument was reduced to a puerile tactical level for which there was not a shred of historical evidence, as when he stated that 'we want, here in Europe, despite all our reservations, strong communist parties because they are at present the only solid guarantee against a return of fascism . . .'.[4]

But there was a more important source of fascination in communism than these prosaic considerations suggest. Mounier saw the analogy between communism and religion which many other critics have also emphasized and, more than most of these critics, he was sympathetic to communism's religious components despite the unacceptable form in which they appeared because of his scrupulously honest criticism of the history of his own Church. What was essential to communism was not the behaviour of communist parties nor even its doctrine; it was its mysterious capacity to win certain men's hearts.[5] Along with its anti-Christian elements it bore 'a share of the Kingdom of God . . .'.[6] The acts of the French communists revealed, among other less worthy qualities, 'the faith of the early Christians'.[7] Even the O.G.P.U. and the Moscow

---

[1] 'Court Traité du catholicisme ondoyant', in *Feu la Chrétienté*, p. 53.
[2] Ibid., p. 63.
[3] 'Débat à haute voix', in *Les Certitudes difficiles*, pp. 190 and 192.
[4] 'Petkov en nous', in *Les Certitudes difficiles*, p. 239.
[5] 'Christianisme et communisme', in *Feu la Chrétienté*, p. 130.
[6] Ibid., p. 131.   [7] Ibid., p. 127.

trials had Christian counterparts in the form of the Inquisition and the trial of Galileo.[1] And if communism were to emerge victorious politically in France, its future course could be measured against the religious past: 'France would undoubtedly see its Gallican tradition reawaken, and the French people would play the same role in the new history that the very Christian kings played in centuries past, before pontifical ambitions toward universal power . . .'.[2]

If communism had its positive side, it also had its negative side, and Mounier was explicit enough about the inadequacies of Marxism and the dangers of communism. He knew that his analogy between communism and a church ended at the point where the liberty of the spirit meets the callousness of power.[3] He argued that the Christian could wonder whether any effort at social liberation could avoid ending in oppression unless it was inspired by 'the auxiliary of a transcendent Love'.[4] In this respect, Marxism fell under the same general condemnation, from Mounier's viewpoint, as liberalism. It was an extension of the rationalism and utilitarianism underlying the bourgeois democratic society which communism presumably opposed.[5] It rejected 'the existence of eternal truths and of values transcendent to the individual, space, and time' and its vision of the world excluded liberty and love.[6]

Mounier believed that the working class had a particular mission, but he knew that its interests could be distorted by a party and those of a party by its leaders.[7] He argued that a Christian could not completely adhere to 'a philosophy which denies or belittles transcendence, devalues the inner being, and tends to combine a fundamental criticism of religion with a just criticism of idealistic escapism'.[8] He knew that the Soviet Union was a dictatorship, which was bad enough, but that it was materialistic and atheistic as well, which struck at the

[1] 'Christianisme et communisme', in *Feu la Chrétienté*, pp. 136–7.
[2] 'Débat à haute voix', in *Les Certitudes difficiles*, p. 210.
[3] 'Christianisme et communisme', in *Feu la Chrétienté*, pp. 136–7.
[4] 'L'Histoire chrétienne', in *Feu la Chrétienté*, p. 112.
[5] 'Court Traité de la mythique de gauche', in *Les Certitudes difficiles*, pp. 113–17 and 125–6.
[6] *Manifeste au service du personnalisme*, pp. 49–50.
[7] 'L'Histoire chrétienne', in *Feu la Chrétienté*, p. 115.
[8] 'Christianisme et communisme', in *Feu la Chrétienté*, p. 133.

fundamentals of his faith.[1] He was disgusted with the Stalinist conformism exhibited by some of France's leading intellectuals of the Congress for the Defence of Culture,[2] which he regarded as an 'outrageous resignation of the intelligence'.[3] He had no illusions about the Soviet Union, a 'so-called popular régime', 'which makes the memory of the Asiatic tyrannies grow pale', or about the Communist Party, 'which tries to make off in the general confusion with the last remnants of the democracies'.[4] As revolutionary as he believed himself to be, he could not permit himself to believe that 'the revolution is always right'.[5] He believed himself to be a socialist, but he wanted 'a socialism which does not crush three generations to save the following ones . . .'.[6] He had nothing but scorn for people who opposed communism out of what he regarded as selfish interests, but he knew that all opposition to communism was not based on 'mystifications of class or of interest'. It stood opposed to two authentic realities: 'the Christian sense of man' and 'an irreducible sense, in the West, of the habits of liberty'.[7]

Mounier constantly displayed this ambivalent attitude towards communism, but from his first main political work until almost literally his dying day he refused either to accept Marxism integrally or to regard communism as a form of government intrinsically superior to liberal democracy. In 1935, he wrote that 'it is difficult to imagine a more inhumane régime than the present one, if a revolution did not risk opening the way today to a communist seizure of power . . .'.[8] Three weeks before his death, he wrote that he could see only two possible substitutes for the existing régime, a fascist or pseudo-fascist one and a communist one. The latter, he wrote, 'would be, in a sense, the best, but, alas, can one still think in the short term of a communism without the totalitarian plague

---

[1] 'Leçons de l'émeute ou la révolution contre les mythes', in *Révolution personnaliste et communautaire*, p. 322.

[2] 'Entretiens VIII' of 29 June 1935, in *Mounier et sa génération*, pp. 167–9.

[3] 'Court Traité du catholicisme ondoyant', in *Feu la Chrétienté*, p. 47.

[4] Ibid., pp. 63–64.

[5] 'Christianisme et communisme', in *Feu la Chrétienté*, p. 136.

[6] 'Débats', in *Les Certitudes difficiles*, p. 297.

[7] 'Débat à haute voix', ibid., p. 223.

[8] 'Confession pour nous autres chrétiens', in *Révolution personnaliste et communautaire*, p. 348.

and Russification?'[1] The key phrase here is 'in the short term'. Mounier's perspective was the perspective of centuries, the result of his deep immersion in the history of his Church and of its relations with various political systems. Mounier almost always spoke more like a leader of a church than like a political theorist. Viewed theoretically, his attitude towards communism suffers from the eclecticism against which, paradoxically, he argued in a different context.[2] But viewed prophetically, his attitude towards communism appears as a striking anticipation of a portion of the Encyclical 'Peace on Earth'.[3] Marxism is a false doctrine in certain fundamentals; the communist movement is idolatrous and rejects all notion of the supernatural. But doctrines succeed one another and political movements become transformed. Mounier was working for the transformation of a movement on which he probably had little if any impact. Like other non-communists, he tried to maintain a dialogue with the French Communist Party, but this never produced any visible effects upon that party's behaviour. His prophetic view was too detached from contemporary experience to be more than an appeal to leave the future open rather than to crystallize antagonisms into permanent ideological differences. One may wonder whether this is adequate for men who need to find their ways in the here and now.

VII   Insights and Deficiencies

It is impossible to characterize with economy the political thought of a man who literally erected ambivalence into a philosophic principle. Mounier regarded the human condition

---

[1] Letter of 1 March 1950 to Xavier de Virieu, in *Mounier et sa génération*, p. 416.

[2] 'Réponse à Semprun', in *Les Certitudes difficiles*, p. 68.

[3] 'It must be borne in mind, furthermore, that neither can false philosophical teachings regarding the nature, origin and destiny of the universe and of man, be identified with historical movements that have economic, social, cultural or political ends, not even when these movements have originated from those teachings and have drawn and still draw inspiration therefrom. Because the teachings, once they are drawn up and defined, remain always the same, while the movements, working on historical situations in constant evolution, cannot but be influenced by these latter and cannot avoid, therefore, being subject to changes, even of a profound nature. Besides, who can deny that those movements, insofar as they conform to the dictates of right reason and are interpreters of the lawful aspirations of the human person, contain elements that are positive and deserving of approval?' *New York Times*, 11 April 1963, p. 19.

as a constant state of tension, with the elements of this tension neither contradictory nor permanently resolvable.[1] The social order is a function of both values and institutions; exhortation alone is a futile instrument of social change, yet institutions are corrupted if they are not infused with the proper values. Mounier's search for a revolutionary formula was conditioned by a simultaneous concern for efficacity and purity, by the eternal dilemma of ends and means. Mounier was essentially a man of peace, and yet he could anticipate violence with equanimity. He knew that there could be no paradise on earth and that no political system could be regarded as an absolute,[2] but he also believed that there were political verities which, however relative they might be to time and place, could be regarded as absolute in the sense of the meaning of truth in experimental science.[3]

Ambivalence is likely to appear in any undogmatic approach to politics and ethics, and it is not in itself a weakness, but it became one in Mounier's thought when combined with his failure to identify the conditions which would permit the tension to be most satisfactorily tolerated. His early Proud-honian suggestions were in some cases naïve, but at least they represented efforts to sketch the institutional guide-lines of a better society. Towards the end of his life, however, Mounier had less to say about institutions, except to indicate his conviction of both the inevitability and the desirability of what he called socialism, and even this conviction was not entirely blind. He had, however, insights into the relativity of ethics which are of importance for the development of contemporary French political thought. He drew a distinction between eternal values, among which he included personal liberty, the family, and even property, and the concrete forms in which they appear historically and consequently variously. Mounier wanted to preserve the values at the same time as he was prepared to accept, indeed as he welcomed, their appearance in new forms.[4] But he never undertook to examine closely the significance of these or other values in the light of contemporary

---

[1] *L'Affrontement chrétien*, pp. 32–33.
[2] Letter of 14 March 1950 to a collaborator, in *Mounier et sa génération*, p. 416.
[3] 'Christianisme et communisme', in *Feu la Chrétienté*, p. 135.
[4] 'Pour une Technique des moyens spirituels', in *Révolution personnaliste et communautaire*, pp. 275–6.

society; this is a task which it was left to Raymond Aron to undertake only a few years after Mounier's death. Nor did he come to grips with the problem of how to distinguish between a value itself and the form in which it is expressed. How much alteration in its 'incarnation', to use Mounier's vocabulary, can a value stand before it ceases to retain its value? Life is a sea of change which threatens the stability of all forms; what are the changes that men should resist, what are the changes that they should welcome?

Mounier also had other important insights which he failed to develop, but which were to be subjected to intensive analysis by other French theorists who grappled with the problems of social and political organization. For all his ambivalence, Mounier seems to have believed that men's goals can sometimes be mutually exclusive in that the pursuit of one objective may affect the social and political system in such a way that it becomes impossible to achieve certain other goals. Writing about the consequences of a nation preparing for total war, he argued that the inspiration of the political system—whether liberal or socialist or anti-totalitarian—would be unavailing, and that the outcome for the system would inevitably be totalitarian, because of 'the internal necessity of its choice'.[1] This idea approximates to a central principle of Simone Weil's early thought—that purposes are less important than the implications of the means employed to achieve them. It also approximates to a major theme developed by Raymond Aron— that political systems are wholes which can be defined by the relationships which necessarily follow from certain fundamental choices characteristic of each system or type of system. But Mounier did not develop this theme either; it is as though he separated war from other human activities, and did not recognize that a method of analysis which applies to one can also be applied to the others.

The one central axis of consistency from which Mounier never deviated, however, and which inspired all his thought, was his insistence on the separation of religion from politics.[2] This meant, because of the particular nature of the links that

---

[1] 'Le Pacte atlantique', in *Les Certitudes difficiles*, pp. 344–5.

[2] This point is emphasized by François Goguel, 'Positions politiques', in *Esprit*, 18 (December 1950), pp. 798–800.

existed between religion and politics in France, essentially an
effort to divorce Catholicism from politically conservative and
reactionary forces, although Mounier was just as insistent that
no political group of any kind should attempt to suggest that
its political recommendations were any more desirable spiritually than others. This view led him to criticize both socialist
groups, with which he was sympathetic on the political plane,
and Christian Democrats, with whom he was at one religiously.
Quite apart from the religious and philosophical merits of
refusing to permit any political group to clothe its temporal
preferences with religious sanction, Mounier's attitude towards
the Christian Democrats had solid practical merit, as the post-
war history of Christian Democratic parties in Western Europe
demonstrates. Only by minimizing their religious preferences
can most Christian Democratic parties hope to win the support
of a majority of voters. In France, the Christian Democrats
remain a minority which may be crushed between larger,
conflicting secular parties; in Germany, the Christian Democrats have sometimes won a majority, but they have done so by
interpreting their Christianity broadly enough to embrace both
Catholics and Protestants; in Italy, where the Christian
Democrats are most closely identified with the Catholic Church,
they won a majority in 1948, but have had to govern for most
of the post-war years in collaboration with anti-clerical
groups.

Mounier always attached qualifications to his central
formula about the indifference of his Church and of Christianity generally to temporal systems. These qualifications can
be reduced to the requirement that the régime must permit
spiritual liberty.[1] It was a profound weakness of his thought that
he never undertook to investigate whether certain forms of
political or social organization might constitute greater threats
to spiritual freedom than others. He was aware that certain
forms of political organization could produce undesirable
results, regardless of the inspiration of their founders, but he
never examined rigorously the possible consequences for

---

[1] Speaking of the condemnations of communism by the Church, Mounier said
in 1949 that 'ce qui semble essentiel et qui relève de son message le plus constant,
c'est la dénonciation d'une société, quelle que soit sa structure, qui se clôt au
surnaturel'. 'Feu la Chrétienté', in *Feu la Chrétienté*, pp. 260–1.

spiritual liberty of different kinds of political organization, so great was the emphasis he placed on the development of proper attitudes. What respective roles are played by institutions and attitudes in shaping the character of a social or political system constitutes, of course, one of the continuing problems of political science. The dilemmas posed by the problem appear clearly enough in the thought of Emmanuel Mounier. They appear even more sharply in the thought of Simone Weil.

4

Simone Weil:
Sociology, Utopia, and Faith

I Two Phases of Thought

WHEN Simone Weil died in 1943, at the age of thirty-four, she was hardly known to the general public. She had been working for the Gaullist resistance organization in London and, like many other young French intellectuals, she had participated in the remarkable wave of political speculation which occurred in France during the thirties. Although she wrote a good deal, she published very little during her lifetime, and what she did publish appeared for the most part in relatively obscure journals.

The years between 1935 and 1938, during which Simone Weil underwent her spiritual conversion, constitute a dividing line between what can be called the two phases of her thought. Prior to 1935, Simone Weil wrote almost exclusively on social and political affairs; her analytical method was materialist; her sociology was functional; her normative theory was strictly secular. In short, she was a rationalist, and her early writings are the product of her rationalist phase. After 1938, she wrote more on religion and the supernatural than she did on social and political organization. Her interest in society and politics continued, however, and some of her last writings are on these subjects. These later social and political writings differ from the earlier ones in that they are spiritual rather than materialist, historical rather than sociological, romantic rather than rationalist. The later writings constitute what may be called Simone Weil's spiritual phase. This is not to say that there is not continuity in the preoccupations which inspire the political works of the two periods, or that there are not perhaps greater points of similarity between them than first readings might suggest. The Simone Weil of the rationalist phase resembles Rousseau more than any other political thinker; she of the spiritual phase resembles Burke; and the resemblance between Rousseau and Burke is greater than the latter, at least, would acknowledge. But there is a difference in tone and emphasis between the works of the two periods, as the titles of the main political essays of the two periods indicate. Each of the two phases of Simone Weil's thought is dominated by a single political essay supplemented by lesser essays inspired by a similar outlook. The main essay of the first phase is 'Réflexions sur les causes de la liberté et de l'oppression sociale'; that of the second phase is *L'Enracinement*.[1]

There has been remarkably little discussion of Simone Weil's early political and social writings. Most of the discussion of her thought has centred on her religious writings and the political writings of her spiritual phase.[2] The main reason for this, probably, is simply that 'Réflexions' was not published until after her later writings had appeared. Almost all of Simone Weil's religious writings[3] and notebooks,[4] as well as her

---

[1] The first essay is in *Oppression et liberté*, Paris, 1955; Eng. tr. by Arthur Wills and John Petrie, *Oppression and Liberty*, London, 1958. The second is book-length in itself; its full title is *L'Enracinement: prélude à une déclaration des devoirs envers l'être humain*, Paris, 1949; Eng. tr. by Arthur Wills, *The Need for Roots, Prelude to a Declaration of Duties toward Mankind*, N.Y., 1952.

[2] For a discussion of *L'Enracinement* which emphasizes its Burkean characteristics, see G. L. Arnold, 'Simone Weil', *Cambridge Journal*, IV (March 1951), 323–43.

There are some studies which include 'Réflexions' in their treatment: the chapter on Simone Weil in Lucien Guissard, *Écrits en notre temps*, Paris, 1961, Marie-Magdeleine Davy, *Simone Weil*, Paris, 1965, and Victor-Henry Debidour, *Simone Weil ou la transparence*, Paris, 1963. Davy states (pp. 20 and 24) that Simone Weil wrote 'Réflexions' after her experience as a factory worker, and Guissard seems to believe so too (p. 95). The evidence indicates, however, that she had written this essay before she became a factory worker. In a letter of 1940 referring to what can only be 'Réflexions', Simone Weil says that it dates from 1934 (*Oppression et liberté*, p. 7), and biographical accounts agree that she started factory work on 4 December 1934. There is a sharp reduction in the number of her periodical publications after December 1933, suggesting that she was working on a major study after that date. Lastly, the germs of the theme of 'Réflexions' appear in two articles published in the fall of 1933.

[3] *La Pesanteur et la grâce*, Paris, 1948; Eng. tr. by Emma Craufurd, *Gravity and Grace*, London, 1952. *La Connaissance surnaturelle*, Paris, 1950. *Intuitions préchrétiennes*, Paris, 1951; Eng. tr. and edited version by E. C. Geissbuhler, *Intimations of Christianity*, London, 1957. *Lettre à un religieux*, Paris, 1951; Eng. tr. by A. F. Wills, *Letter to a Priest*, London, 1953.

[4] *Cahiers*, 3 vols., Paris, 1951, 1953, 1956; Eng. tr. by Arthur Wills, *Notebooks*, 2 vols., London, 1956.

spiritual autobiography,[1] were published between 1948 and 1953. The main essay of her spiritual phase, *L'Enracinement*, which was written just before her death in 1943, was published in 1949, but the main essay of her rationalist phase, 'Réflexions', which was written in 1934, was not published until 1955.[2] Simone Weil herself did not repudiate 'Réflexions', despite the different orientation her thought took after 1938,[3] so it is proper in any analysis of her political thought to take first things first.

'Réflexions' consists of a critique of Marxism, a sociological analysis of the causes of oppression, and the construction of a Utopia. The critique of Marxism is in the main familiar, and it need not be developed except where Simone Weil made an original effort to replace Marxian determinism with a more intelligible theory of social change. The sociology is a mixture of Darwin's concept of the conditions of existence, Mosca's theory of social forces, and Hobbes' psychology, and will be treated in some detail. The Utopia is the product of an imaginative student of Rousseau. This combination of sociology and Utopia is rare, and the use Simone Weil made of it runs counter to the widespread view that Utopias are dangerous and to be identified with millenarianism. Simone Weil was no millenarian. Taken together, her sociology and her Utopia found a theory of democratic self-government, furnish a unique scheme for comparative social and political analysis, and provide an analytical framework which illumines the dilemmas of man's pursuit of freedom.

[1] *Attente de Dieu*, Paris, 1950. Eng. tr. by Emma Craufurd, *Waiting for God*, N.Y., 1951; *Waiting on God*, London, 1951.

[2] In *Oppression et liberté*. Still more recently published works of political interest are *Écrits de Londres et dernières lettres*, Paris, 1957, and *Écrits historiques et politiques*, Paris, 1960. Several of the essays contained in the latter two works appear in English translation in Simone Weil, *Selected Essays 1934–1943*, chosen and translated by Richard Rees, London, 1962. Some of Simone Weil's letters which were first published in *Écrits de Londres et dernières lettres* and in *Écrits historiques et politiques*, as well as others which were published elsewhere or previously unpublished, appear in *Seventy Letters, Some hitherto untranslated texts from published and unpublished sources*, translated and arranged by Richard Rees, London, 1965.

[3] She referred to 'Réflexions' as 'the great work' as late as 1943 (*Écrits de Londres et dernières lettres*, p. 227), and in 1940 she wrote to a friend that she regretted not having published it and that she thought it was *'très actuel'* and worth the trouble of not losing (*Oppression et liberté*, p. 7).

II   The Case for Utopia

Utopian political thought has been subjected to much criticism in recent years.[1] This is so for a variety of reasons, but probably the main one is that tremendous damage can be done to life and human values by groups which engage in what Karl Popper calls 'utopian engineering'—the effort to reconstruct society as a whole according to some presumably rational plan. The intractability of societies before efforts to translate prefer- ences into reality can lead to violence and the contradictory sacrifice of men to a cause conceived for their benefit. But this still leaves us with the problem of how we can properly conceive of our social goals. Even Popper concedes that 'piecemeal engineering'—step by step efforts to reduce or eliminate social evils—of which he approves may be inspired by what he calls a blueprint.[2]

Anti-utopianism is reflected in the large body of contempor- ary literature which proclaims, advocates, or simply asks whether it is true that the Western democracies have reached 'the end of ideology'. People employ the term 'ideology' in a variety of ways, but what they seem most frequently to mean by an ideology is a conception of a good society or political system or both which requires, without exception, certain specific forms of social or political organization. It may be correct that some of this literature expresses a con- servative mood and reflects a narrowing of moral interests.[3] The abandonment of efforts to change society in the pursuit of social ideals might reflect the absence of social ideals and might simply express a conservative mood. But it is also true that suspicion of or antagonism towards ideologies, as defined above, can spring not from inherent conservatism or lack of moral concern but from doubt whether the establishment of the specific forms of organization urged will actually produce the desired results. An effort will be made in later chapters to show

---

[1] See George Kateb, *Utopia and Its Enemies*, N.Y., 1963, for an examination, from an acknowledged utopian bias, of criticisms of utopianism.

[2] Karl Popper, *The Open Society and its Enemies*, 2 vols., London, 1952, Vol. I, Ch. 9.

[3] As suggested by P. H. Partridge, 'Politics, Philosophy, Ideology', *Political Studies*, IX (1961), 217–35.

that the formulations of Albert Camus and Raymond Aron, who are leading contributors to this literature, are not automatically conservative and do not exclude moral concerns. Anti-ideologists urge us not to allow our conceptions of reality to diverge from reality itself, not to pursue goals without regard to circumstances, and not to identify any given society with an ideal society. But this implies no prohibition upon conceptualization, the pursuit of goals, or the formulation of ideals.

Simone Weil's early thought is relevant to these concerns because it dealt with identical problems. She, too, was an ideology slayer. She argued that it was necessary 'to discredit empty abstractions and analyse concrete problems',[1] and that it would be 'an act of public service' to hunt down abstract entities 'in every domain of political and social life'.[2] She was committed to what she called the materialist method, by which she meant 'examining any human fact by taking less account of the goals pursued than of the consequences necessarily implied by the very play of the means put into use'.[3] She anticipated a theme which was to be developed by Isaiah Berlin by arguing that the revolutionary movements of the thirties, of which she was severely critical, assumed that a revolution would automatically solve all problems simply by abolishing them.[4] She was deeply pessimistic; she believed that there were no inherent social forces at work making for progress, and that 'the enlightened good will of men acting as

[1] From a fragment in *Oppression et liberté*, p. 173.

[2] Ibid. A sentence identical to the one quoted from appears in 'Ne Recommençons pas la guerre de Troie (Pouvoir des mots)', in *Écrits historiques et politiques*, p. 272. This volume, like most of the posthumously published volumes of Simone Weil's writings, contains essays published earlier as well as previously unpublished essays. I will not cite the original place of publication, but I will indicate in parentheses the date of first publication for previously published essays or the date of writing, if known, for previously unpublished essays. In this case, the date is 15 April 1937. An English translation of this essay appears in *Selected Essays 1934-1943*.

[3] 'Réflexions sur la guerre', in *Écrits historiques et politiques*, p. 233 (November 1933). Eng. tr. (revised version), 'Reflections on War', *Politics* (N.Y.), 2 (February 1945), 51–55.

[4] 'Examen critique des idées de révolution et de progrès', in *Oppression et liberté*, p. 180 (between 1934 and 1938), and 'Quelques Méditations concernant l'économie', in *Écrits historiques et politiques*, p. 321 (1937?). See Isaiah Berlin, 'Political Ideas in the Twentieth Century', *Foreign Affair* (N.Y.), 28 (April 1950), 351–85.

individuals is the only possible principle of social progress'.[1]
In the conflict between revolution and reform, Simone Weil
was squarely on the side of reform. Yet, at the same time, she
was convinced that a utopian vision was essential, no matter
how far distant it might be from reality.

Simone Weil believed that reformism was based on the
'principle of the lesser evil' and that this was 'certainly emin-
ently reasonable'. 'The formula of the lesser evil', she wrote,
'remains the only one applicable.' But this formula has to be
applied with 'the coldest lucidity', which means defining 'the
worse and the better as a function of a clearly and concretely
conceived ideal' and determining 'the exact margin of possibilities'. If this operation is not performed, she argued, it is
not possible to tell which is the lesser evil. And in the absence of
knowledge of which is the lesser evil, the existing balance of
forces is necessarily and reasonably maintained, necessarily
because it is an unchallenged balance of *forces*, reasonably
'because any real evil is always less than the possible evils
which an uncalculated action always risks producing'. In this
theory, what it is illegitimate to expect a revolution to produce,
it is essential for the mind to conceive. Utopian thought is
necessary if the existing social balance is to be consciously
changed without risk of creating new conditions as bad as, or
worse than, the existing ones.[2]

But if a utopian concept is essential to provide a criterion
for judgement, a knowledge of society is also required to determine the probability of achieving one's goals. Simone Weil is a
particularly interesting utopian because she continually
insisted on the futility of proposing reforms which social
analysis could demonstrate to be doomed to failure. The key
concept of her own social analysis is what she called 'the conditions of existence'. Proposals for reform, in her view, must be
compatible with the conditions of existence of a given society
if there is to be a reasonable expectation of their success. Her
central criticism of Marxism was that she saw no reason to
believe that productive forces necessarily increase and that

[1] 'Réflexions sur les causes de la liberté et de l'oppression sociale', in *Oppression
et liberté*, p. 80. This essay will hereinafter be cited simply as *Oppression et liberté*.

[2] The quotations are from *Oppression et liberté*, pp. 85 and 86, and from 'Médita-
tion sur l'obéissance et la liberté', in *Oppression et liberté*, p. 192 (between June 1936
and 1938).

social institutions automatically adapt to them, eventually producing a good society. She thought that this was a myth which bore the same relation to social science that Lamarck's theory of the propensity of living creatures organically to adapt to their environment bore to biological science, and that the development of social science required an improvement on Marxism equivalent to Darwin's improvement on Lamarck. She interpreted Darwin's improvement on Lamarck as the introduction of the notion of the conditions of existence (actually, the concept of natural selection more clearly conveys the meaning of the distinction Simone Weil wanted to emphasize); living creatures do not organically adapt to their environment, but those creatures which are so organically adapted will survive, while those which are not will perish. Similarly, for social science, Simone Weil argued that there is no single force at work, such as the productive process, which produces social institutions adapted to it, but rather that people continually make all kinds of innovations, some of which will fail because they are incompatible with the conditions of existence, others of which may endure because they are compatible with them. There is, in other words, a process of natural selection among human initiatives. These initiatives are in no way determined by the conditions of existence, but the conditions of existence render ineffective all initiatives not compatible with them.[1]

The conditions of existence include the natural environment; the existence, actions, and competition of other groups; and the way in which society organizes to deal with these two conditions.[2] This means essentially the way in which society equips itself and organizes itself for productive purposes and for warfare. These conditions form the basis of Simone Weil's sociology. It is by means of these conditions that she sought to explain the problem of social change and the existence of oppression, and it is in relation to these conditions that she sought to determine the conditions of liberty.

[1] *Oppression et liberté*, pp. 64–68; 80–84. Simone Weil repeated this argument just before her death in 'Y a-t-il une doctrine marxiste?', in *Oppression et liberté*, pp. 241–6 (1943).
[2] *Oppression et liberté*, p. 84.

III   The Functional Theory of Oppression

Simone Weil did not offer an explicit definition of oppression. She did, however, illustrate it and she did furnish a statement of what she meant by liberty. As oppression appears in her thought in relation to liberty, her interpretation of oppression may be approached by starting from her definition of liberty.

Simone Weil's ideal conception of liberty combines what Maurice Cranston calls 'rational freedom'—self-mastery through reason—and the notion that freedom is a faculty—a power to do what one has decided to do.[1] Simone Weil's ideal of liberty is essentially the capacity for complete self-determination. She conceived of the completely free man as one who would constantly hold 'his own fate in his hands' and who 'would at every moment forge the conditions of his own existence by an act of thought'.

Liberty is not, in this view, defined 'by a relationship between desire and satisfaction, but by a relationship between thought and action . . .'. The free man is self-determining in that he acts after considered judgement with respect both to his goals and to the means by which he will seek to achieve them. The importance of methodical thought to the definition is indicated by Simone Weil's comparison of her notion of ideal liberty with the solution of a mathematical problem which contains all the elements of its solution and which can be solved by a man unaided except by his own judgement.

It is essential to this ideal conception that the action which a man undertakes should follow from his own thought. A man would not be free, but 'would be wholly a slave if all his acts proceeded from a source other than his thought, whether the unreasoned reactions of his body, or the thought of another'. Simone Weil described both the Roman slave and the modern assembly-line worker as approaching 'that miserable condition'. Total liberty, therefore, excludes the subordination of one human being to another as well as action which is routinized or automatic.

This conception of liberty was presented by Simone Weil only as an ideal, inexistent and unrealizable. No man alone can forge the conditions of his existence. But she believed that

[1] Maurice Cranston, *Freedom, a New Analysis*, London, 1953, Part One, Ch. 3.

it was a conception which provided a criterion for the evaluation of situations according to whether they approached or were distant from the ideal. She had no hope of attaining her ideal conception of liberty, but she did hope that it might help men to attain 'a less imperfect liberty than our present condition . . .'.[1]

Oppression appears in Simone Weil's thought as the opposite of liberty. Absolute oppression would be a situation in which none of a man's acts proceeds from his own thought. But while Simone Weil treated liberty as an ideal, which can therefore be defined abstractly, she treated oppression, which she regarded as something only too real, in more concrete terms. In the last analysis, oppression is the deprivation of the power of thought, but its conditions are material and physical. Simone Weil objected to low wages and the economic harm done to the workers by bureaucratic inefficiencies within the factory, especially under the piece-work system, in which a worker suffers if the foremen delay in allocating jobs, supplying materials, and repairing machinery. She was concerned also with the physical aspect of oppression in the forms of fatigue resulting from long hours and dangers resulting from poor working conditions. She burned with indignation at the humiliations to which workers are subjected. Low wages, physical danger, and arbitrary treatment are burdensome in themselves, but what links them to Simone Weil's theory of liberty is that they are neither self-determined nor conducive to the exercise of methodical thought. Her fundamental objection to the material and physical aspects of oppression is that they reduce the capacity and even the desire to think.[2]

Enforced prohibition upon thought was for Simone Weil the supreme humiliation. She found it inhuman that a worker's acts should follow the rhythm of a machine, the pace of an assembly line, an arbitrary set of rules, or a foreman's unexplained command. Liberty is rational freedom and the faculty

[1] The quotations in this and the three preceding paragraphs are from *Oppression et liberté*, pp. 113, 115, 116, and 117.

[2] *La Condition ouvrière*, Paris, 1951, passim. See also Anne Reynaud, *Leçons de philosophie de Simone Weil (Roanne 1933–1934)*, Paris, 1959, pp. 136–8. This volume consists of notes taken by the author when she was a student in a class taught by Simone Weil. The pages cited confirm my interpretation of Simone Weil's concept of oppression.

to make it operative; oppression is subordination to the will
of others.

The core of Simone Weil's sociology is her functional theory
of oppression. The essence of this theory is that oppression
results from the subordination of those who execute to those
who command, and that those who command do so in the
performance of essential social functions. Simone Weil was
not an anarchist. She did not think that subordination could
ever be removed from the social order. She distinguished
between the 'subordination of individual caprices to a social
order' and a degree of constraint that is stultifying physically
and morally.[1] The only time in her early writings that she
indicated how she distinguished between oppression and
legitimate subordination was in connexion with the relationship between subordinates and superiors within the factory.

I conceive of the question of authority on the theoretical level
in the following way [she wrote]: on the one hand, the chiefs
must command, surely, and the subordinates obey; on the other
hand, the subordinates must not feel themselves delivered body
and soul to arbitrary domination, and to this end they must not,
certainly, collaborate in the preparation of orders, but be able to
understand the extent to which the orders correspond to a necessity.[2]

The distinction between legitimate subordination and oppression would seem to lie in the absence or presence of understanding on the part of subordinates of why they should obey.
But what is a necessity? At one point, Simone Weil talks of
'natural necessities', but beyond a certain level of subsistence
the weight of nature becomes a matter of human choice. On
another occasion, again in the context of industrial relations,
she spoke of balancing the legitimate material interests of
production and the legitimate rights of the workers.[3] These,
too, are matters of choice and not necessity, but Simone Weil
believed that these problems had to be settled by compromise,
and the bargaining situation furnishes the most accurate
interpretation of her notion of necessity. The subordinate
understands that his position corresponds to a necessity when
he is rationally persuaded that there is no way, in the prevailing

---

[1] *Oppression et liberté*, p. 79. See also p. 271.
[2] *La Condition ouvrière*, p. 187 (1936–7).   [3] Ibid., p. 208 (1936–7?).

conditions, to satisfy what he and the superior agree to be a necessity except by his subordination. This proposition, that commands should be justified rationally, has broad implications for social and political organization.

The abolition of all constraints, therefore, was in Simone Weil's view neither possible nor even conceivable. What was reasonable, she believed, was to try to find a form of social organization which would not be oppressive. Oppression was not, in her view, the result of conscious human desires but rather the product of necessary social relationships. She approached the problem of reducing oppression by analysing the objective conditions which produce it. The conditions are the conditions of existence which underlie her whole sociology: nature, other social groups, and the ways in which men organize to master nature and to protect themselves from other social groups. But this sociology alone is not adequate to account for oppression; it accounts only for subordination. Her theory of oppression rests also on the dynamic of competition, and this implies a psychology. Simone Weil borrowed her psychology from Hobbes.

The fundamental characteristics of the conditions of existence in Simone Weil's theory are the complexity of knowledge and the division of labour. These two characteristics necessarily produce power holders, i.e., people who dispose of the fate of others, because they both lead, although by different paths, to situations in which large numbers of people are dependent upon smaller numbers of people. The division of labour makes the co-ordinating function necessary, but this is a function which cannot be performed by everyone, in part because it requires specialized knowledge but also because there is only a limited number of co-ordinating positions. The complexity of knowledge gives certain people power over others because as long as the others regard this knowledge as essential, they are dependent upon the people who alone have it. The privileged groups which Simone Weil identified were priests, scientists and technicians, the military, specialists in the organization of economic exchange, and specialists in the aggregation and co-ordination of effort, both in governmental and private affairs. These groups did not, in her view, necessarily all appear at the same historical moment, and she did not claim that the list was exhaustive, but she thought she had listed the main ones.[1] But the exercise of power by groups which perform socially necessary functions is not, by itself, sufficient to account for oppression. The exercise of power becomes oppressive, in Simone Weil's theory, because of competition, or what she called the struggle for power.

Simone Weil's analysis of the struggle for power is similar to, but not identical with, Hobbes' analysis of the natural condition of mankind. Men are active beings who seek to determine themselves; consequently, there is conflict between the power holders and their subordinates. Moreover, the instruments of power, such as arms, wealth, or knowledge, can be acquired by others; consequently, there is conflict between the power holders and their rivals. The privileged seek to conserve their power, their rivals seek to replace them, their inferiors seek to remove them. In part, the power holders act out of a defensive reflex based on a selfish interest: it is a vital necessity for the power holders to conserve their power because it is their power which nourishes them. But power is only a means to an end which is never secure as long as power is threatened, with the result that there is never really power but only a race for power, which goes on 'sans terme, sans limite, sans mesure'. In this race for power, the power holders seek to extend and intensify their control over the human and other resources essential to the maintenance of their power. The result is oppression.[2]

So far, the analysis is essentially Hobbesian. But Simone Weil goes beyond Hobbes and attributes to the struggle for power characteristics which Hobbes sees only in its containment. The privileged do not seek to conserve their power only because of a selfish interest. They hold their privileges because they perform necessary social functions, so the defence of their positions also serves a social interest. The power holders regard it as their duty to defend their privileges because by doing so they also defend the existing social order. The preservation of order is a social necessity; the existing social order is the only one which the power holders can regard with certainty as being possible; and Simone Weil held that they are partly right. The power

---

[1] *Oppression et liberté*, pp. 88–90.
[2] Ibid., pp. 90–98; the quotation is from p. 93.

holders oppress with good conscience.[1] This is what makes a social science necessary, for without one how can any convincing argument for social change be made?

The weakness of this theory is one which is inherent in any purely functional theory of social organization; it cannot alone explain the variations in the organization of different societies. Simone Weil knew, of course, that societies were organized differently, but while she could describe these differences within the framework of her theory (the distribution and combination of power holders, the degree of concentration of power, the degree of accessibility to each functional group) she made no attempt to explain them. If she had, she would have had to go outside her functional framework. Instead, she tended to blur the distinctions among modern societies by producing a 'developmental construct' similar to that of the garrison state which Harold Lasswell was producing at about the same time (and which also rests on a functional theory of social organization).

Subordination, privilege, and power probably do have a functional base (though allowance must be made for the tendency of privilege and power to outlive their functional utility), and the struggle for power has produced and can produce oppression, but whether subordination becomes oppressive or remains legitimate depends upon the way in which the struggle for power is organized and conducted. One striking omission from Simone Weil's theory is an examination of the political organization of society and the non-functional factors which contribute to it. This is surprising in view of the important role that her 'developmental construct' attributed to the state. She thought that there was a tendency almost everywhere for societies to develop totalitarian forms of organization, more or less approximating to the Russian model, in which economic and social activities would be subordinated to the military and all, in turn, would be co-ordinated by (and consequently subordinated to) the state. Yet she had a rather rudimentary notion of a state, which she seems to have regarded essentially as a bureaucratic hierarchy. She did not analyse the institutions which constitute a state, the mechanisms by which

[1] Ibid., p. 157 and a fragment on p. 171 (1933–8). Also see 'Réflexions sur la guerre', p. 239, and 'Ne Recommençons pas la guerre de Troie', pp. 264–5.

it performs the co-ordinating function, or the relationships
between the institutions of the state and social groups. Her
emphasis on the state as a general co-ordinating agency in an
increasingly complex society is surely an improvement on
sociological theories which rely on more automatic processes of
social integration, and it has tended to be confirmed by events,
but the co-ordinating process itself is not and need not be performed in the same manner in all societies.

Simone Weil had a clear notion of how the co-ordinating
process *should* be conducted, however. In a highly bureau-
cratized society, the co-ordinating function logically fell, in her
view, to the state, 'the bureaucratic organization *par ex-
cellence*'.[1] But if co-ordination is the most essential social
function, it is also the function 'most essentially attached to the
individual'.[2] Performed by the state, the co-ordinating function
is anonymous; performed by the individual it is the exercise of
methodical thought. The exercise of methodical thought is
liberty. The ideal society, therefore, is one in which the co-
ordinating function is performed not by the state but by
everyone.

IV   Utopia

Simone Weil's Utopia is essentially a system of production in
which every worker would determine his own behaviour by
reason alone, without reference to any rules, with respect both
to his own role in the productive process and the co-ordination
of his role with the roles of all the other members of the community. In such a society, everyone would be in a position to
control the entire life of the community, so community life
would always be in conformity with the general will. Would this
not put the whole society at the mercy of a single arbitrary
act? The situation is excluded conceptually, because 'there is
only one single, identical reason for all men; they become
foreign and impenetrable to one another only when they depart
from it; thus a society in which the necessary and sufficient
condition of all material life is that everyone should exercise
his reason would be completely transparent to every mind'.[3]

[1] *Oppression et liberté*, p. 151.   [2] Ibid., p. 144.
[3] The Utopia and its conditions are described ibid., pp. 130–2; the quotation is
on pp. 131–2.

Such a society requires special conditions. The technology employed would have to be of a kind which requires the constant exercise of reason; technological knowledge would have to be widespread; there would have to be an analogy among the various specialized tasks so that every worker could understand all of them; the co-ordinating process would have to be simple enough to be understood by all. The community would have to be small, so that its nature and requirements could be understood by everyone, and so that the common interest would be obvious enough to override the temptation to rivalries.

In this Utopia, there can be no privileges based on monopolies of knowledge because specialized knowledge is shared by all. There can be no privileges based on the performance of the co-ordinating function because this function, like knowledge, is shared by all. Simone Weil's particular repugnance for what she felt to be the mentally stultifying effect of performing a limited, specialized task without knowledge of the total productive process is removed by the enlargement of the knowledge and perspective of the worker. In such a society, Simone Weil believed, external constraint would be replaced by self-discipline.

The Rousseauian inspiration of this Utopia is evident, but if the style of reasoning is Rousseauian, the Utopia envisaged is far more 'utopian' than the system produced by Rousseau. Simone Weil's Utopia extends the principle of the general will to all the detailed regulations of economic life with which Rousseau was not concerned, partly because the economy of his day was far less complex than is that of the twentieth century but mainly because he was more interested in producing uniform rules of law than he was in detailed questions of public or private administration. Simone Weil's scheme implies far more mutual dependence among men than Rousseau envisaged; not only governmental acts (which Rousseau permitted a particular group to exercise) but also private acts must proceed from a consideration of their effects upon everyone. Each act is personal and separate from those of other persons, although co-ordinated with them; although Rousseau is ambiguous on the matter of whether there is communication among the citizens in his system, there are at least assemblies;

in Simone Weil's system, there are none. She envisaged the kind of society which Rousseau thought was for gods and not for men.

Simone Weil's system differs from Rousseau's in other ways as well. Rousseau allowed for men to be deceived; Simone Weil allows for no mistakes. There is in Rousseau the possibility of men learning by experience; in Simone Weil's system, one error wrecks the society. The kind of interdependence which Simone Weil conceived takes as given the mutual understanding of the requirements of social life which Rousseau allowed time to produce. Simone Weil's scheme requires the universal application of pure reason, while Rousseau's assumed in addition to the application of reason a kind of mutual sympathy among the citizens as a whole which would inform their reason. Simone Weil's scheme represents a perfect functional harmony; Rousseau's a perfect moral harmony. Rousseau's social contract is the democratization of Hobbes' contract; Simone Weil's Utopia is the democratization of Plato's philosopher king.[1]

V   Social Reform and the Conditions of Existence

Simone Weil did not, of course, offer her Utopia as a description of any society which existed or ever would exist; it is purely an ideal. She thought, however, that her Utopian ideal would be useful as the basis for the analysis of real social systems. The critical variable in her proposed comparative method is the relation between thought and action, or the existence of liberty. Social systems would be analysed from the viewpoint of the extent to which they require or permit the exercise of methodical thought by the citizens and the range of activities which the exercise of thought controls. Any comparative analysis based on graduations in proximity to the ideal would be difficult and complex, but the focus of examination would be the extent to which men are self-determining within the framework of any given social system.

[1] The conditions of the Utopia also relate to a problem which Simone Weil did not discuss in her early writings, but which she did discuss just before her death, in 'Y a-t-il une doctrine marxiste?' This is the problem of particular wills or of group morality. Rousseau tried to solve it by his construction of the general will and by his enigmatic references to associations. Marx tried to solve it by changing the property system. Simone Weil tried to solve it by ending the division of labour.

In the effort to designate the main factors which affect men's opportunities for self-determination, and hence which are critical points of application of the analysis, Simone Weil singled out the nature of their work, the nature and extent of their political participation (directly through the exercise of the co-ordinating functions or indirectly through control of the co-ordinators), and the extent to which they are dependent upon others for their livelihood and for their physical security. Combining these factors, she concluded that 'the least bad society is one in which the common man is most often obliged to think while acting, has the greatest possibilities of exercising control over the whole life of the community, and possesses the most independence'.[1]

Simone Weil was not only interested in analysing and classifying societies; she was also interested in changing them. She was continually preoccupied, however, with the necessity for all proposals for reform to be compatible with the conditions of existence. On the basis of her analysis that oppression is caused by struggles for power among the knowledgeable specialists in the performance of social functions that are essential in a complex society characterized by the division of labour, she reasoned that to abolish oppression entirely would require a return to the kind of primitive society which would have no need for such specialists. Applying her principle of compatibility with the conditions of existence, she immediately pointed out that this would be impossible. An advanced machine-age society cannot return to a primitive form of economic organization, she argued, because it is so dependent on its machines that it would not be able to survive economically without them. Moreover, she argued, any society which attempted such a move backwards would simply put itself at the mercy of any society which did not, with the result that oppression would be imposed from the outside.

The problem, therefore, is not how to abolish oppression, because that is impossible, but how to reduce it. Simone Weil was very pessimistic about the possibilities of doing so. One reason for this was that she did not distinguish adequately between those conditions of existence which place insurmountable barriers before efforts at social or political reform and those

[1] *Oppression et liberté*, p. 136.

which can themselves be reformed. She knew that all the conditions of existence were not beyond men's power of choice. She took the natural environment and the existence of other groups as given, but she thought that the organization and methods which men utilize to deal with nature and other groups are matters over which men might have some control. She held a narrower view of what was possible, however, than in fact was the case.

Simone Weil seems to have believed that no change in economic organization would be acceptable if it did not at least maintain the level of productivity of the existing one.[1] It has been possible to remedy some (but not all) of the factory conditions with which Simone Weil was so directly concerned, while raising the level of productivity. Similarly, while the state may be more than ever necessary as a general co-ordinating agency, there is more than one way to organize a state. Like Mounier, Simone Weil approved heartily of decentralization, but she believed that no centralized power ever decentralized of its own volition and that the centralizing tendencies of a civilization marked by rivalry, conflict, and war were too powerful to be overcome. This centralizing tendency is real, but the experience of western societies indicates that decentralizing devices of various kinds are a condition of the successful performance of the state's co-ordinating function.

Actually, Simone Weil's analysis admits such possibilities. It does not deny that men can enlarge their freedom; it holds only that all of freedom's conditions cannot be maximized simultaneously in an industrial society and in a competitive world. Simone Weil herself thought that some optimum point of equilibrium might be reached,[2] but as this would necessarily be a theoretical point for any dynamic society, her view implies the constant pursuit of freedom through adjustments compatible with the conditions in which men live. In a fashion not generally associated with builders of Utopias, Simone Weil produced a theory which points more to the difficulties of enlarging human freedom than it does to any halcyon society in which men would be freed of all limitations on their capacity for self-determination.

[1] *Oppression et liberté*, pp. 266–7.
[2] Ibid., p. 136.

VI   Sociology and Utopia

There are several implications of Simone Weil's early thought for contemporary politics and political science. In the first place, it demonstrates that the construction of a Utopia is not necessarily a radical act. A Utopia implies the desirability of a different order, but if it is tested against a sociology which reasonably represents the conditions of society it can illuminate the risks of certain attempts at social change and demonstrate the impossibility of pursuing a given goal indefinitely without creating conditions worse than those already existing. Simone Weil's Utopia was an ideal representation of a society in which men are fully self-determining by virtue of their reason alone. Yet the whole bent of her sociological analysis was to emphasize the obstacles in the way of approximating the ideal, in part because she did not distinguish adequately between necessary and dispensable conditions, in part because she ignored purely political arrangements—such as the suffrage—as an instrument for promoting liberty. But we do not need to accept all her conclusions to value the analytical method by which she reached them. The notion that proposed social goals must be analysed against the conditions of existence in order to determine their probable consequences is fundamentally sound. Simone Weil held this notion because she wanted to avoid choices between 'capitulation and adventure'.[1] This suggests a quest for greater certainty than is likely to be attained in human affairs and, in the absence of certainty, Simone Weil tended to treat the conditions of existence more as prohibitions on social reform than as social institutions susceptible themselves of being reformed. But even if the balance had been the other way, adherence to her central scheme of social analysis would have both kept alive the inspiration for reform and guarded against unwarranted social risks.

A second set of implications that follows from Simone Weil's theory is institutional. The only general recommendation she made for legitimizing subordination—by introducing the subordinate to an understanding of why he should obey—was relatively modest, but, here again, the particular form of

[1] Ibid., p. 86.

Simone Weil's own recommendations is less important than the conclusions to which her theory leads. The kind of control over the life of the community which her theory prescribes for the common man calls for devices to require that power holders justify their decisions, institutions to permit popular control over the power holders and methods by which the common man can participate in decision-making himself. Simone Weil was not an ideologist (in the sense of someone who argues on the basis of *clichés*), but these institutional implications of her theory include practices which are historically associated with democracy. Her theory calls for a larger application of these practices, functionally, vertically and horizontally,[1] than any democratic system at present enjoys, but it is not a distortion of her theory to say that it presents a non-ideological argument in favour of the practices of democracy.

Lastly, Simone Weil's suggestion that her concept of liberty be used as the variable for the analysis and comparison of political systems presents an interesting challenge to the comparative study of political systems. To the extent that liberty be regarded as a value, its use would imply an evaluation, and the mode of analysis would have the virtue of emphasizing what is most important about a political system: its consequences. But the use of Simone Weil's concept of liberty as a comparative variable does not require its application as a criterion of evaluation. Simone Weil defined liberty as a relation between thought and action; in this respect it may be regarded simply as a functional category, a way in which social functions are performed.

The utility of Simone Weil's concept of liberty both as a criterion of evaluation and as a functional category for comparison parallels the whole structure of her early thought. She conceived a Utopia, but she knew that pure utopianism could be either idle or dangerous. She constructed a functional sociology, but pure functionalism tends to legitimize any method of performance of a necessary social function.[2] Simone

---

[1] That is, the individual should participate in determining the activities of the functional groups to which he belongs, his decisions should affect operations at all levels of the hierarchies in which he is placed, and the range of his decisions should be as broad as possible.

[2] I apply here the reasoning that C. Wright Mills applied to what he called 'grand theory', in *The Sociological Imagination*, N.Y., 1959, pp. 48–49, n. 19.

Weil combined functional social analysis with a utopian ideal in the effort to find a way of performing essential social functions that would enlarge the possibility of the individual to determine the conditions in which he lives. Only a fool would say that this is easy; functional sociology demonstrates how difficult it is. Without a utopian conception to inspire the task it would be impossible.

VII The Power of Grace

The second phase of Simone Weil's life and thought dates definitively from 1938, after the decisive religious experience of Easter of that year when, as she wrote, 'the thought of the Passion of Christ entered into me once and for all'.[1] From this point on, all her writings consistently testify to her religious preoccupations and they place a continuing emphasis on the supernatural that is absent from her early writings. The spiritual quality with which Simone Weil's later works are suffused gives them a tone and temper which are quite different from the more coolly analytical early writings, but it would not be correct to say that they represent simply a wholesale substitution of faith for reason, and Simone Weil certainly did not lose any of her interest in the problems of social and political organization. What may well be the last essay which she wrote (it is her only essay which ends in the middle of a sentence) is a study of Marxism, in which she qualified as 'ingenious' Marx's notion of 'taking society as the fundamental human fact and studying it, as the physician does matter, with respect to the relations of forces',[2] and said that this was probably also the intention of Machiavelli, '*qui était un grand esprit*'.[3] Simone Weil remained until the end as convinced as she had ever been of the need for a social science, but while she had thought earlier that such a science could be founded wholly upon a mechanistic view which took into account only forces, she now thought that the scientific study of society needed to be integrated with the equally scientific study of the supernatural.[4]

[1] *Attente de Dieu*, p. 75.

[2] 'Y a-t-il une doctrine marxiste?', in *Oppression et liberté*, pp. 225–6 (1943); also see the fragment on p. 215 (1943).

[3] Ibid., p. 236; also see the fragment on p. 216 (1943).

[4] *The Need for Roots*, pp. 294–5. Except where otherwise noted, all translations from and citations of this book refer to the English translation.

Recognition of the supernatural is the main distinguishing theme of the later writings of Simone Weil. Her application of the supernatural to politics consisted in the substitution for what she had earlier stated to be 'the enlightened good will of men acting as individuals', which she had regarded as being 'the only possible principle of social progress',[1] of 'the supernatural intervention of grace'.[2] She came to believe that 'there is no other force on this earth except force',[3] that social morality varies from group to group and its weight reflects the force wielded by the groups which inspire it,[4] that these forces are essentially blind,[5] although they have their origins in the functional requirements of need and warfare,[6] and that the only exceptions to this mechanistic view of society—which is essentially that of the group behaviourist school of contemporary political analysis—are produced by inspirations which have their origin outside of this world and are received through divine grace. She retained the functional sociology of 'Réflexions', in that she continued to believe that everything on earth is matter and hence governed by forces which are presumably measurable, but while she always believed that man had a choice between ceding blindly to the forces of necessity and acting according to his own interpretation of necessity, earlier she had seen the source of the decision for freedom in 'enlightened good will'. Now she saw the only source of the decision as divine grace.

She also remained as convinced as ever that it was necessary to conceive of a perfect form of civilization, not on the ground which she might earlier have adduced, that it is the rational thing to do, but on the ground that it is a Christian truth 'that progress towards a lesser imperfection is not produced by the desire for a lesser imperfection'.[7] She thought that men would

---

[1] *Oppression et liberté*, p. 84. In one of the several outlines of this essay, Simone Weil wrote: 'C'est seulement dans l'homme pris comme individu que se trouvent la clairvoyance et la bonne volonté, uniques sources de l'action efficace.' (*Oppression et liberté*, p. 267.)

[2] 'Y a-t-il une doctrine marxiste?', in *Oppression et liberté*, p. 238. Also see the fragment on p. 218 (1943).

[3] *The Need for Roots*, p. 220.

[4] 'Y a-t-il une doctrine marxiste?', in *Oppression et liberté*, p. 238.

[5] *The Need for Roots*, p. 243.

[6] 'Y a-t-il une doctrine marxiste?', in *Oppression et liberté*, p. 246.

[7] *The Need for Roots*, pp. 217–18.

not produce much of a civilization without religious inspiration, although she did not believe in the establishment of any church, for that would identify religion with a given political system, thereby both tarnishing religion and encouraging state claims to absolute and unconditional loyalty, which is owed only to God. In Simone Weil's view, the 'proper function of religion . . . is to suffuse with its light all secular life, public or private, without ever in any way dominating it'.[1] In fact, Simone Weil never specified that the religious spirit she regarded as necessary should follow the precepts of any particular religion. She personally regarded herself as a Christian, but she never adhered to any church and she spared no church in her criticism, with the exception of the Albigensians, for whom she felt a strong attraction. She thought that when children in France were taught about religion, they should be taught mainly about Christianity, but only in the sense that French children are taught more about French history than any other history. She regarded all religious thought as genuine as long as it was universal, and on this principle she excluded Judaism, which she regarded as linked to a racial conception,[2] and which fell generally under her anti-Semitism, which was partly based on her notion that the Jews had invented the concept of nationalism, to which she was opposed, rather than on the more usual aspect of anti-Semitic prejudice which considers the Jews to be refractory to the claims of a nationalism which is approved.

Simone Weil's itinerary from faith in science to a science of faith is nowhere better illustrated than in her changing attitude towards work. Throughout her lifetime she remained consistent in the belief that society must rest on a conviction of the value of manual labour, but the perspective in which she approached this notion after her conversion was radically different from what it had been before. In her early writings, Simone Weil grounded the supreme value of manual work in her conception of freedom as action proceeding from the actor's thought and she shared the rationalist's confidence in science to master nature;[3] in her later writings she based the primacy of labour on a purely religious foundation. She had earlier thought of

[1] Ibid., p. 119.   [2] Ibid., p. 93.   [3] *Oppression et liberté*, pp. 140–1.

work as 'an act of conscious submission to necessity', but she
believed also that in this submission there could be a kind of
creative joy, provided that the work undertaken came directly
to grips with nature in a fashion that could readily be perceived
both by the worker himself and by everyone affected by his
work. She credited this recognition of work as a human value to
Bacon, whose 'Man commands nature by obeying it' she
regarded as a 'stroke of genius' which ought 'to constitute by
itself alone the Bible of our epoch' and which was a great improvement over 'the ancient and despairing malediction of
Genesis, which made the world appear like a prison and work
as the mark of the slavery and abjection of man'.[1] But Simone
Weil's experience in the factories of Paris directed her to the
fundamentalism which she had denied only a few months
earlier. For her experience in the factories seems to have made
the world a kind of prison for her, and she literally felt like a
slave.[2] Towards the end of her life, she still placed the dignity of
work at the centre of her conception of a good civilization, but
the rational basis of dignity is replaced by a spiritual foundation,
rooted in the supernatural,[3] and her interpretation of Genesis
changed. Work, like death, is God's punishment for man's sin;
it permits man's return to the plenitude of the Good by suffering; when submitted to with consent and without the spirit of
revolt, it is a perfect act of obedience.[4] In the space of a few
years, Simone Weil moved from the pursuit of rational means
by which men might overcome their suffering to the erection of
suffering into a spiritual virtue.

Insistence on the regenerative quality of suffering is hardly
an adequate basis for the elaboration of social and political
theory, if only because it runs counter to the conditions of
existence on which Simone Weil placed so much emphasis
as setting the limits to social reform. If the white race were
as devoid of religious inspiration as Simone Weil claimed it to
be,[5] to require a revival of religion as the main condition of
social and political reform would be futile. But Simone Weil
was given the task by the Free French organization in London

---

[1] *Oppression et liberté*, p. 140.

[2] 'Journal d'usine', in *La Condition ouvrière*, pp. 74, 92, and 106. See also the
Introduction by J. M. Perrin to *Attente de Dieu*, p. 20.

[3] *The Need for Roots*, p. 94.   [4] Ibid., pp. 295–302.   [5] Ibid., p. 219.

of preparing reports on what the Gaullists might do by way of
reorganizing France after the war,[1] and while she ended one
work which seems to have grown out of this assignment with the
glorification of suffering, she also proposed schemes of political
action which demonstrate that she continued to believe that
political theory should be an instrument for policy-makers
and not a futile speculative effort. The report which she
wrote, which is the main political work of her later years,
is *The Need for Roots*, and it is no doubt to this book that she
referred as 'a second "great work" ' in progress in a letter of
May 1943.[2]

The Need for Roots of 1943 displays certain lines of continuity
with the 'Réflexions' of 1934. It is essential to try to create
order in the sense that people do not have incompatible
obligations, although it is by no means certain that the conception of such an order is not simply a fiction;[3] there must be
liberty, regarded as the real ability to choose, under few,
general, and stable laws whose necessity can be understood
by everyone;[4] men should have the responsibility for making
decisions over the broadest possible range of activities.[5]
The concentration of power in a centralized state is still
regarded as a dangerous evil, although Simone Weil now
launched her attack against the idolatry of power rather than
against the consequences of state power. 'Present-day patriotism consists in an equation between absolute good and a
collectivity corresponding to a given territorial area, namely
France . . .',[6] while what is needed is a conception of patriotism
as compassion for one's country,[7] which should be regarded
only as a vital medium and which need neither be protected
from foreign influences nor regarded as excluding local and
regional loyalties.[8] She continued to be 'utopian' in the sense
that she made recommendations which she herself believed
exceeded existing possibilities, and she also continued to
believe that it was absolutely essential to do so if there was to
be any chance that the necessarily imperfect decisions which

[1] Jacques Cabaud, *L'Expérience vécue de Simone Weil*, Paris, 1957, p. 376, and the
enlarged, English version of this principal biography of Simone Weil, Jacques
Cabaud, *Simone Weil, A Fellowship in Love*, N.Y. and London, 1964, p. 327.

[2] *Écrits de Londres et dernières lettres*, p. 237.

[3] *The Need for Roots*, p. 10. [4] Ibid., p. 12. [5] Ibid., pp. 15–16.
[6] Ibid., p. 144. [7] Ibid., p. 170. [8] Ibid., pp. 161–3.

men would make would also be good decisions.[1] But at the same time as *The Need for Roots* carried forward some of the notions contained in 'Réflexions', now subordinated to the pervasive influence of Simone Weil's spirituality, it also broke new ground not covered in the earlier work. 'Réflexions' is essentially an analysis of the mechanics of society and a statement of the necessary conditions of an ideal form of society, but it deals only inferentially with the concrete problems of government in the here and now. Parts of *The Need for Roots* amount to no less than a set of recommendations for the art of government. While 'Réflexions' can be regarded as an effort to state how society should be organized, *The Need for Roots* can be regarded, in part, as a statement of how political power should be exercised.

VIII   The Art of Government

The crucial conception in Simone Weil's approach to the art of government is that political action has to be regarded as a means of education of the citizens. In this respect, her view of politics follows in the tradition of Plato, Rousseau, and John Stuart Mill, all of whom found it impossible to separate politics from education. Her inspiration was primarily Platonic, for she found in Plato the same conception of the world that is held by Christianity, but in fact her specific recommendations fit much less closely into the Platonic scheme of political organization than they do into the political frameworks built by Rousseau and Mill.

By education, Simone Weil meant providing the motives for action, and she believed there were five ways in which political activity could operate as a means of education in this sense:

First, fear and hope, brought about by threats and promises.
Suggestion.
Expression, either officially or under official sanction, of some of the thoughts which, before ever being publicly expressed, were already in the hearts of the people, or in the hearts of certain active elements of the nation.
Example.
The modalities themselves of action, and those of organizations created for purposes of action.[2]

---

[1] *The Need for Roots*, p. 217.   [2] Ibid., p. 190.

Simone Weil regarded the first method, which is the early utilitarian formula for government, as the 'crudest' and the one which was always used. The second method, of course, was Plato's, but Simone Weil overlooked that fact, and simply described it as 'the one in the handling of which Hitler has displayed such genius'.[1] The other three she regarded as unknown,[2] although by saying this she directly denied the value of democratic self-government as an instrument of education, which was the logical implication of the argument she had presented in 'Réflexions'.

In asking that there should be official expression of the unspoken thoughts of the people, Simone Weil was probably asking for the impossible. It is true that peoples everywhere look to their political leaders for a kind of moral leadership, and that this is sometimes achieved, but it is almost always after considerable prodding precisely in the form of the expression of what Simone Weil thought of as unexpressed thoughts. In order to make this recommendation, Simone Weil had to contradict a proposition she had expressed earlier, for in stating how this educational method might be employed at the time she was writing she said that it required the ability to place oneself in the position of others,[3] while in 1936 she had written that 'men never know how to put themselves in the place of one another'.[4] And if Simone Weil thought of this as essentially a religious function, which is possible, her qualification that it should be done under official sanction runs counter to her insistence that Church and state should remain separate.

Simone Weil did not state explicitly how the force of example might operate, but there is much in her later writings which bears on it. The problem here, of course, is to provide the motives for the rulers to set a good example, but the best that Simone Weil could produce here was an application of precisely what she described as the crudest form of education: establishing fears and hopes by threats and promises. One of her more spectacular recommendations for political organization was to establish a system whereby rulers would be held criminally responsible for mistakes made in the conduct of office, with

---

[1] *The Need for Roots*, p. 190.   [2] Ibid.
[3] Ibid., p. 199.
[4] 'Lettres à un ingénieur directeur d'usine', in *La Condition ouvrière*, p. 131.

penalties ranging to that of death,[1] and she even argued that de
Gaulle should be guided by the terms of a fundamental declaration for a limited period after which he should stake his life
before a special court designated to judge his adherence to it.[2]
She did not take into account the possibilities that such a
system would create for base acts of vengeance, and, in failing
to do so, she also failed to adhere to what she herself said about
the modalities of political action and political organizations as
instruments of education in those passages of *The Need for Roots*
which constitute the most systematic elements of her later
political thought.

Simone Weil's view of government took literally the banal
phrase, 'the art of government'. In her conception, politics
had a close affinity to art in that it involves 'simultaneous
composition on several planes at once' and requires intense
concentration if the results are to be good.[3] Every political
choice must be decided, whenever possible, only after careful
consideration of the problem involved and the alternate courses
of action. For Simone Weil, this meant essentially a consideration of all the possible effects of both the words used by government and the actions government requires or encourages among
the citizens. Otherwise, there is a real risk that one may actually
produce what one wants to avoid. Simone Weil's illustration of
this necessity was that of the pacifists after the First World
War, who appealed to the desire for security and comfort in
order to win supporters, in the hope that they could thereby
gain enough influence to control French foreign policy in the
interests of peace. They did not, however, consider what would
happen if their appeals to security and comfort were heeded
widely, although not widely enough to give them control of
foreign policy. If they had considered this, according to Simone
Weil's argument, they would have understood that they were
doing nothing to prevent war but simply making it possible
for the more aggressive side to win.[4]

With respect to action, as opposed to words, Simone Weil
thought that there was an additional factor to be taken into

[1] 'Idées essentielles pour une nouvelle constitution', in *Écrits de Londres et dernières
lettres*, pp. 93–97.

[2] 'Légitimité du gouvernement provisoire', in *Écrits de Londres et dernières lettres*,
pp. 69–71.

[3] *The Need for Roots*, p. 216.   [4] Ibid., pp. 201–2.

account. This is what she called 'the transference mechanism, which attaches the miser to his treasure'.[1] This mechanism can be described as the transformation of a means into an end, something which Simone Weil thought was the more likely to happen if there is not a close link between the means employed and the original motive for employing it. The examples she gave of how this mechanism might work politically were the acquisition of a taste for murder as a result of killing German soldiers in order to serve France and, by way of contrast, the acquisition of a taste for helping people in misfortune as a result of helping workmen to avoid deportation to Germany, again out of the original motive of serving France. The problem for the policy-maker is to select 'methods of action which contain in themselves an impulsion toward the good' and this should surely be done when all other things are equal and even, often, when all other things are not equal.[2]

There is a parallel between Simone Weil's conception of the art of government and what, in her early writings, she had called the materialist method: concern with the consequences implied by the means employed rather than with the goals pursued. But if the two conceptions are analogous, there is also a fundamental difference between them. In her early use of the materialist method, which she applied principally to production and warfare—the two main categories of the conditions of existence which were so central to her sociology—she thought of consequences exclusively as the patterns of social relations produced by efforts to provide for functional necessities in societies characterized by the struggle for power. In this view, capitalism may be undesirable because the workers are exploited, but workers are also exploited under socialism regardless of the goals at which socialists may be aiming; war may be nationalistic or revolutionary, imperialistic, defensive, or preventive, but whatever its goal, warfare requires certain oppressive forms of organization and requires that soldiers be massacred.[3] Goals are not identical with motives, but Simone Weil's early analytical method would seem to have to regard motives, as well as goals, as irrelevant to the outcome of any

[1] Ibid., p. 212.　　　　　　　　[2] Ibid.
[3] See especially 'Réflexions sur la guerre', in *Écrits historiques et politiques*, pp. 229–39 (1933).

course of social action. But when Simone Weil spoke of the consequences of governmental words and commands in *The Need for Roots*, the consequences she had in mind were precisely the motives which the government's words or commands would arouse. This was consistent with her view of politics as educational and with her view of education as a supplier of motives, but it was incompatible with the method of social analysis which she had employed in her early writings.

The emphasis on motives in Simone Weil's later writings reflects the ethical theory which she had come to hold. This theory is simply that the goodness of an act depends entirely upon the motives behind it. The goodness of a thing, in this view, consists solely in the goodness of the motives behind the effort which produces it. She recognized that it is never possible to be absolutely certain of people's motives, but she thought that the way in which any given act is conceived is generally known and is compatible with some motives but not with others, and that it would be possible to discriminate morally among acts on the basis of the motives implied or excluded by their conception.[1] Unfortunately, she gave no concrete illustrations of this operation.

An ethical theory which relies exclusively on motives as the criterion of evaluation is inadequate in social affairs. The evaluation of acts which have social consequences may sometimes be difficult and complex, but men are justified in giving more weight to their consequences than to the motives behind them. An act which produces a disaster remains a disastrous act, regardless of the motives which produced it. Even in private life, everyone can think of good intentions which have gone astray. Charity inspired by the best of motives may legitimately be resented by the man who prefers to provide for himself. Simone Weil herself did not rigorously adhere to this ethical theory. She was critical of the extirpation by the Catholics of what they regarded as the Albigensian heresy,[2] but she did not question the motives of the Church, she criticized the means employed and lamented the consequences.

---

[1] *The Need for Roots*, pp. 251-2.

[2] 'L'Agonie d'une civilisation vue à travers un poème épique', in *Écrits historiques et politiques*, p. 73, and 'En Quoi Consiste l'inspiration occitanienne?', ibid., p. 83. Both essays were originally published in 1943 and appear in English in *Selected Essays 1934-1943*.

Simone Weil did not establish any concrete hierarchy of motives but, despite a certain ambiguity in her presentation, when she came closest to doing so she suggested that she believed that in many cases the consequences of acts, viewed as other than the motives they inspire, are a necessary concern of governments. She distinguished between completely pure and spiritually good motives, medium-quality motives, and evil motives. Pure motives should always be invoked, evil motives should always be rejected, regardless of expediency. In the case of medium-quality motives, however, expediency is a legitimate consideration.[1] Accordingly, Simone Weil's rule for policy-makers included the requirement that when government was to invoke medium-quality motives, it should be asked:

> . . . This motive can produce effects in this, that, or the other group; and in what other groups as well? It can produce effects in this, that, or the other domain; and in what other domains as well? This, that, or the other situation can be produced; and what other situation as well? In each case, what effects would it be likely to produce in each group, in each domain, immediately, later and later still? In what respects would each of these possible effects be advantageous, in what respects harmful? What seems to be the degree of probability of each possibility?
>
> We must carefully consider each of these points and all of these points together; suspend for a moment all inclination towards a choice; then decide; and run the risk of error, as in every human decision.[2]

If it be reasonable to assume that most of the motives invoked by governments are of 'medium quality', then Simone Weil presented a guide for political choice which considers consequences as well as motives, without completely separating them. The guide is simple, but powerful. Emmanuel Mounier, also, had tried to establish what he called 'the technique of spiritual methods'. His efforts were directed primarily at discovering the proper forms of behaviour for a dissident body of citizens without direct political power who wanted to create a new moral climate, just as Simone Weil's prescriptions were

---

[1] *The Need for Roots*, p. 201.
[2] My translation of *L'Enracinement*, pp. 173-4. See *The Need for Roots*, p. 202.

for the use of the Free French Resistance movement, which had an official character, in an attempt to breathe new life into France. Simone Weil's scheme displays the greater intellectual rigour. It applies to all groups, whether governmental or social. It has regard for goals, but not to the exclusion of conditions. It contains a check-list across space and time of the factors to be taken into account. And when combined with her additional prescription that the institutions employed for carrying out acts be in harmony with their purpose, it constitutes as useful a guide to government as anyone has produced without specific reference to the content of policy itself.

Simone Weil was ambiguous as to whether the methods she recommended could be applied generally or were appropriate only to the particular moment in French history when she was writing. At one point she suggested that the opportunity for their successful implementation was fleeting: 'It must be done now. Once victory is attained, in the irresistible unleashing of individual appetites seeking happiness or power, it will be absolutely impossible to start anything of the kind.'[1] But this statement is in the context of her desire to inspire the purest spiritual motives. Elsewhere, in a context which suggests a hierarchy of motives, she spoke of the possibility of deriving a method of making men and peoples better, without regard to the immediate circumstances of the war and the occupation,[2] and her several references to government as an art suggest that she may have thought some continuing implementation of her scheme was possible. The method of calculating possibilities and probabilities is always possible, and the writings of Raymond Aron contain specific applications of this method. For the type of political thought characteristic of Simone Weil's early writings and of those sections of her later writings which can stand independently of her spirituality also appears in amplified form in the political writings of Raymond Aron, who is less explicit methodologically but more extensive and concrete in his political analyses than Simone Weil was. In this respect, Simone Weil's work stands in the best tradition of rigorous political sociology. It also had an impact on a French

[1] *The Need for Roots*, p. 214.
[2] Ibid., p. 252.

thinker who was not a sociologist but a moralist. The man who personally supervised the posthumous publication of many of her works described Simone Weil in 1951 as 'the only great spirit of our time'.[1] That man was Albert Camus.

[1] *L'Express*, 11 February 1961.

5

Albert Camus: Liberal Moralist

I The Political Man of Letters

ALBERT CAMUS is a representative of that character-istically French phenomenon, the politically preoccupied man of letters whose message may be expressed in the novel or the drama as often as in the essay or the treatise, and whose work is therefore laid bare with the tools of literary criticism at the same time as it is scanned for its social or political significance. France is not alone, of course, in produc-ing great literary figures who deal with political themes in their works of fiction, or who devote part of their lives to political matters. Russia's Dostoievsky is probably the single most important source of inspiration for Camus' political speculation, apart from his own personal experience, and from time to time any country may produce a Thomas Mann or a George Bernard Shaw or a Ralph Waldo Emerson. France, however, is unusual in the historical regularity with which literary figures have appeared prominently in political contexts and in the public attention which is given to their political pronounce-ments. Voltaire, Chateaubriand, Hugo, Zola, Malraux, Mauriac, Sartre, and Camus all share a common tradition which is without counterpart elsewhere. It was, perhaps, un-usual even for France when André Malraux, Minister of Information, proposed to send a committee consisting of French holders of the Nobel Prize for literature to investigate charges of the use of torture by the French forces in Algeria,[1] but the full measure of the unusualness of the situation, at least com-pared to United States practices, can be seized by trying to

---

[1] André Malraux made this proposal at a press conference shortly after Charles de Gaulle's return to power in 1958. See *Le Monde*, 26 June 1958, p. 3. The French Nobel Prize winners were Roger Martin du Gard, François Mauriac, and Albert Camus.

imagine that in 1958 John Steinbeck was a member of the Cabinet who proposed to send a committee consisting of Pearl Buck, William Faulkner, and Ernest Hemingway to investigate, let us say, charges of police brutality in certain states.

There is, ordinarily, a special difficulty in dealing with the political ideas of literary figures, simply because they express themselves in works of fiction. In fiction, the most stimulating dialogues are as likely as not to terminate in dilemma, if not enigma, rather than in resolution, and authors may rarely if ever be identified with any of their characters, with the result that interpretation of the author's meaning, which is difficult enough even in the case of the essay, risks becoming more an exercise of the critical literary imagination than the elucidation of a political argument. In the case of Camus, however, this problem is not serious. Camus expressed his main political ideas in essays, and while his fiction may be taken as illustrative of these ideas, the ideas themselves do not depend on it.[1]

Camus is also immune from another difficulty which often attaches to politically-minded men of letters. His political ideas are not casual pronouncements upon political themes to which attention is directed principally because of the literary reputation of their author. Camus' political essays would be worth attention even if he had never written a novel or a play. His political ideas are the fruit of the exercise of methodical thought and, in this sense, it is quite appropriate to treat him as a political philosopher.[2]

In his maturity, after he had achieved fame, Camus disclaimed the role of philosopher. 'I am not a philosopher and I have never pretended to be one,' he said in 1952.[3] He had also said the same in 1945, both publicly and in his private journal.[4] But one may question whether this was really so. After all, he

---

[1] One student of Camus has suggested that Camus' art precedes his philosophy, that his novels seem to represent the working out of philosophical positions which he only later clarified in essays. Thomas Hanna, *The Thought and Art of Albert Camus*, Chicago, 1958, p. 162.

[2] This argument is put forth by Richard Wollheim, 'The Political Philosophy of Existentialism', *Cambridge Journal*, VII (October 1953), pp. 3–5.

[3] 'Entretien sur la révolte', in Albert Camus, *Actuelles II, Chroniques 1948–1953*, Paris, 1953, p. 63.

[4] Albert Camus, *Théâtre, récits, nouvelles*, pp. 1929 and 1886.

chose to study philosophy rather than literature at the university.[1] In 1936, he wrote that one must write novels to be a philosopher[2] and in 1938 he repeated the point: 'A novel is never anything but a philosophy set into images.'[3] And some jottings in his journal for 1936 and 1937 indicate that at those times he was thinking of political theory, in one case linked with the Mediterranean, in the other case linked with theology.[4] These may simply be youthful scribblings, but there is a continuity between Camus' early journal notations and the later development of his work and thought that at least suggests that political theory may never have been very far from his thoughts. But he was intellectually unsuited to writing a political treatise of the kind produced by a Hobbes or a Locke or a Rousseau, if only because such a work implies abstraction, and Camus fought against abstractions throughout his entire life.

II   The Danger of Abstraction

Camus developed early a suspicion of what in 1936 he called 'general ideas'.[5] This is evident from his Algerian newspaper articles, which generally avoided starting out from 'hazardous principles'.[6] In his early review of Silone's *Bread and Wine*, which foreshadows the main argument of Camus' *The Rebel*, he spoke of turning from 'an abstract philosophy of revolution' to 'the bread and to the wine of simplicity'.[7] He claimed in 1945 not to 'believe enough in reason to believe in a system'.[8] He coined the phrase 'the end of ideologies'[9] to designate a

---

[1] According to his teacher and friend, Jean Grenier, because in addition to aspiring towards the truth, Camus did not like the excessive role given to history and biography in the literature programmes. *Le Figaro Littéraire*, 26 October 1957, pp. 1 and 5.

[2] Albert Camus, *Carnets, Mai 1935–Février 1942*, Paris, 1962, p. 23. Eng. tr. by Philip Thody, *Notebooks: 1935–1942*, New York, 1963.

[3] *Théâtre, récits, nouvelles*, p. 1886. See also *Carnets, Mai 1935–Février 1942*, p. 250.

[4] *Carnets, Mai 1935–Février 1942*, pp. 50 and 85.

[5] Ibid., pp. 37 and 39.

[6] 'Misère de la Kabylie, IX, L'Avenir politique; les centres communaux', *Alger-Républicain*, 13 June 1939. Reprinted in Albert Camus, *Actuelles III, Chronique algérienne, 1939–1958*, Paris, 1958.

[7] *Alger-Républicain*, 23 May 1939.

[8] *Théâtre, récits, nouvelles*, p. 1929.

[9] 'Ni Victimes ni bourreaux', in *Actuelles, Chroniques 1944–1948*, Paris, 1950, p. 154. The articles are dated November 1948 in this volume, but Philip Thody

situation in which people would no longer accept with equanimity any action, however murderous, in order to promote an absolute Utopia defined by substituting 'a logical succession of reasoning for living reality'.[1] Ideologies and abstractions were one and the same for Camus, and he regarded them as dangerous because it was in their name that people killed one another. 'We have seen lying, degradation, killing, deportation, and torture,' he wrote in 1946, 'and, each time, it was not possible to persuade those who did it not to do it, because they were sure of themselves and because one does not persuade an abstraction, that is, the representative of an ideology.'[2]

Earlier, during the German occupation, Camus had given a different formulation to the same general notion. Writing in the clandestine *Les Lettres Françaises* about the execution of Pierre Pucheu, a businessman who served in several posts during the Vichy régime, including that of Minister of the Interior, and who was arrested by the Giraud government in Algiers and later tried and executed, Camus argued that Pucheu had been condemned because he did not have enough imagination to understand that he served an abstraction and that, by the same token, he should not be judged on the basis of any abstract principle. This text, which does not seem to be well known, deserves to be cited at some length.[3]

Il [Pucheu] a cru, par exemple, qu'un gouvernement de défaite était un gouvernement comme les autres et que les mots ministre, pouvoir, lois, condamnation, ne changeaient pas de sens quand la

points out in *Albert Camus 1913–1960*, New York, 1961, p. 233, that they actually appeared in *Combat* in November 1946. They appeared in an English translation by Dwight Macdonald as 'Neither Victims Nor Executioners', in *Politics* (New York), 4 (July–August 1947), pp. 141–7.

The sentence 'Nous refusons de mettre sur le même plan les bourreaux et les victimes' appeared in an article in *L'Aube* by Georges Bidault which was reprinted in *Le Soir Républicain*, the Algerian newspaper of which Camus was editor, on 28 November 1939. In Simone Weil's *L'Enracinement*, p. 204, the following sentence appears: 'Dans la catastrophe de notre temps, les bourreaux et les victimes sont, les uns et les autres, avant tout les porteurs involontaires d'un témoignage sur l'atroce misère au fond de laquelle nous gisons.' These references to victims and executioners indicate clearly what the world looked like to some French men and women during the war.

[1] 'Entretien sur la révolte', in *Actuelles II*, pp. 60–61.

[2] 'Ni Victimes ni bourreaux', in *Actuelles*, pp. 142–3.

[3] 'Tout ne s'arrange pas', in *Les Lettres Françaises Clandestines*, réédités en fac-similé, Paris, 1947, No. XVI, May 1944, p. 4.

France elle-même changeait de visage. Il a cru que tout pouvait continuer, qu'il était toujours dans le système abstrait et administratif où il avait toujours vécu, où l'on se poussait, où l'on intriguait, où l'on signait ces lois derrière lesquelles rien ne s'imaginait. Et ces lois qu'il signait dans le décor de tous les jours . . . il n'a pas eu assez d'imagination pour voir *réellement* qu'elles allaient se transformer en petits matins d'agonie pour des Français innocents qu'on mènerait à la mort. Pour ce genre d'hommes, c'est toujours la même abstraction qui continue et je suppose que le plus grand de leurs crimes à nos yeux est de n'avoir jamais approché un corps, fût-il supplicié comme celui de Politzer,[1] avec les yeux du corps et la notion que j'appellerai physique de la justice.

*   *   *

. . . Il faut qu'on sache dans toute la France (et dans tous les Ministères) que le Temps de l'abstraction est terminé. Tout maintenant a un sens et ce sens peut être mortel . . . ce n'est pas le jugement d'une classe ou d'une idéologie, ce n'est pas le verdict porté au nom d'une Abstraction qui fonctionne ici. C'est le cri général, l'appel, le langage plein de chair et d'images vraies, la revendication de tous les inculpés que nous sommes depuis quatre ans, devenus soudain assez forts pour juger leurs juges eux-mêmes et pour le faire sans haine, mais sans pitié.

Camus was later to change his views about the punishment of collaborators,[2] but this wartime article—which was greeted with less than enthusiasm by some of the other contributors to *Les Lettres Françaises*[3]—contains some of the main elements of his

---

[1] Georges Politzer was a French communist philosopher who was killed by the Germans in 1942.

[2] Shortly after the liberation, Camus became engaged in a polemic with François Mauriac over the punishment of collaborators, Camus supporting it in the name of justice and Mauriac opposing it in the name of charity. In 1948, Camus said that on the central point of the controversy, Mauriac had been right. See 'Morale et politique', VIII, in *Actuelles*, pp. 70–74, and 'L'Incroyant et les Chrétiens', in *Actuelles*, pp. 212–13. The latter article appears in English in Albert Camus, *Resistance, Rebellion, and Death*. Translated from the French and with an Introduction by Justin O'Brien, N.Y., 1961. Camus also argued against what he regarded as the injustices committed during the post-liberation purges: see, for example, 'Morale et politique', X, in *Actuelles*, pp. 78–81.

[3] Paul Éluard and Claude Morgan, both communists at the time, wrote that 'several of our friends, in accord with the author's general thesis, nevertheless insist on stating that this convenient lack of imagination of which he speaks still appears to them, and particularly in the case of Pierre Pucheu, voluntary. It is voluntarily that a criminal like Pucheu, desirous above all of indulging his hatreds, has no conscience.' 'La Volonté de nuire', in *Les Lettres Françaises Clandestines*, No. XVI, May 1944, p. 4.

political thought. No man should act either on the basis of routine or on general principles, without regard to circumstances or without regard for the consequences of his acts. When men do act in such a fashion, however, they are not to be judged with reference to groups, general principles, ideologies, or other abstract ideas. What counts as a criterion of action and of judgement is what happens to the lives of men and women, regarded as the flesh-and-blood creatures which they are. Justice has to do with what happens to people's bodies. By keeping people in the forefront of one's thoughts, it may be possible to avoid harming them. But the risks of doing harm are great if one thinks in terms of abstraction; abstractions are the foundation of 'logical crime'.[1]

Camus' hostility toward abstractions is the main link between his own thought and the thought of Simone Weil, for it is the most important fundamental attitude which they held in common. Antagonism to what Simone Weil called '*entités vides*'[2] and to what Camus called variously 'general ideas', 'abstractions', or 'ideologies' formed the basis of each thinker's analytical method. To be sure, their outlook converged on a number of other points as well. Camus referred approvingly to Simone Weil's notion of functional oppression,[3] he relied on her account of her experience with factory work to describe the impact on the worker of the rationalization of labour,[4] he came to share her early enthusiasm for political syndicalism,[5] and he expressed ideas about the necessity for a union of manual

---

[1] Albert Camus, *L'Homme révolté*, Paris, 1951. Except where otherwise noted, all translations from and citations of this book refer to the English translation by Anthony Bower, *The Rebel*, New York (Vintage Books), 1956. In this case, the reference is to p. 3.

[2] 'Ne Recommençons pas la guerre de Troie (Pouvoir des mots)', in *Écrits historiques et politiques*, Paris, 1960, p. 271. An English translation of this essay appears in *Selected Essays 1934–1943*.

[3] *The Rebel*, p. 215. The translation omits the footnote in the French edition (p. 266) which refers to Simone Weil's 'Allons-nous vers une révolution prolétarienne?', in *Révolution Prolétarienne*, 25 April 1933. The date which Camus gives is incorrect; it should be 25 August 1933. The essay was reprinted in Simone Weil, *Oppression et liberté*, pp. 12–38.

[4] *The Rebel*, p. 216.

[5] Ibid., pp. 217; 297–300. Shortly after the publication of *The Rebel*, Camus complained that reviewers had neglected his reference to revolutionary syndicalism and said that it was that revolutionary tradition which had inspired his essay. 'Entretien sur la révolte', in *Actuelles II*, p. 57. See also 'Révolte et romantisme', in *Actuelles II*, p. 81.

labour and intellectual labour[1] similar to those which Simone
Weil had inherited from both the syndicalist and the Marxist
traditions, but none of these ideas was fundamental to his
thought.[2] On certain central points, Camus and Weil actually
diverged quite widely. Part of Camus' hostility towards
abstractions was a distrust of what he called 'systems', but
there are no more systematic writings in modern French
political thought than the early writings of Simone Weil, and
her early writings are the only ones which Camus ever cited
in his own work, although he was familiar with her later
writings as well. Simone Weil's less systematic, later writings are
permeated with a spiritual quality which Camus could respect
but certainly did not share. And Simone Weil eventually came
to believe that justice could appear only through grace, while
Camus thought that the question facing men in the twentieth
century was precisely 'how to live without grace and without
justice'.[3]

    Certainly authors do not have to agree to respect and admire
one another's work, and Simone Weil's integrity alone could
have been a sufficient attraction to persuade Camus to super-
vise personally the publication of five volumes of her writings,
but it may well be that their common hostility to abstractions
accounts for Camus' particular interest in Simone Weil's work.
Indeed, while it is generally recorded that Camus discovered
Simone Weil's work in 1946,[4] it is quite possible that he had
read some of her articles while he was still in Algeria, before
the war. In *Alger-Républicain* of 4 July 1939, Camus called the
attention of his readers to a French journal called *Nouveaux
Cahiers*, which he admired for its precision, objectivity, and
effort to understand reality. 'Many of us say that we love the
truth,' he wrote. 'But to love it is nothing, one must accept it.
And in the light of common sense, many truths are difficult to

---

[1] 'Le Pain et la liberté', in *Actuelles II*, pp. 168–71. An English translation of this
article appears in *Resistance, Rebellion, and Death*.

[2] Simone Weil's suggestion that writers should be liable to criminal prosecution
for not telling the truth (*L'Enracinement*, pp. 39–40) also had a milder parallel in
Camus' proposal for a daily newspaper which would be published later than the
other papers and which would evaluate the 'probable element of truth in the other
papers' main stories, with due regard to editorial policies and the past performance
of the correspondents' (*The New Yorker*, 16 January 1960, p. 2).

[3] *The Rebel*, p. 225.

[4] Albert Camus, *Théâtre, récits, nouvelles*, p. xxxiv.

accept. The reading of this publication therefore demands that one should rid himself of a certain number of habits of thought and of prejudices.' An unsigned editorial of 7 November 1939 in *Le Soir Républicain*, of which Camus was the editor, also referred most warmly to the *Nouveaux Cahiers*. This was the publication of a study group to which Simone Weil belonged,[1] and she contributed several articles to the journal, including her 'Ne Recommençons pas la guerre de Troie (Pouvoir des mots)',[2] in which she elaborated her objection to empty abstractions. There is no public record which indicates whether Camus had read any of Simone Weil's articles around the time they were published, but it is clear that he already felt a special bond of sympathy with writings which tried to deal with current problems in as concrete a fashion as possible and without regard to preconceived general principles.[3]

Simone Weil's response to the challenge of abstractions took the forms of a ruthless dissection of the meaning of such concepts as revolution, capitalism, and socialism, in order to uncover the prosaic realities to which they refer,[4] the construction of a functional sociology by means of which society might be understood, and, eventually, ultimate reliance on the power of divine grace to enlighten men's motives.[5] Camus' response

---

[1] Jacques Cabaud, *L'Expérience vécue de Simone Weil*, pp. 179–81.

[2] *Nouveaux Cahiers*, 1 and 15 April 1937. The essay is reprinted in Simone Weil, *Écrits historiques et politiques*, pp. 256–72.

[3] Camus refers in his notebooks, apparently some time between June and September of 1943, to an article of Simone Weil entitled 'En Quoi Consiste l'inspiration occitanienne?' which he had read in the *Cahiers du Sud* of August-September-October 1942. The article had been published under the pseudonym Emile Novis, however, and there is no reason to believe that Camus knew the real identity of the author. Albert Camus, *Carnets, Janvier 1942–Mars 1951*, Paris, 1964, p. 101. The only studies I know which deal with both Simone Weil and Albert Camus are Marie-Josèphe Rustan, 'La Notion de limite chez Simone Weil et chez Albert Camus', in *Terre Humaine*, 3e Année (February 1953), pp. 32–43, and Marie-Madeleine Davy, 'Camus et Simone Weil', in *La Table Ronde*, No. 146 (February 1960), pp. 137–43. The former is a highly perceptive analysis which emphasizes differences in their thought; the latter a more general account which emphasizes their common intellectual integrity; but neither refers to the common hostility towards abstractions which I find.

[4] 'Si l'on analysait de cette manière tous les mots, toutes les formules qui ont ainsi suscité, au long de l'histoire humaine, l'esprit de sacrifice et la cruauté tout ensemble, on les trouverait tous sans doute pareillement vides.' 'Ne Recommençons pas la guerre de Troie (Pouvoir des mots)', in *Écrits historiques et politiques*, p. 269.

[5] See Chapter 4.

was different. He was inclined neither to sociology nor towards religion. For Camus, society was just another abstraction, and he regarded it less as something for men to analyse than as something with which they had to come to grips in their daily lives. While he held that he would 'never start from the supposition that Christian truth is illusory', he nevertheless held also that he 'could not accept it'.[1] Camus' method of avoiding the generalizations which he believed to be potentially murderous was to emphasize men rather than society and doubt and error rather than truth. And men act at different times, in all kinds of circumstances, and in all kinds of ways. The key to understanding the human situation, therefore, lies neither in the analysis of society nor in deductions from universal truths, but in the extraction of whatever meaning can be found in the direct experience of individuals.

III   The World of Experience

Camus' observation of the history he had lived, his particular artistic talent, and his early philosophical assumptions all led him away from abstractions and into the world of concrete individual experience. Even when he speculated, he did so within a framework which ruled out in advance the kinds of assumptions which would have encouraged generalization. This appears clearly in his youthful essay, *Le Mythe de Sisyphe*, in which Camus developed his concept of the sentiment of the absurd. This sentiment is described as the perpetual tension involved in man's efforts to understand, seize, and control a universe which stubbornly refuses to yield its secrets and which has no ultimate rational justification or principle of explanation.[2] It is the Faustian urge intensified and restated as 'the desperate encounter between human inquiry and the silence of the universe'.[3] H. J. Blackham has argued that if one starts out by holding that existence is inherently unintelligible, the objects of knowledge can be approached only through the

---

[1] 'L'Incroyant et les Chrétiens', in *Actuelles II*, p. 212. The translation I cite appears in *Resistance, Rebellion, and Death*, pp. 69–70.

[2] *Le Mythe de Sisyphe*, Nouvelle édition augmentée d'une étude sur Franz Kafka, Paris, 1942, pp. 31–37. Eng. tr. by Justin O'Brien, *The Myth of Sisyphus and Other Essays*, New York, 1955.

[3] *The Rebel*, p. 6.

interpretation of experience in all its varied and concrete forms.[1] Although this comment is made in an analysis of existentialist thought, of which Camus always denied being a representative, it surely applies to him. 'Our desire to understand, our nostalgia for the absolute', he wrote in *The Myth of Sisyphus*, 'are explicable only to the extent precisely that we can understand and explain many things. It is vain to deny reason absolutely. It has its domain in which it is effective. This is precisely that of human experience.'[2] This perspective on the world is reflected not only in Camus' choice of the media of the drama and the novel—which are the normal vehicles for the expression of conflict in human experience—for his exploration of situations in which men are at grips with forces which threaten to overwhelm them. In his essay, *The Myth of Sisyphus*, Camus also illustrates ways in which men may seek to overcome the absurdity of their situation by the fanciful, but concrete, cases of the Don Juan, the actor, the adventurer, and the creative artist. Even in *The Rebel*, which is a work of theoretical and historical analysis, Camus remains as close as he can to specific cases, as in his discussion of the Russian terrorists during the Czarist régime, and particularly of those 'fastidious assassins',[3] who considered the potential consequences of their acts in terms of individual persons and who acted out of convictions that were shaded to the end with doubt.[4] One may wonder whether Camus did not feel some tinge of regret that when he published the collection of his articles under the title *Actuelles*, Sartre had already pre-empted for his own collection the more appropriate title *Situations*.[5]

It is, of course, totally impossible to speculate about the meaning of anything without resort to generalization, and any work of theoretical or historical analysis can hardly avoid abstraction, in the sense that the meaning of an argument or a situation which is extracted from the specific case necessarily is couched in general terms. This is a process in which Camus

[1] *Six Existentialist Thinkers*, New York, 1952, pp. 153–4.
[2] *Le Mythe de Sisyphe*, p. 55.
[3] This rendering by Anthony Bower of Camus' 'meurtriers délicats' surely ranks among the most felicitous translations.
[4] *The Rebel*, pp. 164–73.
[5] Three volumes of Sartre's *Situations* were published in Paris, in 1947, 1948, and 1949, before the first volume of Camus' *Actuelles* was published in 1950.

continually engages in *The Rebel*. There is intelligible ground
between the absent single principle which would both justify
and explain the universe and the infinite variety of human
experience. Camus undervalued the capacity of science to
understand the world, even in the absence of any single
explanatory principle.[1] Camus has been criticized for asking
too much—indeed, for raising a false problem—by suggesting
that men seek to understand the necessity of the matters of
fact which make up the universe.[2] The criticism is warranted,
but in the end it is irrelevant because Camus' ideas do not
depend on the actual existence of a sentiment of the absurd in
anyone but Camus himself, and there is nothing wrong with
asking an impossible question if one comes up with important
propositions in the course of trying to answer it. In fact, Camus
had already anticipated this criticism before he even wrote
The Myth of Sisyphus. In his journal, at what appears to be
November 1939, he wrote that 'one can despair of the meaning
of life *in general* but not of its particular forms, of existence,
since one has no power over it, but not of history where the
individual can do everything'.[3] Individuals can do anything
and, as Camus repeatedly pointed out, they had succeeded in
killing, uprooting, or enslaving seventy million human beings
in fifty years. How had this come about? How could similar
disasters be avoided in the future? Is it possible to find a rule
of conduct for men, in a universe which they will never completely understand, and without reliance upon absolute rules
of any kind, which will prevent human beings from murdering
one another?

[1] The only commentary on Camus that I know which gives more than passing
attention to his opposition to abstractions is Emmanuel Mounier's 'Albert Camus,
ou l'appel des humiliés', in *Carnets de route*. Vol. 3, *L'Espoir des désespérés*, Paris,
1953. Mounier is generally critical of Camus' position. He understands Camus'
fundamental point: 'Il est plus commode de servir une abstraction, voire de se
faire tuer pour elle en aveugle (outre que l'aveuglement préfère encore tuer) que
de servir des hommes, surtout les vaincus, qui ne gonflent pas le coeur d'éloquence
et de fausse ambition' (p. 104). But 'general insurrection against the abstract' is
itself an abstraction. And the abstract 'is also at the origin of all the great periods
of thought, art, and faith, whether it be pre-Roman art, Greek logic, discussions of
the Trinity and of Hypostatic union or of Cartesian science. It is at the origin of all
social life' (p. 138).

[2] See A. J. Ayer, 'Novelist-Philosophers—VIII: Albert Camus', in *Horizon*,
XIII (March 1946), pp. 155–68.

[3] *Carnets, Mai 1935–Février 1942*, p. 181. Italics in the original.

IV   Man and the Universe: *The Myth of Sisyphus*

These are the questions to which Camus addresses himself in *The Rebel*, which is his only major political essay and was written between 1947 and 1951 and published in the latter year. *The Myth of Sisyphus*, which appeared in 1942, already contained some of the elements of the answers he was later to give to these questions. On the one hand, he spoke there of revolt, by which he meant the refusal to surrender before the unknowable and the overpowering, a kind of defiance of the universe that is a spectacle of human pride.[1] Revolt is, of course, the central theme of *The Rebel*, and in it Camus remarks that 'the astonishing history evoked here is the history of European pride'.[2] On the other hand, in *The Myth of Sisyphus* he also suggested the stoicism so often remarked by students of Camus, the patient, ceaseless endurance in the face of obstacles that is reflected in the title of the book itself, with its evocation of Sisyphus, condemned eternally to push to the mountain's top the rock which regularly rolls back to the base.[3] Here is the forerunner of Dr. Rieux in *The Plague*, for whom the only means of fighting the plague is 'common decency', and for whom common decency means simply doing his job.[4]

If *The Myth of Sisyphus* already contained the germs of themes which Camus was to develop more fully later on, it also lacked a crucial element which was to acquire central importance for Camus as his thought progressed, and particularly as it was affected by the circumstances of the war and the occupation. Each of the heroes in *The Myth of Sisyphus*— Don Juan, the actor, the adventurer, and the creative artist— is treated as a solitary figure. Camus is concerned only with the passions which motivate them and with the impact of their acts upon themselves. There is no consideration of the consequences of their behaviour for others. Camus argues that

[1] *Le Mythe de Sisyphe*, pp. 76–79.

[2] *The Rebel*, p. 11.

[3] Is still another bridge between Camus' thought and Simone Weil's to be found in the parallel between Camus' evocation of Sisyphus and Simone Weil's final interpretation of physical labour as a daily death?

[4] Albert Camus, *La Peste*, Paris, 1947. Eng. tr. by Stuart Gilbert, *The Plague*, New York, 1948, p. 150. All page references to and translations from *The Plague* rely on this English language edition.

what he calls the absurd is not a reason for despair; a kind of exhilaration actually results for the person who decides to pick up the gauntlet and revolts lucidly against his condition. Camus argues in *The Myth of Sisyphus* that if we cannot understand the world, we can at least experience it, and that one experience is as good as another as long as our awareness of it is sharp and clear.[1] When he speaks of experience serving or not serving man, he means only the relationship of a man to his own acts and not the relationship of those acts to others. This kind of reasoning could not stand up under the impact of the war and the occupation. In fact, there is reason to believe that Camus regarded *The Myth of Sisyphus* as incomplete even as he wrote it. The introduction to the book points out that it is a point of departure rather than a conclusion, and, well before he wrote it, he noted ideas in his journal which reflect very different kinds of considerations. While in *The Myth of Sisyphus* he wrote about the 'profound inutility' of 'absurdist creation' (which seems in the context to embrace not just the creative artist but all Camus' absurdist heroes),[2] he had already written in his journal, apparently in November 1939, of 'a useful task to accomplish'. As though addressing the author of a book like *The Myth of Sisyphus*, but against the background of the outbreak of war, he wrote of the possibility of preventing injustices.

Each man disposes of a more or less wide sphere of influence. . . . Do not push anyone to revolt. We must spare the blood and liberty of others. But you can persuade ten, twenty, thirty men that this war was not and is not inevitable, that means of stopping it that have not yet been tried still can be used, that they must say so, write it when they can, shout it if they must. These ten or thirty men in turn will say it to ten others who will repeat it. If laziness stops them, so much the worse, begin again with others. And when you have done what you must do in your sphere, on your own ground, stop and despair at your leisure.[3]

In a short essay which was not published until 1954 but which was written in 1940, and therefore completed before *The Myth of Sisyphus*, which was not finished until 1941, Camus also departed from the inward, exclusively individualistic theme of *The Myth of Sisyphus*.

[1] *Le Mythe de Sisyphe*, p. 96.   [2] Ibid., pp. 157–8.
[3] *Carnets, Mai 1935–Février 1942*, p. 181.

Nous savons que nous sommes dans la contradiction, mais que nous devons refuser la contradiction et faire ce qu'il faut pour la réduire. Notre tâche d'homme est de trouver les quelques formules qui apaiseront l'angoisse infinie des âmes libres. Nous avons à recoudre ce qui est déchiré, à rendre la justice imaginable dans un monde si évidemment injuste, le bonheur significatif pour des peuples empoisonnés par le malheur du siècle.[1]

The war brought about Camus' confrontation with history, and in this new context he became sharply aware that acts not only reflect private attitudes but also have social consequences. It was not until Camus moved his heroes from the abstract context of struggle with what he called the universe into the real conflicts of human history that he could express the complete meaning of revolt.

V   Man and History: *The Rebel*

The main argument of *The Rebel* is that revolt, which Camus had considered in *The Myth of Sisyphus* only as an act affecting the actor, is the only means by which intolerable social situations can be improved but that it also can lead and has led to the creation of intolerable social situations. The form of the argument is partly historical and partly analytical. It is historical in the sense that Camus tries to follow the succession of ideas and practices which constitutes the evolution to the contemporary situation in which men massacre one another in the name of abstractions which have lost all contact with the men they presumably were designed to serve. In each case, he finds revolt at the origin of the idea or practice, in that each new idea or practice is the result of someone's revolt against his condition, although, in every case also, that revolt produced consequences which were disastrous for man's condition. But revolt remains the only way of overcoming disaster because it remains the only impulse contrary to man's condition and it is through revolt that values are affirmed. Hence the analytical parts of the book are directed towards the elaboration of a philosophy of revolt which would enable men to exploit its liberating potentiality without suffering from its hitherto murderous consequences.

[1] 'Les Amandiers', in *L'Été*, Paris, 1954, pp. 71–72.

The notion of revolt with which Camus is concerned has a specific origin and takes place in a clearly defined context. It originates at the time when men decide whether they live in a society based on religious faith, which Camus calls the sacred, or whether they will seek to forge their destiny in exclusively human terms. This means that the revolt at the origin of all the succeeding revolts which the western world has experienced took place during the Enlightenment, the period which Paul Hazard characterized as 'the crisis of the European consciousness'. Men may opt for the sacred, which for Camus is a society in which there are no real problems because the answers have all been given in advance, and where there are no questions but rather 'only eternal answers and commentaries'.[1] Men have, however, opted for the exclusively human, or what Camus calls the world of revolt, where questions are continually being asked and where they must be answered reasonably.

Camus holds that revolt originally implies the defiance of God. It consists of the simultaneous germination in the mind of the rebel of his rejection of an intolerable situation and his affirmation of a value in opposition to which the situation is defined for him as intolerable. By revolting against his condition and challenging the grounds on which that condition is justified, man is also revolting against the power which compels him to live in that situation.[2] Camus does not make it clear why the rebel may not also ground his revolt on the power of God. If God is responsible for man's situation, is he not also responsible for the revolt which is part of that situation? Men, on the whole, have been much more prone to revolt against churches than against God, and one great revolution, the Puritan revolution in England, was the work of deeply religious men. But Camus insists that while revolt is not equivalent to atheism, it necessarily brings into question the power of God to maintain a human order. This task then falls upon the shoulders of the rebel, who has implicitly assumed responsibility for maintaining a different order. But how is the rebel to justify the new order without reference to the God he has defied?

The greater part of Camus' analysis in *The Rebel* is devoted to a study of the various ways in which men have answered that

---

[1] *The Rebel*, pp. 20–21.   [2] Ibid., pp. 23–25.

question and to the consequences which have flowed from the answers that they have proposed. The theoretical underpinnings of the answers Camus calls metaphysical rebellion; the violence that has been unleashed in their name he calls historical rebellion. The argument is not always easy to follow in its details: artists and terrorists, philosophers and politicians follow one another across Camus' pages in episodic fashion. But the main lines of the analysis are clear. When faced with the problem of justifying a human order, without reliance on divine destiny, men have invented three different solutions. The first one historically was to replace eternal truths with abstract principles: this is the solution of bourgeois democracy. The second was to reintroduce destiny in the form of history: this is the Marxist solution. The third was to hold that if nothing is forbidden, everything is permissible: this is the Nazi solution. Camus is critical of all three solutions, either for their logic or for the values that they imply or both, and, in all three cases, for their contributions to what Camus regarded as the nihilism of the modern era.

The adoption of the position that if nothing is forbidden, all is permissible, is the choice that leads most directly to nihilism. Camus sees this choice at work in the minds and practices of such otherwise diverse figures as the Marquis de Sade, the surrealists, and Hitler; in each case the assumptions are the same even if their consequences differ vastly in scale. The position denies all morality and leads to the conclusions that there is nothing in the world but the individual and his desires and that there is no limit to the means that he may employ to satisfy them. It is irrational because it represents a demand for a total freedom that is impossible, and it is destructive because the efforts to satisfy the impossible demand can mean only the unremitting pursuit of power. Reason gives way before instinct, fulfilment means domination, and the effort to dominate dehumanizes. The logic of the position leads to 'a complete totalitarianism, universal crime, an aristocracy of cynicism, and the desire for an apocalypse'.[1] The fantasies of de Sade and the gratuitous acts of the surrealists become the 'unadulterated dynamism' of the nazi state. And because the only value is complete success, there can be no discrimination

[1] *The Rebel*, p. 46.

among degrees of failure, with the result that a Hitler could deliberately lead his country to total disaster.[1]

The bourgeois, democratic path of revolt from the sacred society is different from the one that leads through de Sade to Hitler. The essence of the bourgeois solution is to replace the eternal truths of God with the abstract principles of reason, which becomes, in effect, the new Supreme Being. But the reign of reason, which Camus dates from the French Revolution, gets off to a bad start. The Revolution, whose leaders at first declare against the death penalty, ends by claiming thousands of lives. The law which should be based on reason ends up by reflecting the arbitrary will of legislators.

It is true that the formal principles established by the Revolution are still principles and that they are set above the march of history. In this respect, justice, reason, and truth could have served as guides to men as they confronted the problems of government. But, in Camus' view, the bourgeoisie of the nineteenth century governed hypocritically. It invoked formal virtue but acted on contrary principles, thereby discrediting the principles in the name of which it acted. And in a condemnation that Camus places in the present tense, he describes the bourgeois aspect of contemporary nihilism as the willingness 'in the name of formal principles, to find all direct violence inexcusable and then to sanction that diffuse form of violence which takes place on the scale of world history'.[2]

The third path of revolt for men who have abandoned the notion of a divine destiny is to retain the notion of destiny, but to anchor it in history rather than in God. This is the path which has led to contemporary communism, and Camus follows its course from Hegel through Marx, across the disillusionment following upon the violation by the bourgeoisie of its formal principles, through Lenin, and into the concentration camps of the Stalinist régime.

With Hegel, the ideas of justice, reason, and truth, which appear as guides in their original bourgeois conception, now become goals. The notion is broadcast that men should not act on the basis of principles, but only in view of goals. 'The

[1] *The Rebel*, pp. 36–47 (on de Sade); pp. 88–99 (on surrealism); and pp. 177–87 (on Hitler).

[2] Ibid., p. 169; on the bourgeois revolt generally, see pp. 112–32.

movement which starts with Hegel, and which is triumphant today, presumes . . . that no one is virtuous, but that everyone will be.'[1] 'Values are thus only to be found at the end of history' and 'all morality becomes provisional'.[2] Marx adopted the Hegelian perspective and translated it into a secularization of the Christian prophecy; the inevitable is defined in advance. While the Marxist prophecy conflicts with the historical facts, at least the values that it presumes lie at the end of history are still values, and the survivors are therefore to be served. With Lenin, however, the decision is made to hasten the inevitable. The conditions of the inevitable are established, and everything is sacrificed in order to create those conditions. Instead of waiting for the values to come, revolution itself is made the supreme value, and it becomes even more important than the people it is presumed to serve. The dream ends with Lenin's assertion that ' "it has never been vouchsafed to any socialist to guarantee the advent of the higher phase of Communism" '.[3] With this, freedom is dead.

The death of God, then, has led to several strands of thought and practice. One can, like Saint-Just, replace God with formal virtue and kill in its name. One can, like Hitler, defy destiny in the pursuit of power, or, like Lenin, pursue power to encourage destiny. All three paths lead to nihilism and terror. Is it possible to chart another course which, while preserving what is valid in the movement of revolt itself, can avoid the murderous consequences which revolt has so far produced?

VI   The Philosophy of Revolt

Camus' reply to this question is posed modestly as the kind of philosophy which might be founded on revolt, if revolt could be the foundation of a philosophy. This is a philosophy of moderation, sustained by an awareness of man's ignorance, the relativity of values, the inevitability of injustice and suffering, but at the same time by an awareness of the necessity of seeking to transcend one's condition.[4]

[1] Ibid., p. 136.   [2] Ibid., p. 142.
[3] Ibid., p. 231; the analysis from Hegel through Stalin appears in many places, especially pp. 133–48, 188–245.
[4] Ibid., pp. 289–90.

The rebel is indispensable to the service of mankind. It is through rebellion that values are affirmed. These values, however, are common, not private, because, by risking death, the rebel proves that he is willing to sacrifice himself for a cause more important than himself.[1] That is why the demand for freedom at the origin of de Sade's revolt becomes a corruption when it extends into a demand for total freedom. For Camus, values are never absolute, but they are universal; the rebel's demand for freedom is limited by everyone else's claim to freedom.[2]

The values of rebellion, according to Camus' conception, are neither formal nor historical;[3] they are, rather, concrete and immediate. They are concrete in that they are affirmed within the context of specific situations. They are immediate in that they are affirmed contemporaneously with the flow of events. Camus' theory of rebellion, therefore, rejects both the 'bourgeois humanism'[4] which he believed rested on the 'disembodied and formal values' of the French Revolution[5] and the notion of the reign of history which attributes absolute value to some event that is presumed to come.[6] 'Real generosity toward the future', Camus wrote, 'lies in giving all to the present.'[7] The bourgeois places values above history and the cynic identifies them with history; Camus sees the relationship differently. Through rebellion, values appear in history at the same time as they interrupt history. When the rebel says 'No', he opens a breach with the present. But the interruption of history is itself an historical act which cannot fail to have consequences. The rebel must look closely to his behaviour, for historical acts are full of risks.

Where the risks of action are great in that the probability of murder—and of murder on a large scale—is high, the responsible intellectual attitude is doubt and the responsible form of behaviour requires moderation. It has already been pointed out that Camus was greatly impressed as early as 1939 with the attitude of Ignazio Silone's hero, Pietro Sacca, in *Bread and Wine*, that 'great revolutionary work'.[8] At that time, Camus

---

[1] *The Rebel*, p. 15.   [2] Ibid., p. 284.   [3] Ibid., p. 252.
[4] 'Entretien sur la révolte', in *Actuelles II*, pp. 56–57.
[5] 'Révolte et servitude', in *Actuelles II*, p. 100.   [6] *The Rebel*, p. 16.
[7] Ibid., p. 304.   [8] See Chapter 2, pp. 37–38.

wrote that 'the militant who is too quickly convinced is to the true revolutionary what the bigot is to the mystic. For the greatness of a faith is measured by its doubts.'[1] Similarly, the only hero of *The Rebel* of 1951 is the Russian terrorist Kaliayev, who doubted to the end. But doubt does not mean paralysis; it implies caution about others. The rebel must remember that he is not God even if he has defied him, and that however noble the goal which it is his intention to achieve, it will not be salvation and there will be a price. For Camus, the unadulterated virtue of Saint-Just can be as lethal as unpurified cynicism. 'Any historical enterprise can therefore only be a more or less reasonable or justifiable adventure. It is primarily a risk. In so far as it is a risk it cannot be used to justify any excess or any ruthless and absolutist position.'[2]

Camus' argument, therefore, involves a triple plea: for the maintenance of what has been called elsewhere the 'open society';[3] for the reduction of violence; and, most fundamentally, for the adoption by every person of an attitude of moral responsibility. Discontent is inevitable in a world where the notions of liberty and equality are propagated but in which actual conditions fail to fulfil the promise of such noble values. This is as it should be, because it is only through active discontent—what Camus calls rebellion—that closer approximations to the fulfilment of this promise can be achieved. But achievement will never be more than approximation, so the way must be left open for succeeding waves of active discontent. This implies the right to freedom of criticism,[4] which does not exist in a system like that of the Soviet Union, which reflects the conviction that the future is assured by what already has been done, or like that of nazi Germany, which rejected all values other than the unremitting pursuit of power.

Camus' plea for the reduction of violence does not contain the expectation that violence can be totally removed from human affairs. He believed that violence was both inevitable and unjustifiable, but he also distinguished between the violence that is unavoidable in certain circumstances and the systematic use of violence which is legitimized by reference to

[1] *Alger-Républicain*, 23 May 1939, p. 2.   [2] *The Rebel*, p. 289.
[3] Karl Popper, *The Open Society and Its Enemies*.
[4] *The Rebel*, pp. 290–1.

some general principle.[1] The distinction is valid, even if it must necessarily blur at some point where general principles must be relied upon to define the circumstances which make violence unavoidable. Camus is no more able than anyone else to solve the problem of violence permanently; it becomes a dilemma: violence is unjustifiable but it may be necessary, absolute non-violence leaves the way open for the violent.[2] His main effort to deal concretely with the problem leads him into inconsistency. Camus admires Kaliayev not only because he doubted even as he acted, but also because he willingly accepted death in retribution for his act of murder.[3] It is surely morally superior to give one's life in a cause than to urge others to risk theirs while protecting one's own. But the principle of a life for a life is inconsistent with Camus' philosophical opposition to both suicide and the death penalty.[4] And when murder is committed for the sake of ideas, acceptance by the murderer of the principle of a life for a life does not imply, as Camus suggests, the refusal to place any idea above human life because it equates the value of lives;[5] it implies only that the value of the idea is placed above two human lives rather than above one.

Camus does not succeed in resolving the dilemma of violence, but the special attention he pays to Kaliayev and the other 'fastidious assassins' does reflect his central concern with the necessity for the individual to assume personal responsibility for his acts rather than to rest them on some general principle.[6] This is, in essence, his message for the bourgeois democratic society which, unlike the Soviet one or the Nazi one, does permit

---

[1] 'Première Réponse', in *Actuelles*, p. 184; also *The Rebel*, p. 169.

[2] *The Rebel*, p. 291.   [3] Ibid., p. 173.

[4] Camus' notebooks for 1947 indicate that he was not entirely happy with the life-for-a-life argument. 'La grande pureté du terroriste style Kaliayev, c'est que pour lui le meurtre coincide avec le suicide. . . . Une vie est payée par une vie. Le raisonnement est faux, mais respectable. (Une vie ravie ne vaut pas une vie donnée.) Aujourd'hui le meurtre par procuration. Personne ne paye.' *Carnets, Janvier 1942–Mars 1951*, p. 199.

Camus' argument against suicide appears in *The Myth of Sisyphus*, pp. 15–23, and his argument against the death penalty appears in *Resistance, Rebellion, and Death*, pp. 175–234. See also *The Rebel*, pp. 6 and 292.

[5] *The Rebel*, pp. 169–70.

[6] Tarrou, in *The Plague* (p. 227), says 'I learned that I had had an indirect hand in the deaths of thousands of people; that I'd even brought about their deaths by approving of acts and principles which could only end that way.'

the existence of multiple sources of social and political change and does guarantee freedom of criticism. Camus was usually extremely critical of bourgeois, democratic society,[1] but he did acknowledge that 'the few democratic liberties which we still enjoy are not illusions without importance, which we could permit to be stolen from us without protesting'.[2] It is an important step forward to achieve an open society, but Camus also believed that for it to work well required the presence of open minds.

It is this aspect of Camus' thought which justified his argument, in the face of critics who held that *The Rebel* was essentially an attack on communism, that he gave parallel treatment to 'the bourgeois and formal revolution of 89' and 'the cynical revolution of the 20th century . . .'.[3] Camus' critics are correct up to a point. His main charge against the bourgeoisie of the nineteenth century is that it did not practise what it preached; it professed but did not use as guides the principles which it could have so used. His main charge against the communists is that while they practise what they preach, what they preach is wrong. In the case of communism the failure is intrinsic, in the case of bourgeois democracy the failure is not necessary.[4] But Camus himself is also correct in his claim that he gives communism and democracy parallel treatment in that he criticizes both of them from the viewpoint of his philosophy of rebellion, and while this accepts democratic principles it does not coincide with them.

Camus' philosophy of rebellion is not identical with democratic principles because they are formal principles and Camus wants to apply them rather than to repeat them. Their application depends on individual judgement, however, and not on any principle. Men make their own choices and they cannot attribute responsibility to the principles they invoke for

[1] 'If there were something to conserve in our society, I would not see anything dishonourable in being a conservative. Unfortunately, there is nothing.' 'Révolte et conformisme', in *Actuelles II*, p. 41.

[2] 'Le Pain et la liberté', in *Actuelles II*, p. 166.

[3] 'Révolte et servitude', in *Actuelles II*, pp. 100–1.

[4] I borrow this distinction between an intrinsic and an extrinsic failure from Raymond Aron's comparative analysis of the imperfections of constitutional régimes and single-party systems in *Démocratie et Totalitarisme*, Paris, 1965, pp. 346–7. See Chapter 8, pp. 236–7.

the uses that they make of them. To rest one's case on principle confers a comfort that is unreal. The person whom Camus calls the rebel does not experience this comfort. Because he believes he is right he must act, but he must act as though he might be wrong. The tension in which Camus places the rebel is reminiscent of the world of Emmanuel Mounier.[1] Rebellion is moderation and moderation 'is nothing but pure tension'.[2]

VII   A Morality for Our Time

If a moralist is a thinker with an ethical theory but without a sociology, concerned with individual behaviour but not with institutions, Camus was a moralist. In this respect, his thought differs from Emmanuel Mounier's and Simone Weil's, for they both tried to reconcile their views of how men ought to behave with the conditions of society and they were concerned with the establishment of proper political institutions. Camus' thought almost totally disregards political, social, and economic structures. Yet Camus is a moralist with a difference, and his theory of rebellion has its descriptive as well as its prescriptive values. There is little conventional moralizing in Camus' works; in fact there is an austere irony in his fiction which mocks the conventional moralist. Why else would Camus' narrator tell us that if *The Plague* has a hero, it is Joseph Grand, the man who cannot express himself?[3] And the theory of rebellion is not simply a rule to govern behaviour, it is an

[1] The only comment on Mounier's writings that I know of which is certainly by Camus appears in his notebooks, apparently between May and July of 1949. 'Mounier me conseille dans 'Esprit' de me détourner de la politique, n'ayant pas la tête à cela (cela, en effet, est évident) et de me contenter du rôle bien assez noble et qui m'irait si gentiment d'avertisseur. Mais qu'est-ce qu'une tête politique? la lecture d'Esprit ne me l'apprend pas. . . .' *Carnets, Janvier 1942–Mars 1951*, p. 274. There is also the following remark, in an unsigned editorial which appeared in *Le Soir Républicain* of 9 November 1939: '*Esprit* reparaît. A bien des égards, il semble avoir perdu dans la guerre la lucidité dont il se faisait honneur. Cependant le fonds demeure et il nous est possible de citer cet extrait d'un article d'Emmanuel Mounier. . . .' Mounier, on the other hand, wrote an excellent essay on Camus (see p. 132, note 1).

[2] *The Rebel*, p. 301.

[3] *The Plague*, pp. 43 and 126. Camus wrote in his notebooks in 1950 that all his work was ironical and that he always had to fight against the temptation of cynicism. *Carnets, Janvier 1942–Mars 1951*, p. 317.

instrument for the interpretation of history.[1] It is surely not a sociological instrument, although it contains an invitation to found one. Camus' reading of history does not take place against a background of challenges and responses, rising and falling social forces, or great cultural upheavals. It is, at bottom, Carlylean, although there is nothing in Camus—quite the contrary—to suggest that he thinks of great men only as those whose names are long remembered. The men who rebel 'at the appropriate moment' advance the interests of mankind.[2] It is the 'at the appropriate moment' which is the invitation to a sociology. What is the appropriate moment for rebellion?

As soon as one raises this question, one is tempted to think of the history of rebellion which Camus did not write. He never provides an historical example of an appropriate and effective act of rebellion, with the single exception of the French Resistance, and that is not mentioned in *The Rebel*.[3] Moreover, it is not demonstrated that what Camus calls historical rebellion—the movement into action with all its attendant violence—has not advanced mankind's interests. Unless one ventures into the realm of might-have-been's, historical rebellion must be judged by its consequences. Yet the tracing of consequences is a never-ending, cumulative effort, and the criteria of judgement are multiple. Do we judge the French Revolution, for example, by the blood it caused to be shed or by the egalitarian impulse it set in motion, thereby contributing to the democratic liberties which Camus valued and which he regarded as representing 'exactly what remains to us of the great revolutionary conquests of the last two centuries'?[4]

Camus' historical range is limited to continental Europe; he is almost Machiavellian in his lack of regard for the impact of social forces on men's behaviour; he sometimes escapes into rhetoric. For all of that, there is a persuasiveness about the main bent of his argument that commands attention and respect.

---

[1] This thought was suggested to me by the convocation address entitled 'Civil Disobedience' which was delivered at Earlham College on 7 February 1961 by Leslie W. Dunbar.

[2] *The Rebel*, p. 302.

[3] 'La Chair', in *Actuelles*, p. 90. An English translation of this article appears in *Resistance, Rebellion, and Death*.

[4] 'Le Pain et la liberté', in *Actuelles II*, p. 166.

For one thing, Camus' thought is more in harmony with his age and his universe than is that of either Emmanuel Mounier or, in her later years, Simone Weil. There is in Camus little inveighing against modernity: the Enlightenment is not presented as a kind of sin. The demise of the era of faith was followed by colossal tragedies, and Camus does not flinch from acknowledging the disasters which have led some people to despair of ever being able to prevent the recurrence of similar events, but he does not despair. Nor does he look to a revival of faith as the only means by which the future may be made secure. The age of reason created massive problems, but it also provided the instrument by which men can recognize them, analyse them, and seek to solve them.

To the extent, then, that there is a kind of historical pessimism at large, Camus can remain in communication with its representatives because he does not deny the evidence on which this pessimism is based.[1] But Camus is personally enough of a child of the Enlightenment to refuse to share the pessimism itself. 'Man can master in himself everything that should be mastered,' he wrote in *The Rebel*,[2] and as early as 1940 he spoke of the need to appease 'the infinite anguish of free souls'. 'Naturally,' he went on, 'it is a superhuman task. But one calls superhuman the tasks that it takes men a long time to accomplish, that's all.'[3] Camus did not believe in any linear or dialectical notion of progress, but he subscribed to just enough optimism about man's capacity to order the world[4] to enable him to communicate also with those of his contemporaries whose confidence in man's ability to control his destiny was greater than his own.

Camus is also in tune with his century in that he refused to erect suffering into a virtue, as Simone Weil, for example, was eventually to do. Human suffering is precisely what Camus hoped to limit. He believed that suffering could never be totally eliminated, but he steadfastly held that men must seek

---

[1] See the comment by Angus Wilson: 'J'ai beaucoup de reconnaissance envers Camus pour son testament d'humaniste, particulièrement parce qu'il est peut-être le seul des humanistes contemporains à ne pas refuser de voir toutes les preuves accumulées contre l'homme.' 'Albert Camus', in *La Nouvelle Révue Française*, Numéro Spécial, Hommage à Albert Camus, No. 87 (March 1960), pp. 547–8.

[2] P. 303.   [3] 'Les Amandiers', in *L'Été*, pp. 71–72.   [4] Ibid., p. 71.

to limit the suffering that they cause one another. Men will, of course, suffer in the very process of trying to limit suffering. The state of mind of the rebel is never comfortable and the physical risks he runs are extreme. But the rebel does not enter into these tensions out of any philosophical asceticism; they are, rather, the result of a choice that is ultimately inspired by a very different kind of philosophy—one which acknowledges human happiness as good. Camus' rebel is a hero, but on Camus' scale of values heroism comes after happiness.[1] The pursuit of happiness, however, requires the kind of heroism which risks happiness while cherishing it.[2]

[1] At least, if Dr. Rieux in *The Plague* speaks on this point for Camus (p. 126).

[2] 'Considérer l'héroisme et le courage comme des valeurs secondaires—*après avoir fait preuve de courage.*' *Carnets, Janvier 1942–Mars 1951*, pp. 123–4. Italics in original. Also see p. 128.

6

Jean-Paul Sartre: Existential Marxist

I Camus and Sartre

ALBERT CAMUS is linked in the public mind with Jean-Paul Sartre. Men can be associated in the minds of others by what distinguishes them as much as by what they have in common if the distinction is sufficiently dramatized, and this is true of Camus and Sartre. Their public quarrel in the pages of *Les Temps Modernes* during the summer of 1952 served to guarantee that for a long time to come the name of one of them could not fail to evoke that of the other.

The two men, however, share a number of features in common. They acquired literary prominence more or less simultaneously as the major new talents of post-war France. Camus received the Nobel Prize for literature in 1957; it was not until 1964 that the prize was awarded to Sartre, who declined to accept it, but Sartre's influence upon the young French post-war generation may have been, at least for a time, considerably greater than that of Camus.[1] Both men, of course, belong to the long French line of politically-minded men of letters, which Sartre apparently entered into with a certain self-consciousness.

There was always a good deal of common ground between the two and in the formative periods of their thought they

---

[1] In 1957, a sample of persons born between 1927 and 1939 were asked: 'If you had to designate one of the following authors as having particularly struck the mind of people of your age, whom would you choose?' A larger percentage of the respondents (20 per cent.) selected Sartre than anyone else; 9 per cent. selected André Gide, and 9 per cent. selected François Mauriac; only 5 per cent. selected Camus. Each of the other six authors listed (Alain, Aragon, Bernanos, Breton, Malraux, and Maurras) was designated by fewer than 5 per cent. of the respondents. See Françoise Giroud, *La Nouvelle Vague, Portraits de la jeunesse*, Paris, 1958, and *L'Express*, 5 and 12 December 1957.

adopted a number of common assumptions. There was enough similarity at least of mood, tone, and theme in their early writings to suggest more of an identity of outlook between them than their later works were to display, but associations once established are not easily undone, and the public vaguely identified them both with the emerging and popular current of thought loosely known as existentialism.

It was Sartre, of course, who was most instrumental in popularizing existentialism in France, and Camus denied being an existentialist, saying that he believed existentialist conclusions to be false,[1] but Camus was certainly preoccupied with the same themes that concern French existentialists like Sartre and Simone de Beauvoir. To some extent, after their discovery of each other's kindred works, they may also even have inspired one another.[2] Camus and Sartre both expressed the view that life is gratuitous or contingent and they found it difficult to justify one mode of existence more than another. One year before Sartre wrote that 'it amounts to the same thing whether one gets drunk alone or is a leader of nations',[3] Camus had written that it is all the same if one is a conqueror or a substitute postman.[4] Both men are preoccupied with

[1] 'Le Pessimisme et le courage', in *Actuelles, Chroniques 1944–1948*, Paris, 1950, p. 111.

[2] Camus reviewed Sartre's *La Nausée* and his *Le Mur* in *Alger-Républicain* of 20 October 1938 (p. 5) and 5 March 1939 (p. 5) respectively; Sartre wrote an 'Explication de *L'Étranger*' of Camus in February 1943 (see Jean-Paul Sartre, *Situations I*, Paris, 1947, pp. 99–121).

The adventurer, the Don Juan, and the writer of Camus' *Le Mythe de Sisyphe* also appear in Simone de Beauvoir's *The Ethics of Ambiguity* (translated by Bernard Frechtman, New York, 1948), pp. 57–73. Both writers may have derived these characters directly from Hegel's models of the four types of men; Simone de Beauvoir tells us that her descriptions were 'obviously influenced by those of Hegel' (*La Force des choses*, Paris, 1963, p. 80; Eng. tr. by Richard Howard, *Force of Circumstance*, N.Y., London, 1965), but her discussion can be read as a criticism of Camus' *Le Mythe de Sisyphe*.

There is also a reference in *The Ethics of Ambiguity* (p. 137) to 'the unknown person who throws himself into the Seine and whom I hesitate whether or not to fish out . . .'. Clamence, of Camus' novel *The Fall*, is haunted by his failure to try to help a woman whom he knows has thrown herself into the Seine.

[3] Jean-Paul Sartre, *L'Être et le néant, Essai d'ontologie phénoménologique*, Paris, 1943. Eng. tr. by Hazel E. Barnes, *Being and Nothingness, An Essay on Phenomenological Ontology*, New York, 1956. All references are to the Barnes translation except where otherwise noted; in this case the quotation is from p. 627.

[4] Albert Camus, *Le Mythe de Sisyphe*, Nouvelle édition augmentée d'une étude sur Franz Kafka, Paris, 1942, p. 96. Eng. tr. by Justin O'Brien, *The Myth of Sisyphus and Other Essays*, New York, 1955.

complicity in evil; both men claim to reject theological absolutes and formal principles; both men insist on the ultimate
responsibility of each man for his own behaviour; both men
have a predisposition in favour of change, expressed in the
notion of transcendence of the existing situation. Even the
sources of their moral outlook are similar: Sartre, as we will
see, derives motivation from the viewpoint of society's least-
favoured group; Camus wrote in *The Rebel* that 'those who
find no rest in God or in history are condemned to live
for those who, like themselves, cannot live: in fact, for the
humiliated'.[1]

For all these points of similarity, however, Camus and Sartre
arrived at quite different political conclusions. Camus produced
a theory of political moderation which sought to combine the
necessity for moral intransigence with the need to accept only
approximations to ideals, on a basis of respect for the rights
of free expression, and he was severely critical of both Marxism
and the political practices of the Soviet Union. Sartre, on the
other hand, eventually came to adopt a version of revolutionary Marxism and to confer a favourable prejudice on the
Soviet Union as opposed to the western democracies, attitudes
which Camus deplored.

Sartre's effort to wed Marxism to existentialism is not a
wholly fortuitous development. There are certain analogies
between existentialism and Marxism, if only because both
philosophies reflect their common ancestry in the writings of
Hegel, but the analogies between the two bodies of thought are
perhaps less important than the fact that they tend to comple-
ment each other. Existentialism generally, and Sartre's early
philosophical writings in particular, are concerned essentially
with the individual to the exclusion of the social phenomena
with which politics is associated. Existentialism lacks a sociological component; indeed, it has been contrasted with
sociology as an analytical perspective.[2] It implies an historical
dimension but it lacks an historical theory. It is a dynamic
philosophy, with a built-in stimulus to action, but it is totally
without any ingredients that might give direction to the action

[1] Eng. tr. by Anthony Bower, New York, 1956, p. 304.

[2] See Edward A. Tiryakian, *Sociologism and Existentialism, Two Perspectives on the Individual and Society*, Englewood Cliffs, N.J., 1962. The volume concludes by suggesting that the two perspectives can be viewed as complementary.

it compels. In these circumstances, existentialism by itself does not lead to any concrete political conclusions. It is an analytical scheme which desperately needs help if it is to be of any use to anyone except writers with a penchant for un-resolved dilemmas. By combining Marxism with existentialism, Sartre has tried to give political content to the highly schematic and nearly empty existentialist framework, and at the same time reject, as Simone Weil rejected, the unseen hand of economic determinism.

In this union of Marxism and existentialism, it is not always clear which is the dominant partner. Sartre describes Marxism as the only valid philosophy of the present historical era, and he refers to existentialism only as an ideology, a sort of parasite which feeds on the body of Marxism at the same time as it contributes to Marxism's explanatory power.[1] In general, when Sartre discusses persons, existentialism is still his chief tool of analysis,[2] but when he discusses contemporary politics, Marxism dominates the field.

Camus, in a sense, saw all this coming. When he addressed his letter to 'the director of *Les Temps Modernes*' at the end of June 1952, the immediate occasion was not something that Sartre had written but rather an unfavourable review of *The Rebel* which had been written by Francis Jeanson, a disciple and former secretary of Sartre.[3] The main point of Camus' letter was that Jeanson had seemed to be arguing from Marxist

[1] Jean-Paul Sartre, 'Question de méthode', in *Critique de la raison dialectique* (*précédé de Question de méthode*), Tome I, *Théorie des ensembles pratiques*, Paris, 1960, pp. 17–18, 29. This essay was first published in two parts under the title 'Questions de méthode' in *Les Temps Modernes*, 13 (September 1957), pp. 338–417, and 13 (October 1957), pp. 658–97. Hazel Barnes has written an introduction to and translated 'Question de méthode' under the title *Search for a Method*, New York, 1963.

[2] 'Valéry est un intellectuel petit-bourgeois. . . . Mais tout intellectuel petit-bourgeois n'est pas Valéry.' 'Question de méthode', in *Critique de la raison dialectique*, Tome I, p. 44.

[3] Jeanson's review appeared under the title 'Albert Camus ou l'âme révoltée', in *Les Temps Modernes*, 7 (May 1952), pp. 2070–90. Camus addressed his reply on 30 June 1952 (Albert Camus, *Actuelles II*; *Chroniques 1948–1953*, Paris, 1953, p. 85, n.) and it was published as 'Lettre au directeur des "Temps Modernes"', in *Les Temps Modernes*, 8 (August 1952), pp. 317–33. Sartre's 'Réponse à Albert Camus' and Jeanson's 'Pour tout vous dire' appeared in the same number, on pp. 334–53 and 354–83 respectively. Sartre's 'Réponse à Albert Camus' was reprinted in Jean-Paul Sartre, *Situations, IV*, Paris, 1964, pp. 90–125. Eng. tr. by Benita Eisler, *Situations*, N.Y., 1965.

assumptions, without asserting them explicitly, while failing to meet the objections to Marxism which Camus had raised in his book. Even Sartre's earliest post-war writings are punctuated with Marxist categories,[1] but it was in the same month that Camus wrote to him that Sartre drew closer to the communists than he had been since the end of the war and embarked on a major effort to combine existentialism and Marxism.[2] Camus' criticism of Jeanson, therefore, was also (to use the language of existentialism) a criticism of what Sartre was to become.

Camus' argument was an interesting one: he claimed that existentialism and Marxism were incompatible. If the existentialism were shed and only the Marxism retained, it would be open to the objection that Camus had raised in *The Rebel* against the kind of reasoning which sacrifices the present for values

[1] Notably 'Présentation des temps modernes', 'Qu'est-ce que la littérature', and 'Matérialisme et révolution'. The first essay originally appeared in *Les Temps Modernes*, 1 (October 1945), pp. 1–21; the second ibid., volume 2, from February to the end of June 1947; and both were reprinted in Jean-Paul Sartre, *Situations, II*, Paris, 1948, pp. 9–30 and 57–330. The second essay has been translated by Bernard Frechtman under the title *What is Literature?*, New York, 1947. The third essay originally appeared in *Les Temps Modernes*, 1 (June 1946), pp. 1537–63 and 2 (July 1946), pp. 1–32. It was reprinted in Jean-Paul Sartre, *Situations, III*, Paris, 1949, pp. 135–225; an English translation by Annette Michelson appears in Jean-Paul Sartre, *Literary and Philosophical Essays*, London, 1955, pp. 189–239.

[2] Sartre apparently went through a severe period of self-questioning, from the outbreak of the Korean War in 1950 until the middle of 1952, about what his attitude towards the Soviet Union and the French Communist Party should be. He reports that the precipitating cause of his decision to align himself with (but not to join) the communists was the arrest in June 1952 of the French communist leader, Jacques Duclos. 'Les derniers liens furent brisés, ma vision fut transformée: un anticommuniste est un chien, je ne sors pas de là, je n'en sortirai plus jamais . . . après dix ans de ruminations, j'avais atteint le point de rupture et n'avais besoin que d'une chiquenaude. En langage d'église, ce fut une conversion. . . . Au nom des principes qu'elle m'avait inculqués, au nom de son humanisme et de ses "humanités", au nom de la liberté, de l'égalité, de la fraternité, je vouai à la bourgeoisie une haine qui ne finira qu'avec moi.' (Jean-Paul Sartre, 'Merleau-Ponty vivant', in *Les Temps Modernes*, 17 (Numéro Spécial), 1961, p. 347), reprinted in Jean-Paul Sartre, *Situations, IV*, pp. 189–287. Sartre's ambivalence is illustrated by his writing, some time after Duclos' release, that his release was the result of Montesquieu's separation of powers principle applied by a proud and scrupulous judge. ('Les Communistes et la paix [II]', *Les Temps Modernes*, 8 (October–November 1952), p. 708. Reprinted in Jean-Paul Sartre, *Situations, VI* ('Problèmes du marxisme', 1), Paris, 1964). Camus probably knew something of Sartre's ruminations, as they were personally acquainted.

For Simone de Beauvoir's account of Sartre's uncertainty between 1950 and 1952 and of the relations between Camus and Sartre, see her *La Force des choses*, pp. 249–52, 260–2, 275, 278–82.

presumed to lie in the future. Camus did not say what the result would be if the Marxism were shed and only the existentialism retained, except that in that case his book could not be condemned absolutely. Is it unreasonable to believe, however, that Camus, who denied being an existentialist, thought that existentialism was more likely to lead to his own philosophy of moderation than to any other?

II   Sartrean Existentialism

The main philosophical work in which Sartre set forth his existentialist theory is *L'Être et le néant*.[1] This work is large, abstract, and cast in a peculiar vocabulary without indulgence for the reader, but while it is obscure on some points its main themes are clear enough. The work is a study in ontology, which deals with the nature of being, and it is a discussion of the human being and of the human being's relation to the world and to other human beings. The principal concepts which Sartre employs in discussing these themes are freedom, responsibility, situation, and conflict.

The central argument of Sartrean existentialism is that each man is individually and totally responsible for what he is and does, and for all the world and all that the world contains. There is no such thing as a human nature, which would define in advance what man is or what he might become if all his potentialities were realized. Each man creates his own essence in a lifelong process of making choices which cumulatively contribute to what he is at any point in time, and it is only at his death, when no more choices are open to him, that a determination of what his essence was can be made. According to this view, man is always in a process of becoming. What he becomes depends upon what he does, and what he does depends upon what he wants to be, or what Sartre calls his 'project'. And in the selection of his 'project', as well as in the succession of choices through which his project is manifested (or which manifest changes in his project), man is completely free. Man is free to constitute his own essence; in fact, he cannot do otherwise than exercise this freedom which is inescapably his.

Sartre's concept of freedom must be understood in this

[1] See p. 149, note 3.

special sense, although he also uses the term in other senses.[1]
In the existentialist sense, freedom means simply the capacity
to make a choice in every situation (or not to make a choice,
which is a form of making a choice). This view of freedom
is quite different from other concepts of freedom which conceive of it as rational, in the sense that only the rational man
is free, or as a faculty, in the sense that freedom depends
upon the absence or relative absence of constraints upon one's
behaviour. It would not be correct to say that Sartre is unconcerned with why people make the choices that they do,
because a substantial portion of his work—what he calls
existential psycho-analysis—is concerned precisely with trying
to identify individual persons' projects as they are revealed by
their succession of choices,[2] but for Sartre, freedom has nothing
to do with the rationality of the choices one makes. Freedom
means only that a choice is always possible. Similarly, freedom
has nothing to do with the absence or presence of constraints
upon one's behaviour, because even in the face of constraint,
man is still free to choose more than one course of action.
In fact, according to this existential view of freedom, it is
precisely a man's attitude towards a situation which establishes
whether or not, or the extent to which, a situation is constraining. Freedom has nothing to do with the success or failure of the
course one adopts, or with the extent to which the outcome of
an action may be determined in advance by the situation.
Freedom refers simply to the autonomy of the choice.[3]

[1] The discussion of freedom in the existentialist sense in *Being and Nothingness*
is summarized on pp. 476–81. Also see p. 483. For more orthodox uses of the word
freedom as external constraints upon one's behaviour, see 'Qu'est-ce que la
littérature', in *Situations, II*, where Sartre says 'the freedom to write implies the
freedom of the citizen' (p. 113), and speaks of militating 'in favour of the freedom
of the person' (p. 298) and of denouncing 'violations of formal and personal freedoms' (p. 306).

[2] On existential psycho-analysis, see *Being and Nothingness*, pp. 626–7. For Sartre's
biographical analyses, see *Baudelaire*, Paris, 1947 (Eng. tr. by Martin Turnell,
London, 1949, Norfolk, Conn., 1950) and *Saint Genet, comédien et martyr*, Paris, 1952
(Eng. tr. by Bernard Frechtman, *Saint Genet: Actor and Martyr*, N.Y., 1963). See
the shorter account of Flaubert, in which existential psycho-analysis is combined
with Marxist materialism, in 'Question de méthode', in *Critique de la raison dialectique*, Tome I, pp. 89–95. And see Sartre's autobiographical account, *Les Mots*,
Paris, 1964 (first published in *Les Temps Modernes*, 19 (October 1963), pp. 577–649,
and 19 (November 1963), pp. 769–834. Eng. tr. by Bernard Frechtman, *The
Words*, N.Y., 1964.

[3] *Being and Nothingness*, p. 483.

Such a view of freedom is radically incompatible with any form of determinism. Sartrean existentialism rejects both the kind of economic determinism which holds that certain choices are necessarily produced by the economic circumstances in which people find themselves and the psychological determinism which holds that a certain choice necessarily follows from a given state of the unconscious, without regard to a person's real intentions. Man is not compelled to be a slave either of his economic condition or of his passions; if he appears to be either, in the Sartrean view, it is because he chooses to be. No choice is determined; for Sartrean existentialism, there is no such thing as a freedom which is not total and absolute.

To say that man is always completely free in that he is always free to make a choice is not to say that he is always free to choose *anything*. The choices that one makes are always, to use the word which Sartre employs in *L'Être et le néant*, 'conditioned' by the situation in which one finds oneself.[1] The situation may make it impossible to make some choices, but it never makes it impossible to make any choice at all. The situation of the prisoner is such that he is not free to walk out of the prison, but he is free to choose between trying to escape and not trying to escape.[2] The situation of a person, however, is not something that is wholly external to that person. Any situation may include what is external to the person—what Sartre calls the 'brute existent'—but it also includes that person's relationship to the elements of the situation which are external to him. It is precisely this relationship which determines what Sartre, borrowing from the French philosopher, Gaston Bachelard, refers to as the 'coefficient of adversity' to be found in things.[3] This coefficient of adversity, that is, the extent to which the external elements of a person's situation appear to be constraining, is a function of the end which that person has freely chosen. 'The rock will not be an obstacle if I wish at any cost to arrive at the top of the mountain . . . it will discourage me if I have freely fixed limits to my desire of making the projected climb.'[4] It is in this sense that constraint has nothing to do with freedom within the context of Sartrean existentialism; it is freedom which determines whether or not constraints exist.

[1] Sartre discusses the concept of the situation in *Being and Nothingness*, pp. 481–9.
[2] Ibid., pp. 483–4.   [3] Ibid., p. 324.   [4] Ibid., p. 488.

This view of freedom as choice exercised within but not determined by the situation is the foundation of Sartre's conception of responsibility. There are two facets of responsibility in Sartre's analysis: what for convenience may be called the private and the public (although Sartre makes no such explicit distinction and employs no such labels). The private facet of responsibility holds that each man is responsible for his acts in that he may not attribute them either to some external constraint or to some internal disposition. The public facet of responsibility holds that through his acts each man is responsible for all the world. Responsibility in this context is to be taken in a declarative and not a normative sense: 'we are taking the word "responsibility" in its ordinary sense as "consciousness (of) being the uncontestable author of an event or of an object" '.[1]

The private facet of responsibility, therefore, means simply that everyone is totally responsible for his own behaviour. To hold otherwise, in Sartre's view, is to give way to what he calls the 'spirit of seriousness' and to evidence what he calls 'bad faith'. To be 'serious', in Sartre's interpretation of the term, is to attribute 'more reality to the world than to oneself'.[2] It is to believe that the world requires one to choose as one does, rather than to accept the reality that one always makes one's own choices regardless of what the world is like, and that it is by making one's choices that one makes the world. To be in 'bad faith' is to say that one could not do otherwise, when it is always true that one could have done otherwise if one had wanted to. The spirit of seriousness denies the reality of human freedom and bad faith is the alibi for the evasion of responsibility. On the other hand, to display a consciousness of one's responsibility, to acknowledge one's own freedom, is to display good faith. The person in good faith recognizes that he is what he is because he has wanted to be what he is, and who recognizes that whatever he does, he does because he chooses freely to do it.

The private facet of responsibility concerns its locus; the

---

[1] *Being and Nothingness*, p. 553. But Sartre precedes this statement with the comment that 'the considerations which are about to follow are of interest primarily to the ethicist...', and his whole discussion of responsibility is shot through with language which conveys moral connotations; see pp. 553–6.

[2] Ibid., p. 580.

public facet concerns its range of application. This range is vast. Sartre holds that each person is responsible for all the world, and by this he means that personal responsibility extends as far as the range of a person's consciousness. There appear to be two grounds for this assertion. One is that nothing which happens in the world has any meaning for a person except as a function of that person's project. Things happen for a person *through* that person; nothing happens *for him* if he does not perceive its happening; hence, that person is the *author* of whatever he perceives to happen.[1] The second ground is that a person is always free to try to alter what exists. If he does so, he is rejecting something and in this case he is not choosing it. But if a person makes no effort to change the situation, he thereby demonstrates that he chooses it.

If I am mobilized in a war, this is *my* war; it is in my image and I deserve it. I deserve it first because I could always get out of it by suicide or by desertion; these ultimate possibilities are those which must always be present for us when there is a question of envisaging a situation. For lack of getting out of it I have *chosen* it. This can be due to inertia, to cowardice in the face of public opinion, or because I prefer certain other values to the value of the refusal to join in the war (the good opinion of my relatives, the honor of my family, etc.). Anyway you look at it, it is a matter of a choice. This choice will be repeated later on again and again without a break until the end of the war. . . . If therefore I have preferred war to death or to dishonor, everything takes place as if I bore the entire responsibility for this war. Of course others have declared it, and one might be tempted perhaps to consider me as a simple accomplice. But this notion of complicity has only a juridical sense, and it does not hold here. For it depended on me that for me and by me this war should not exist, and I have decided that it does exist. . . .[2]

The last of the main elements essential to Sartrean existentialism is conflict. Every person's situation includes the existence of other persons and, of course, each person in any given situation is free in the existentialist meaning of the term. The inescapable consequence of the juxtaposition of free human beings is conflict.[3] In fact, Sartre argues that it is from the simplest forms of human communication that the notions of guilt and sin may derive. According to his argument, it is

[1] Ibid., p. 554.   [2] Ibid., italics in the original.
[3] Ibid., pp. 364 and 408-10.

impossible for anyone to treat another person as other than an object, with the result that the very existence of other people produces guilt. And in the eyes of another person—'beneath the Other's look'—a person is necessarily something which he has not personally chosen to be. On the level of the most elementary human relationships, such phenomena as guilt, misunderstanding, and conflict are inevitable.

On the level of more complex social relationships, which have a more direct relevance to political organization, the consequences are the same, for these more complex relationships are always variations of the more fundamental ones.[1] According to Sartrean existentialism, it is absolutely impossible for people—regardless of their intentions—to treat others according to the Kantian dictum.[2] People cannot be treated as ends; they are, for others, inevitably objects, and this means that they are inevitably treated as means. Every effort to organize a situation in such a way as to treat other people as ends is still designed to act upon other people and does in fact act upon them. The organization of a situation is the creation of a means to an end, and other people are necessarily integrated into the situation instrumentally. Society, according to Sartrean existentialism, appears to be a web of different organizational efforts characterized by the desire of some people to produce effects on others and by the desire of others to escape the intended effects.

III Existentialism and Politics

The existentialist view of the ubiquity of freedom and the consequent impossibility of avoiding responsibility for one's acts is in some ways a stirring doctrine, all the more as Sartre employs such words as 'engagement' to designate the conscious confrontation of a person with the external aspects of his situation, and 'good faith' to designate the attitude of the person who is lucidly aware that he and he alone is responsible for the

---

[1] *Being and Nothingness*, pp. 420–3.

[2] Ibid., p. 408. Yet Sartre has said that the equivalent of Kantian good will can be achieved between reader and writer, and he has indicated that the same kind of mutual confidence can and must be established between doctor and patient. 'Qu'est-ce que la littérature', in *Situations, II*, pp. 105 and 293; 'Question de méthode', in *Critique de la raison dialectique*, Tome I, p. 70 n.

choices that he makes. It is conceivable that people who are excessively committed to routine and who accept without reflection the standards set by others can be led to a fuller and more self-determining existence by exposure to this doctrine. There is a certain liberating potentiality in the notion that existentialist 'conversion' is always possible.

At the same time, there is nothing in the existentialist doctrine to provide a guide for behaviour in the real world. In fact, there is little in it which is even directly descriptive of the real world. Three of the four main analytical categories of existentialism—freedom, conflict, and responsibility—are strikingly formal.[1] There is no doubt a tendency towards a high degree of abstraction inherent in any study of ontology, for the subject of the study itself—the nature of being—is already abstract, but Sartre pushes the tendency to the extreme. Freedom, conflict, and responsibility are all treated as absolute and undifferentiated conditions, and each condition is used to cover such a variety of phenomena that the descriptive usefulness of the terms themselves is cast into doubt. A definition of liberty which places in the same category the freedom of the prisoner to choose to try to escape or not to try to escape and the freedom of the mountain climber to choose to try to reach the summit or not to try to reach it is highly formal, and the meaning of freedom becomes obscured in the possibly infinite number of situations in which men may find themselves.

Conflict, also, is an absolute concept in the Sartrean system. Sartre holds that conflict may assume a variety of forms, but these forms are always reducible to the homogeneous category of the impossible attempt of one person to substitute his own volition for that of someone else. There is no consideration of the varying degrees of intensity of conflict which may appear in the normal conduct of human relations, nor is there any discussion of the possibility that conflicts may somehow be reconciled. Similarly, responsibility, in both what may be called its private and its public forms, is regarded as absolute. The private responsibility of a person for his behaviour is total, just as his public responsibility for what surrounds him extends to the limits

---

[1] It is pointed out by Robert G. Olson, in *An Introduction to Existentialism*, New York, 1962, passim, that this kind of criticism of existentialism reflects the pragmatist's view.

of his consciousness of the world. It would be a harsh penal code that rested on the Sartrean notion of private responsibility. The existentialism which Sartre once argued was a humanism holds people responsible even for their emotions,[1] and there would seem to be no place even for the notion of insanity in the doctrine. The difficulty of applying the existentialist concept of private responsibility to such a concrete problem as juvenile delinquency, for example, appears overwhelming. And the notion that each man is responsible for all the world, quite apart from the flimsiness of its foundations, and regarded only with respect to the operative effect it might have on each man's stance before the world, is so overwhelming in its generality that it is as likely to produce bewilderment and paralysis as it is to produce understanding and considered action. The Sartrean concept of public responsibility is important for its moral implications, and it will be discussed later more fully; for the moment it is enough to emphasize that if a man is to take his responsibilities seriously and try to affect the world of which he is held to be the author, he requires an understanding of the structure of the world, if only in terms which identify the points at which he may reasonably expect to affect it.

The Sartrean concepts of freedom, responsibility, and conflict are not meaningless, but they are highly formal and abstract. They take on concrete meaning only when the situations in which they apply are specified. It is this fourth existentialist concept, the situation, which is really the focal point of existential analysis, because without knowledge of the situation, it is not possible to know in what the exercise of freedom consists, what the person is responsible for, or what forms the ubiquitous human conflict takes. Just as Camus' theory of rebellion is an invitation to a sociology which would indicate those crucial moments when the rebel can affect the course of history, so the existentialist concept of the situation is an invitation to a sociology of choices, responsibilities, and conflicts.

---

[1] In his *Esquisse d'une théorie des émotions*, Paris, 1939, Sartre was slightly less categorical on this point than he became in 1943. See the Eng. tr. by Philip Mairet (with a Preface by Mary Warnock), *Sketch for a Theory of the Emotions*, London, 1962, p. 79, and compare with *Being and Nothingness*, pp. 444–5.

The difficulties involved in trying to apply the existentialist concept of freedom to politics without a close analysis of the situation can be illustrated by reference to a comment which Sartre made in an important early post-war article. At that time, he said that it was necessary to 'délivrer' the free man 'by enlarging his possibilities of choice. In certain situations, there is room only for one set of alternatives, of which one course means death. It must be arranged so that man can, in every circumstance, choose life.'[1]

It is not clear from the context whether Sartre was referring here to two separate but related aims—enlarging the possibilities of choice generally and avoidance of alternatives in which one course leads to death in particular—the second of which would be a specific and important application of the first, or whether he was thinking essentially of avoiding death among alternatives and believed that this was more or less identical with enlarging possibilities of choice. In either case, however, the statement raises a number of questions which Sartre does not answer.

The notion of generally enlarging possibilities of choice is superficially appealing. Everyone can think of choices which he does not now have but which he thinks he would like to have. One can also think of specific social applications of the principle of enlarged choice which would be beneficial: increasing the possibilities for educational and career choices for people whose opportunities are limited is an obvious example. Other choices which everyone does not now have might be added to the list: workers might want to have a choice of employers and citizens might want to have a choice of rulers. But the abstract notion of enlarging the possibilities of choice is not even analytically clear, for the simple reason that there are some kinds of choice which necessarily involve only one set of alternatives: one votes or one does not, one goes to church or one does not, one marries or one does not. It is true, of course, that the choices open to the voter, the churchgoer, or the bachelor might be enlarged: there might be more candidates, more churches, or more potential marriage partners than there are in any given situation. But this kind of enlargement of the possibilities of choice is not automatically beneficial. Whether these enlarged possibilities of choice are individually or socially beneficial would depend on a number of concrete considerations, such as the effect of a multiplicity of candidates upon the functioning of the political system, the effect of a multiplicity of churches upon the capacity of any one of them to satisfy its adherents, the effect of a multiplicity of potential marriage partners upon the possibility of a person making a personally satisfying choice. The number of choices available to a person may, in certain situations, be excessive, just as the indefinite multiplication of choices is, in the end, inconceivable because of the limits of human communication. Sartre's reference to enlarging the possibilities of choice is too general to be a serviceable criterion for social action. Too much depends upon what the choices are.

Sartre is somewhat more concrete in his reference to choices which do not have death as one of the alternatives, but in the article in which he made the reference he did not actually specify the kinds of situation he had in mind. In a later writing he refers to the situation of the worker who either accepts the terms of employment prescribed by his employer or starves, but he has also written that the necessity of working for a living is part of the human condition, so it is difficult to see how the alternative of death can be removed from this particular choice.[1] Of course, the problem can be approached as one of enlarging the worker's possibilities of affecting favourably the conditions under which he will work. In so far as experience is a guide, the establishment of conditions favourable to the worker generally requires a rising standard of living, institutions which tend to equilibrate the power of the workers with that of the employers, such as independent trade unions and universal suffrage, labour mobility, easily accessible information about jobs, and the like. Sartre, however, does not discuss remedies of this sort or even view the problem in this fashion. Instead, he has taken a dogmatic stance in favour of socialism: 'the liquidation of the capitalist social structure, otherwise

---

[1] 'Voyez le libre contrat, pièce maîtresse de la mécanique: comme il combine heureusement la menace de mort et la liberté du travail; l'ouvrier est un homme qui signe librement sous peine de mort.' 'Les Communistes et la paix [II]', p. 757. Sartre refers to working for a living as part of the human condition in his *Réflexions sur la question juive*, Paris, 1946, pp. 76–77. Eng. tr. by George J. Becker, *Anti-Semite and Jew*, N.Y., 1948.

known as what one calls revolution'.[1] Sartre's conception of freedom prevents him from accepting the economic determinism of orthodox Marxism, but in almost every other respect he speaks the language of Marxism and regards the abolition of capitalism and the establishment of socialism as the indispensable prerequisite for a good society.

IV   Responsibility and Revolution

There is no necessary connexion between Sartrean existentialism and Marxism, even when Marxism is shorn of its economic determinism. Marxism is a call to action of a specific sort, because that action is held to be right, and Sartrean existentialism—at least if it is to be equated with the argument set forth in *L'Être et le néant*—is morally indifferent. *L'Être et le néant* is a study in ontology, and 'ontology itself can not formulate ethical precepts'.[2] The only ground for judgement implied in this work is the one which underlies all rational inquiry: the distinction between truth and error, and in a work where Sartre came as close to laying down ethical precepts as he ever has, he indicated that there is a distinction between a logical judgement and a moral judgement.[3]

Some scholars have introduced elements of a moral theory into Sartre's ontology. It has been suggested that authenticity, the awareness of one's freedom and of one's responsibility for

[1] Jean-Paul Sartre, David Rousset, and Gérard Rosenthal, *Entretiens sur la politique*, Paris, 1949, p. 40. In 'Qu-est-ce que la littérature', *Situations, II*, p. 302, Sartre described revolution as 'un phénomène historique comportant à la fois le changement du régime de la propriété, le changement du personnel politique, et le recours à l'insurrection . . .'.

[2] *Being and Nothingness*, p. 625.

[3] 'Mais on peut juger, cependant, car . . . on choisit en face des autres, et on se choisit en face des autres. On peut juger d'abord (et ceci n'est peut-être pas un jugement de valeur, mais c'est un jugement logique), que certains choix sont fondés sur l'erreur, et d'autres sur la vérité. On peut juger un homme en disant qu'il est de mauvaise foi . . . je n'ai pas à le juger moralement, mais je définis sa mauvaise foi comme une erreur.' Jean-Paul Sartre, *L'Existentialisme est un humanisme*, Paris, 1946, pp. 80–81. Eng. tr. by Bernard Frechtman, *Existentialism*, N.Y., 1947.
   Francis Jeanson cautions readers against relying on this work to the exclusion of Sartre's other writings, because it 'manifeste une position qui est précisément l'inverse de l'attitude méthodologique adoptée par Sartre dans tous ses autres ouvrages philosophiques', and reports that Sartre regarded it as an 'error'. *Le Problème moral et la pensée de Sartre*, Paris, 1947, p. 46.

one's own behaviour and for the world, is an existentialist value,[1] and authenticity has been equated with moral responsibility.[2] It is easy to understand why this interpretation has been offered. Sartre regularly uses language that is loaded with moral implications; the very expression 'bad faith' suggests moral censure. But Sartre has explicitly stated that the terms 'authentic' and 'unauthentic' (which were employed by Martin Heidegger) 'are dubious and insincere because of their implicit moral content'.[3] The authentic person faces the facts; the person who displays bad faith does not. Other men may see a basis for moral judgement here; Sartre does not.

But even if one were to concede these points, there is still nothing in the existentialist doctrine to govern the kind of choices men should make. Existentialism alone provides no justification for any particular act, not even for action designed to enlarge man's possibilities of choice.

It is true that by defining man as constantly becoming what his project signifies he will be, Sartrean existentialism contains an inner principle of dynamism which can serve as an incitement to action, at least for those people who, accepting the doctrine, choose to make their behaviour conform to its definitions. But there is more than one form of action and more than one way of envisaging the future. Reform is a way of transcending the present as much as revolution is. Sartre was quite explicit on this score in his early post-war comments on the United States: 'For a Frenchman to denounce an abuse is to speak ill of France, because he sees it in the past and as unchangeable. For an American, it is to prepare a reform, for he sees his country in the future.'[4] His description of American cities unmistakably reflects the dynamism he attributes to the human being in *L'Être et le néant*.[5] Yet, when discussing the alternatives before the worker in an important essay of the same period, he limited them to resignation and revolution and

[1] Marjorie Grene, 'Authenticity: An Existential Virtue', *Ethics*, LXII (July 1952), pp. 266–74.

[2] Olson, op. cit., p. 145.

[3] *Being and Nothingness*, p. 531. See also Sartre's *Réflexions sur la question juive*, where he writes that 'authenticity demands much courage and more than courage' (pp. 116–17) but where he also states that the term unauthentic implies no moral blame (pp. 120–21).

[4] 'Présentation', in *Situations, III*, pp. 131–2.

[5] 'Villes d'Amérique', ibid., p. 101.

made no reference to reform.[1] In a more recent work, Sartre seems to bow to historical facts and admit the possibility of reform where it has occurred,[2] but in the same volume he also repeats his earlier argument that the worker can display his liberty under capitalism only by negating the capitalist order.[3] Sartre's personal detestation of the bourgeoisie and his propensity to identify motion with thrust[4] (which compares with Bergson's notion of the *élan vital*) have got the better of his logic.

To say that revolutionary Marxism does not necessarily follow from existentialism is not to say that there is no intelligible relationship between the two. In fact there is, and Sartre's combination of an ethically neutral philosophy with a political theory which demands the complete overthrow of the existing social order and the establishment of socialism is more comprehensible than at first glance it might appear to be.

The main link between Sartre's existentialism and his revolutionary Marxism is in his concept of responsibility, which holds that each man's responsibility extends to the limits of his consciousness. Sartre explicitly uses the term responsibility in a descriptive and not a normative sense, but the implications of the vastness of the range of responsibility are highly significant for anyone who chooses to try to act morally. Existentialism is morally neutral, but existentialists do not have to be. Existentialist man, the man who lives in good faith, bears the burden of knowing that he is the author of all the world, including, of course, all the world's evils. If he has any moral sense at all,

---

[1] '. . . it is he [the worker] who, freely, gives to the proletariat a future of humiliation without respite or of conquest and victory, according to whether he chooses himself as resigned or revolutionary'. 'Présentation des temps modernes', *Situations, II*, p. 28. See also 'Matérialisme et révolution', in *Situations, III*, p. 209.

[2] *Critique de la raison dialectique*, Tome I, pp. 737–8.

[3] Ibid., p. 703.

[4] 'La vitesse ne se marque pas tant, à mes yeux, par la distance parcourue en un laps de temps défini que par le pouvoir d'arrachement.' *Les Mots*, p. 193. Compare with this statement of liberty from 'Question de méthode', in *Critique de la raison dialectique*, Tome I, p. 95: 'Cette relation immédiate . . . avec l'Autre que soi, cette perpétuelle production de soi-même par le travail et le *praxis*, c'est notre structure propre. . . . C'est ce que nous nommons l'existence et par là, nous n'entendons pas une substance stable qui se repose en elle-même mais un déséquilibre perpétuel, un arrachement à soi de tout le corps. Comme cet élan vers l'objectivation prend des formes diverses selon les individus, comme il nous projette à travers un champ de possibilités dont nous realisons certaines à l'exclusion des autres, nous le nommons aussi choix ou liberté.'

this knowledge of the extent of his complicity in evil is bound to be agonizing, and it is more than likely that he will try to make a better world.

The problem of the extent to which one is personally implicated in the evils that surround one is very real; to use a Sartrean term somewhat out of context, it 'haunts' every person of conscience, as it certainly haunted Emmanuel Mounier, Simone Weil, and Albert Camus. Mounier at one time recommended abstention from the economic practices which he believed were peculiarly associated with the capitalism which he regarded as an evil; Simone Weil sought literally to identify herself with the victims of oppression. Camus wrestled continually with the problem of complicity in evil through silence or inaction; the theme is prominent in *The Plague* and dominates *The Fall*. Each man meets this situation in his own way, and Sartre is right in his insistence that what one does or does not do rests on a free choice. The authentic man grasps the nettle; that much is clear. What is less clear is which nettle to grasp. The world is full of evils; where does one start to try to overcome them?[1]

In this domain, as in so many others, most men follow the principle of the division of labour. They select relatively limited fields in which to work, and these areas of concern as well as the methods employed to deal even with identical areas of concern differ from person to person. This specialization results from the differing orders of priority which men give to social needs and from their differing estimates of the probabilities of achievement. There is a variety of human sensibilities. The distribution of causes to which people attach or dedicate themselves reflects the diversity of passions which people can generate. And even when some situations are regarded by many people with relatively equal degrees of compassion, indignation, or revolt, there still will be differences among those

[1] What existentialists call the 'anguish' of freedom is generally held to refer to the awareness that each person is responsible for his actions and cannot shift this responsibility to anyone else or any thing. In the light of the interpretation I offer above, it may also be referred to the problem of deciding at what points of the complex social structure to exercise one's responsibility. It is in this light that one may probably most accurately interpret the sentence in *Les Mots* (p. 211) where Sartre says he 'ne sait plus que faire de sa vie'. Confirmation is lent to this interpretation by Sartre's interview with Jacqueline Piatier in *Le Monde*, 18 April 1964.

people as to which is the most pressing problem with which to deal.

Considerations of efficiency operate also, with respect both to people's estimates of their own talents and to their estimates of the likelihood of their achieving the social goals they set. Some people may think that one way of tackling a problem is the most likely way of bringing about substantial results; others may have a different view. Whether the cause be their passions or their reason, most men who choose to act limit their roles, try their best, are aware of how limited their contribution to a better world is, but while they may be humbled and distressed by their awareness of how much they have left untouched and unimproved, they remain on their chosen path because it is the only way they can see to make any contribution at all.

Some people are less patient and more ambitious than the rest, however, and Sartre must be counted among them. He wants to eliminate all evils and he wants to act on society on a scale consonant with the ambitiousness of the goal. These objectives virtually define the revolutionary attitude. It envisages a *tabula rasa* on which one can build anew, thereby avoiding the troublesome effort of making continual adjustments in the innumerable elements of the social situation which shock the moral conscience. A revolutionary outlook is not an inevitable consequence of the Sartrean notion of responsibility, but it is at least intelligible as a consequence of the frustration which must befall anyone whose philosophy implicates him in all the world's evils and whose moral conscience requires him to seek to do all he can to abolish all those evils.[1]

[1] 'J'ai vécu deux guerres, l'occupation, tous les conflits où la France a été entraînée, l'antagonisme des deux blocs. De l'ensemble de cette histoire violente, nous devons considérer que nous sommes tous responsables. Chacun de nous, ne serait-ce qu'à un degré très leger, car nous avons blâmé cette violence, chacun de nous est responsable de cette violence. Elle a eu lieu malgré nous, et nous avons été entraînés. Nous sommes qualifiés par elle. . . .' Jean-Paul Sartre, in an interview entitled 'Entretien', in *L'Express*, 3 March 1960, p. 29.

'Je lutterai non seulement pour un niveau de vie amélioré, mais aussi pour des conditions de vie démocratiques pour chacun, pour la libération de tous les exploités, de tous les opprimés.' Ibid., p. 30.

In the interview given to Jacqueline Piatier, Sartre spoke of the need for *all* men to become men and for 'the liberation of man', and raised the question of what literature means in a hungry world. *Le Monde*, 18 April 1964.

Simone de Beauvoir cites the following from unpublished notes of Sartre, at the time of his break with Camus in the summer of 1952: 'J'étais victime et complice de la lutte des classes: victime puisque j'étais haï d'une classe entière. Complice

Still, one needs to know what kind of a revolution to promote
and one needs an instrument with which to promote it. It is at
this point that Sartre borrows from Marxism, for this theory
conveniently provides a sociology of the situation in terms of
capitalist exploitation and class struggle, designates a revolutionary class—the proletariat—and prescribes a general social
remedy—socialism.

Another key link between Sartre's position and that of
Marx is in Sartre's argument that the true character of a
society is revealed to that society's least-favoured group and
that if social evils are to be attacked they must be attacked
from this perspective.[1] The notion that there is a truth to a
society is purely arbitrary, but Sartre is dealing here with a
moral problem and we have seen that while existentialism
permits moral choices it requires none. It does, however,
insist on distinguishing truth from error, so the reference to
truth suggests an obligation to act which would be unfounded
without it. As a source of moral perspective, the concept of
'the eyes of the least-favoured' is admirable. It is difficult
to conceive of a better criterion for establishing priorities for
social action. And if we take Simone de Beauvoir's interpretation of Sartre's thought as equivalent to his own,[2] one
can easily agree that when men inflict suffering on others on

puisque je me sentais responsable et impuissant.' *La Force des choses*, p. 280. Earlier
in the same work (p. 262), she cites another relevant passage from Sartre's notes:
'Car cette liberté que j'étais impliquait celle de tous. Et tous n'étaient pas libres.
Je ne pouvais pas sans craquer me mettre sous la discipline de tous. Et je ne pouvais
pas être libre seul.'

[1] 'Pour délivrer les masses du sentiment de leur infériorité, il a fallu liquider
systématiquement toutes les valeurs socialistes d'avant-guerre; il a fallu leur faire
comprendre qu'elles offraient à tous les hommes la chance de regarder l'homme
et la société *dans leur vérité*, c'est-à-dire avec les yeux du plus défavorisé; puisque
l'evolution de la technique aboutissait à disqualifier le travail, cette ultime supér-
iorité de l'homme sur l'homme, il a fallu montrer à cette jeune barbarie, contre
toutes les morales et toutes les élites, que les "supériorités" sont des mutilations, que
la seule relation humaine est celle de l'homme *réel*, total avec l'homme total et
que cette relation, travestie ou passée sous silence, existe en permanence au sein
des masses et n'existe que là. . . .' Jean-Paul Sartre, 'Les Communistes et la paix
[III]', *Les Temps Modernes*, 9 (April 1954), pp. 1792–3 (reprinted in Jean-Paul
Sartre, *Situations, VI*).

[2] 'La pensée synthétique de Marx, comme celle de Sartre, considère que
l'exploitation pervertit la société dans sa totalité: elle mesure les valeurs à la
lumière de l'oppression; c'est ce que signifie chez Sartre l'appel . . . au regard du
plus défavorisé.' Simone de Beauvoir, 'Merleau-Ponty et le pseudo-sartrisme',
Les Temps Modernes, 10 (June–July 1955), p. 2119.

a social scale they spread a corrupting influence throughout the entire society. The difficulty with Sartre's position does not lie in either his moral perspective or the moral diagnosis which Simone de Beauvoir attributes to him, but in the excessive potential for the improvement of the human condition which he attributes to the prosaic socialist remedy which he prescribes. He simply expects too much from socialism. Whether the least-favoured group he has in mind is the proletariat of industrial societies or the peasantry of the underdeveloped societies,[1] he treats capitalism as the basic evil from which oppression derives and calls for the only visible opposite, which is socialism. This is presumed to end the oppression of the proletariat (or the peasantry). Sartre does not to my knowledge explicitly say that socialism will also emancipate the entire society from the corruption which spreads from oppression, although it is implied in Simone de Beauvoir's interpretation, but Sartre makes it clear that he believes that only socialism provides the chance for such a general liberation, and while Sartre criticizes the policies of socialist states, he does not do so from the perspective of the least-favoured group within those states.

Raymond Aron has repeatedly pointed out[2] that this argument parallels in its fundamentals the argument which appears in the early writings of Karl Marx, in which he developed a philosophy to demonstrate the logical necessity of a proletarian revolution as the means to the liberation of all mankind.[3] It was only after producing this philosophical

[1] See Sartre's preface to Frantz Fanon, *Les Damnés de la terre*, Paris, 1961, where, however, it is not always clear whether Sartre is summarizing Fanon's position or also adopting it on his own account. Eng. tr. by Constance Farrington, *The Wretched of the Earth*, N.Y., London, 1965. Sartre's preface is also reprinted in his *Situations, V, Colonialisme et néo-colonialisme*, Paris, 1964, pp. 167–93.

Sartre has also written that 'the socialist revolution is necessary and sufficient to eliminate the anti-Semite . . .'. *Réflexions sur la question juive*, p. 195.

[2] See 'La Grande Peur du mal-pensant', in *Polémiques*, Paris, 1955, pp. 34–38, and *L'Opium des intellectuels*, Paris, 1955, pp. 67–68.

[3] A clear statement of this early Marxist argument appears in Karl Marx and Friedrich Engels, *The German Ideology, Parts I and III*, edited with an Introduction by R. Pascal, N.Y., 1947, pp. 67–78.

The parallel between Sartre's argument and Marx's can be illustrated by this quotation from the First Manuscript of Marx's *Economic and Philosophical Manuscripts*: 'From the relation of alienated labour to private property it also follows that the emancipation of society from private property, from servitude, takes the political form of the *emancipation of the workers*; not in the sense that only the latter's

argument that Marx set out to try to prove that a proletarian revolution was also historically inevitable on the basis of economic determinism. The early Marxist writings, which do not rely on economic determinism, are more compatible with the existentialist doctrine than are the later ones, and they have exercised a strong influence over Sartre, just as they exercised a lesser, though still considerable, influence over Emmanuel Mounier. Sartre has written that after reading Marx he was overwhelmed by 'the proletariat as the incarnation and the vehicle of an idea'.[1] He has also indicated that a decisive influence in his intellectual development was Maurice Merleau-Ponty's manuscript of *Humanisme et terreur*,[2] in which the early Marxist themes are expounded. Merleau-Ponty was eventually to become a critic both of Sartre and of the Marxist arguments he had helped to propagate,[3] but Sartre clung firmly to the one revolutionary philosophy which promises to end all conflicts.

In this regard, it should be emphasized that for anyone with a revolutionary attitude who seeks a revolutionary philosophy, Marxism is the only one available. The meaning of the word revolution is not settled, of course, and it is customary for historians and political scientists to distinguish among national, political, and social revolutions, but only the last necessarily entails an upheaval in social relationships. A national revolution means only a change in the nationality of the rulers and by itself is without necessary social implications. A political revolution implies only a sudden and non-constitutional change in the leading personnel of a political system. A social revolution, however, which is usually combined with either a national or a political revolution, involves by definition some

emancipation is involved, but because this emancipation includes the emancipation of humanity as a whole. For all human servitude is involved in the relation of the worker to production, and all the types of servitude are only modifications or consequences of this relation.' Karl Marx, *Early Writings*, Translated and Edited by T. B. Bottomore, London, 1963, pp. 132–3. Italics in original.

[1] 'Question de méthode', in *Critique de la raison dialectique*, Tome I, p. 23. 'Ce prolétariat . . . nous fournissait la preuve . . . que *tous* les conflits n'étaient pas résolus.' Ibid.

[2] 'Merleau-Ponty vivant', pp. 322–4. This essay is reprinted in Jean-Paul Sartre, *Situations*, *IV*, pp. 189–287. Merleau-Ponty's book was published in Paris in 1947.

[3] See 'Sartre et l'ultra-bolchévisme', Chapter V of his *Les Aventures de la dialectique*, Paris, 1955.

significantly new structural organization of society. For all the efforts that men have devoted to political and social theory for some two thousand years, the range of conceptions that they have produced as to how society might be structurally changed has been remarkably limited. New social structures are not created easily; indeed, they are not even easily conceivable. What happens in periods of great social change is usually discovered after it has happened rather than deliberately created in advance. In a world of private property, two of the main appeals of socialism are simply that it is different and that it is possible. Anyone looking for a way of radically and suddenly reorganizing society is limited in the choices available to him. Unless he is willing to accept revolutionary theories like nazism or fascism, which promise conflict rather than harmony, and permanent hierarchy rather than equality, socialism is the only theory at hand. If and when men invent some new way of organizing society which promises to be dramatically different from the existing structures, men with revolutionary attitudes will advocate it precisely because it is revolutionary.

V   Socialism as Monster and Socialism as Myth

In curious but intelligible fashion, Sartre starts from a philosophy which poses no goals and no principles of action and which, in any case, is not designed to pose any, only to end up adopting a political position which holds that there is only one way to reach what is presumed to be a desirable end. This itinerary from complete freedom of moral choice to political dogmatism is staggering, but perhaps what strikes one most forcefully is the extreme abstractness of the argument. It is a construction built wholly of ideas and belongs to the realm of prophecy rather than experience.

The explanation for this is that Sartre is enough of an existentialist in political matters to make such choices as he makes not on the basis of things as they are but on the basis of things as he wants them to be. For Sartre, as for Marx, socialism is an ideal at the same time as it must be the antithesis of bourgeois democracy. But Sartre is confronted with a problem which did not exist for Marx. Marx might have made an effort to anticipate the problems that could emerge from a socialist organization of society, and it was tragic that he did not do so, but he wrote well before the leaders of the Soviet Union claimed to have put his doctrine into practice and he never had the opportunity to confront the socialist ideal with historic experience. He could neither compare socialist institutions with the socialist ideal nor compare them with other institutions. Sartre can do both, and his critics, Albert Camus and Raymond Aron, have asked him to do so.

Sartre, however, is not really interested in comparing existing institutions; he is interested in future social states. For a long time he held that to make a choice between the Soviet Union and the western democracies would be a manifestation of 'Manicheanism'.[1] Indeed, from his perspective, the alternatives are singularly unattractive. He writes that the western democracies have nothing to offer; he writes of the socialist camp in terms of 'errors', 'monstrosities', and 'crimes', and, referring to the Stalinist régime, he writes: 'Faut-il appeler socialisme ce monstre sanglant qui se déchire lui-même? Je réponds franchement: oui. C'était même *le* socialisme à sa phase primitive. . . .'[2] Socialism can be a monster, but it is also a myth. Socialism remains for Sartre, as it was for Marx, the symbol of a system in which all men will live in justice and liberty. And the best hope for realizing this ideal, according to Sartre, lies with the communist movement. '. . . Nous dirons donc pour commencer que le communisme nous apparaît, malgré tout, comme le seul mouvement qui portre encore en lui les chances du socialisme.'[3]

Sartre uses an incredible assortment of arguments in support of the favourable prejudice which he confers on communist régimes,[4] but the main reason he gives for the privileged status

---

[1] 'Merleau-Ponty Vivant', *Les Temps Modernes*, loc. cit., pp. 335, 342, 344.

[2] 'Le Fantôme de Staline', *Les Temps Modernes*, 12 (January 1957), pp. 678, 644. Reprinted in Jean-Paul Sartre, *Situations, VII* ('Problèmes du marxisme', 2), Paris, 1965. Italics in original.

[3] Ibid., p. 582.

[4] Sartre refers to China as 'l'effort concerté de six cent millions d'hommes pour supprimer la misère et la faim. Dans quelle démocratie bourgeoise trouvera-t-on cet élan vers l'avenir, cette action consciente et soutenue, cette unité vivante?' (Ibid, pp. 676–7.) The 'living unity' is unfounded rhetoric; Hitler represented an 'élan vers l'avenir', but Sartre has always condemned Hitlerism; conscious and unflagging action can take many forms, from the sweatshop to the army, and in the abstract it is hardly a civic virtue. That leaves us only the battle against hunger

of the socialist camp is that its leaders *intend* to establish socialism. What he calls 'the enterprise' of socialist construction 'wants to give all men justice and liberty' and is therefore radically distinguishable 'from all policies which seek to establish or to conserve the domination of a class over the whole of society'.[1] The entire proposition rests on attributions of motives which are unverified and unverifiable. But even if the motives ascribed were in fact held, men would still be justified in preferring to choose on the basis of results rather than intentions. The only reasonable way of evaluating a political system is by examining the consequences of its practices. But Sartre's approach to what he calls socialism remains impervious to experience. At one point he suggests that acts count: 'Qu'importe, en effet, ce qu'un gouvernement croit faire; ce qui compte, c'est ce qu'il fait.'[2] But at another point in the same article, he tells us

qu'on le veuille ou non, l'édification socialiste *est privilégiée en ceci* qu'on doit, pour la comprendre, épouser son mouvement et adopter ses objectifs; en un mot on juge de ce qu'elle fait au nom de ce qu'elle veut, de ses moyens au nom de sa fin, tandis qu'on apprécie toutes les autres entreprises sur ce qu'elles ignorent, sur ce qu'elles négligent ou sur ce qu'elles refusent. Ce privilège en explique un autre: seuls peuvent et doivent juger ceux qui participent, à l'Est et à l'Ouest, au mouvement du socialisme.[3]

This double standard for the evaluation of political systems does not leave the socialist camp above reproach. It means essentially that socialists, and only socialists, may and must criticize the policies and leaders of the socialist camp when (as in the case of the Russian intervention in the Hungarian revolt of 1956) they weaken confidence in socialism, because Sartre

and misery. Perhaps China will succeed in this effort better than India, about which Sartre has nothing to say; perhaps not. But the relevant comparison to be made here is between China and countries like India, not between China and the bourgeois democracies.

Sartre also writes that, by planning, the communist leaders assume 'full responsibility for the régime in its grandeur and in its faults', while the bourgeois liberal pleads that he only obeys 'the pitiless laws of the economy'. (Ibid., p. 631.) But western democratic governments act so as to get the results they want from such economic laws as they recognize, and Sartre has referred to the Russian 'bureaucracy which did not want to acknowledge its errors . . .'. (*Critique de la raison dialectique*, Tome I, p. 25.)

[1] 'Le Fantôme de Staline', p. 676.
[2] Ibid., p. 588.   [3] Ibid., p. 677. Italics in original.

believes that socialism remains men's only hope for justice and
liberty, while anyone may criticize the western democracies for
any fault, because they are not socialist. But more important
than what the standard means is the basis on which it rests.
It rests more on Sartre's evaluation of the philosophies which
he believes inspire the two sets of régimes than it does on what
each set of régimes has done. The abolition of capitalism by the
socialist states is of course important—it demonstrates that they
operate on the right philosophy—but it is the socialist doctrine itself which is the yardstick for the measurement of political systems.

Depuis plus d'un siècle, sous des formes qui changent au cours de
l'Histoire, un seul mouvement entraîne les exploités, à réclamer pour
eux et pour tous la possibilité d'être hommes pleinement et totalement;
un seul mouvement découvre la société même dans toute sa réalité
et définit la bourgeoisie par l'exploitation quand tous les autres en
font la classe universelle; un seul produit à travers l'action et par
elle une idéologie qui lui permet de se comprendre soi-même et de
comprendre les autres: c'est le mouvement socialiste pris dans son
ensemble. . . .[1]

Sartre reverses the only possible rule of verification; he does not
test his doctrine in the light of experience but judges experience
in the light of his doctrine. One can agree with Sartrean
existentialism when it argues that man should not confer more
reality upon the world than he does upon himself, but one
cannot agree that one should confer more reality upon a
doctrine than upon either man or the world.

VI   Existentialism and Marxism

Sartre combines existentialism with Marxism. The two
philosophies are complementary, and it is possible to understand how, in certain circumstances, an existentialist may be
attracted to revolutionary Marxism. But are the two philosophies compatible? Can one adhere to the tenets of both of
them at the same time?

Sartrean existentialism is not a political theory, and all its
implications for politics are by no means immediately evident.
It is not certain, for example, that—as Sartre argues—his
doctrine excludes that liberal doctrine which holds that a good

[1] 'Le Fantôme de Staline', p. 580.

society automatically follows from the liberation of man from all political constraints,[1] but as few if any liberals now subscribe to that view (if indeed any ever did), the question need not be examined further. It is true that his doctrine excludes economic (or any other kind of) determinism, and this is the main point over which he differs from the exponents of current Marxist orthodoxy, which proclaims economic determinism, although it is banal to point out that every Marxist revolution has been carried out by people who acted as though the movement of history required considerable assistance from them. The only positive implication for politics which follows directly from existentialism is that if one wants to affect the kind of choices which people may freely make, one has to act on their situation.

At first sight, therefore, it might appear that existentialism is compatible with both contemporary liberalism and Marxism, in that both theories hold that a good society depends upon the existence of a certain kind of situation, although the situations they prescribe are quite different. Liberals are less dogmatic than Marxists in their situational requirements, and the focus of their attention is different from that of the Marxists. Liberals focus attention upon power relationships, while Marxists focus attention upon property relationships. Liberals are concerned with the creation and maintenance of institutions through which power can be controlled and diffused, while Marxists are concerned with abolishing private property in the means of production. Of course, liberals take into account the effect of the property system upon the distribution and control of power, and some Marxists (but only a small minority of those in power) show some interest in the problem of controlling and diffusing power, but the concern of the former with controlling power and the concern of the latter with abolishing private property are fundamental distinctions.

This is because liberals believe that political conflicts cannot be avoided, while Marxists believe that political conflicts derive from private property in the means of production. Accordingly, liberals concentrate on finding ways and means of equilibrating the strength of the forces in contention and on establishing institutions and procedures by which settlements among the contending forces can be reached. Marxists argue

[1] 'Présentation des temps modernes', in *Situations*, *II*, p. 25.

that with the abolition of private property conflicts will cease altogether and man will be completely reconciled with all his brothers.

In his celebrated 'Lettre au directeur des *Temps Modernes*', Camus argued that the notion that all men will eventually be reconciled with one another implied that history is moving towards a goal or an end. He argued further that the sacrifices demanded by the Soviet régime throughout its history could be justified only on the ground that this experience was necessary in order to bring about the final historical goal. But, Camus went on, existentialism cannot accept the notion that history has an end or a goal; it 'would be threatened at its very foundation if it accepted the idea of a predictable end of history'.[1]

Presumably, Camus meant that the concept of an end to history strikes at existentialism at two vital points. If history has an end, the accomplishment of this end can be made the common purpose of all men, and one would therefore have the equivalent of an eternal principle on the basis of which to justify one's acts. (Indeed, one might add, one would need such a principle in order to establish that the end is in fact a happy one.) But existentialism denies the existence of eternal principles. In the second place, there is no suggestion in the existentialist doctrine that the conflict which it holds to be intrinsic to human relations will ever come to an end; quite the contrary, conflict is rooted in the very nature of being.[2]

When Camus addressed his letter to Sartre, Sartre had not yet explicitly conferred any privilege on the Soviet Union, but he was eventually to do so in terms that have already been described. Sartre acknowledged 'the errors, the monstrosities, and the crimes' which were part of the Soviet experience, but he also saw in the communist movement the best hope for a good society. He did not explicitly accept the notion that history has an end, but his argument is intelligible only on the assumption that some singularity of the communist movement—like the power of the Communist Party or the socialization of the means of production or both together—is essential if there is to

---

[1] *Les Temps Modernes*, 8 (August 1952), p. 330.

[2] 'Car après tout, si l'homme n'a pas de fin qu'on puisse élire en règle de valeur, comment l'histoire aurait-elle un sens dès maintenant perceptible? Si elle en a un, pourquoi l'homme n'en ferait-il pas sa fin? Et s'il le fait, comment serait-il dans la terrible et incessante liberté dont vous parlez?' Ibid.

be any possibility of bringing about a desirable end. Sartre, in other words, must regard some communist institutions as necessary if the historical outcome is to be a good one, even though he refused to concede that history has an end. Let us ignore the problem of how anything can be regarded as necessary in the absence of an end. Perhaps Sartre has escaped the dilemma which Camus sought to place him in; perhaps there is no contradiction between existentialism and Marxism over the (futile) question of whether history has an end.[1] But Sartre himself took Camus' challenge seriously, for in subsequent years his thoughts turned to the question of whether history does have an end.

VII History and Ethics

In the course of his letter to Sartre, Camus urged him to define his conception of history. He also suggested one way in which he thought that Sartre could reconcile Marxism and existentialism. This could be done, he wrote, if Sartre could 'demonstrate this difficult proposition: history has no end, but it has a *sens* which, however, is not transcendent to it'.[2] In his reply to Camus, Sartre avoided discussing whether or not history has a meaning or an end: 'L'Histoire a-t-elle un sens? demandez-vous, a-t-elle une fin? Pour moi, c'est la question qui n'a pas de sens . . . le problème n'est pas de *connaître* sa fin mais de lui en *donner* une.'[3] Commenting on this reply, Raymond Aron asked how it would be possible to choose history's goal without reference to either eternal principles or knowledge of the whole historical process.[4] Aron's point is easier to understand than Camus'. If one admits no principles

[1] The most illuminating accounts of the problem of the relationship between existentialism and Marxism are by Raymond Aron. See his 'Remarques sur les rapports entre existentialisme et marxisme', in *L'Homme, le monde, l'histoire*, Paris (Cahiers du Collège Philosophique), 1948, pp. 165–95. For an account of the Camus-Sartre exchange, see his *L'Opium des intellectuels*, pp. 62–69. For a discussion of the notion of the 'sense' of history, with special reference to Marxism and existentialism, see 'La Notion du sens de l'histoire', Chapter II of his *Dimensions de la conscience historique*, Paris, 1961.

[2] *Les Temps Modernes*, 8 (August 1952), p. 330. The best translation for *sens* here is probably meaning. Karl Popper uses this term when he discusses similar questions in *The Open Society and Its Enemies*, Vol. II, Ch. 25.

[3] *Les Temps Modernes*, loc. cit., p. 352. Italics in original.

[4] *L'Opium des intellectuels*, p. 67.

of action, then every choice is arbitrary unless one knows what the whole course of history is to be. Camus' point is not wholly clear; he may have meant simply that an argument' which demonstrated that a socialist revolution was inevitable at some point in the historical process, because of what men autonomously do, would justify advocating it and still preserve existentialism's rejection both of eternal principles and the idea that history has an end. If this is what Camus meant, to advocate a socialist revolution would imply a general rule in favour of advocating the inevitable, and this would seem to run counter to Sartre's avoidance of general principles, as well as fail to account for the symbolic importance of his conception of socialism. It appears, however, that Camus would have been satisfied with some such argument as that. 'This perilous reconciliation [of existentialism with Marxism] is perhaps possible,' he wrote, 'and I ask only to read it.'[1]

Camus died before the publication of Sartre's *Critique de la raison dialectique*. This is the main work in which Sartre combines existentialism and Marxism, and viewed against the kind of questions which Camus posed for Sartre (as well as the questions raised by Aron in his commentary on the exchange of letters between the two men), the book may be regarded as a sequel to their debate. *Critique de la raison dialectique* is a large, difficult, opaque, and exasperating book, but, in so far as it is intelligible, it appears to be the start of an effort to discover whether it is possible to reach a total understanding of the historical process. It attempts to discover whether there is a direction or meaning to history, on the assumption that there is one. If history had a meaning, history would be a succession of points of development, each one of which would, at the end, represent an intelligible totalization of all previous and all concurrent historical facts in the light of their relationships to the end.[2] The volume he has delivered so far, which is subtitled 'Theory of Practical Wholes', deals mainly with the

---

[1] *Les Temps Modernes*, 8 (August 1952), p. 330.

[2] '. . . l'Histoire est intelligible si les différents pratiques qu'on peut découvrir et fixer à un moment de la temporalisation historique apparaissent à la fin comme partiellement totalisantes et comme rejointes et fondues dans leurs oppositions même et leurs diversités par une totalisation intelligible et sans appel.' *Critique de a raison dialectique*, Tome I, p. 754.

'Le problème de la dialectique pour moi est celui de la totalisation. Y-a-t-il

definition of social formations. A second volume, which is promised, is to deal with the more properly historical questions. It is the next volume which will try 'to establish that there is *a* human history with *a* truth and *an* intelligibility'.[1] It is to be feared, however, that the promised second volume may be as abstract as the first,[2] for it is not to deal with 'the material content of this history', but rather will seek to show that a totalization process must in fact take place in history.[3]

Judgement must be suspended until Sartre produces his next volume, in which he will presumably set forth his interpretation of the meaning and direction (and possibly also the end) of history. It may be hoped that the next volume will be clearer than the first one. Sartre's principal contention is that the historical process is dialectical, but he does not define closely what he means by the dialectic.[4] If it means essentially that 'nous trouverons peut-être quelque chose comme un sens à l'évolution des sociétés et des hommes si nous envisageons que les rapports réciproques des groupes, des classes et, d'une manière générale, de toutes les formations sociales (collectifs, communautés) sont *fondamentalement pratiques* c'est-à-dire se réalisent à travers des actions réciproques d'entraide, d'alliance, de guerre, d'oppression, etc., quel que soient d'ailleurs le type

des vérités en Histoire ou *une* vérité? Si l'Histoire doit avoir une seule vérité, si nous sommes obligés de tout mettre en liaison synthétique, si je comprends n'importe quel fait, nous pouvons parler d'une vérité historique. Il y a dialectique si l'Histoire est une totalisation, si à chaque instant des faits humains sont rattachés entre eux, de sorte que chacun d'eux est, à sa manière, l'ensemble des choses. A mon avis, tous les faits accidentels, telle notre recontre, expriment une totalité. Et vous le voyez d'ailleurs par nos différentes questions qui mettent en cause la classe ouvrière et le capitalisme. Il y a donc dans cette rencontre quelque chose de plus qu'un étudiant venu voir un écrivain.' Jean-Paul Sartre, in an interview entitled 'Entretien', in *L'Express*, 3 March 1960, p. 30.

[1] *Critique de la raison dialectique*, Tome I, p. 156.

[2] 'Notre but est de déterminer les conditions formelles de l'Histoire; nous n'irons pas insister sur ces rapports de réciprocité matérielle entre des classes *dans leur développement historique réel*.' Ibid., p. 743. Italics mine. See also the comments of Jean-Daniel Reynaud, 'Sociologie et "Raison dialectique" ', in *Revue Française de Sociologie*, II (January–March 1961), p. 57.

[3] *Critique de la raison dialectique*, Tome I, p. 156.

[4] At one point he refers to 'a dialectical movement' only as 'contradictions, dépassement, totalisations'. 'Question de méthode', ibid., p. 32. Elsewhere he says: '. . . si la Raison dialectique existe, il faut qu'elle se définisse comme l'intelligibilité absolue d'une nouveauté irréductible *en tant* que celle-ci est une irréductible nouveauté. C'est le contraire de l'effort positiviste et analytique qui tente d'éclairer les faits neufs en les ramenant à des faits anciens.' Ibid., p. 147.

et la mode de réalisation de ces actions . . .',[1] it involves a type of analysis which every historian and even the most analytically-minded social scientists already employ, and leaves entirely open the problems of determining which social formations are relevant to historical explanation at any given time and how to explain the causes and consequences of the varied relationships among them.

Sartre tries in this work to produce what one might call an existentialist sociology: an explanation of groups and organizations on the basis of individual behaviours. He is concerned with the problem of how collections of separate individuals become organized groups and he is particularly concerned with the definition of social class. The latter is defined as a complex relationship among separate individuals, groups in the process of formation, and existing organizations which provide leadership for the individuals' action.[2] The definition is, therefore, neither literally Marxist nor based on statistical categories, although it is quite compatible with Lenin's notion of the relationship between the Communist Party and the workers.

In his effort to develop a theory of the state and society,[3] Sartre mixes existentialist and Marxist themes, sometimes rejecting elements of orthodox Marxism, sometimes paralleling them.[4] The main new concept which Sartre introduces is scarcity, but it, of course, also figures importantly in the writings of Marx, who made abundance a condition of the end of social conflict, both in his early and in his later writings. But Sartre does not advance an understanding of the importance of scarcity to social organization in any fundamental way. He does not probe the concept in detail. He employs it with reference to vital material necessities and to manpower, but not to such other possible referents as luxury, prestige,

---

[1] *Critique de la raison dialectique*, Tome I, p. 731. Raymond Aron interprets Sartre's conception of the dialectic in this work as suggesting a perpetual alternation between popular alienation and revolution and, hence, as not Marxist. See *Le Figaro Littéraire*, 29 October–4 November 1964, p. 6.

[2] *Critique de la raison dialectique*, Tome I, pp. 647, 652, 661–2, 736. See also Aimé Patri, 'Le Marxisme existentialisé', in *Preuves*, 10 (August 1960), p. 66.

[3] *Critique de la raison dialectique*, Tome I, pp. 562–631.

[4] The very idea of the dictatorship of the proletariat is 'absurd', ibid., p. 630. '. . . Le problème réel qui se pose, c'est celui du dépérissement progressif de l'État au profit de regroupements de plus en plus vastes des sérialités extéro-conditionnées.' Ibid.

or power, with the result that its full implications for politics are not approached.

At the same time as *Critique de la raison dialectique* raises the question of the interpretation of history and tries to develop a sociology, it is an attempt to bring closer together what Sartre calls the philosophy of Marxism and what he calls the ideology of existentialism. The main ontological categories of *L'Être et le néant* are evident in *Critique de la raison dialectique*, but Sartre is not wholly correct in asserting that existentialist principles are not 'touchés' by his analysis,[1] at least if 'touchés' is to be construed to mean affected rather than completely countered. While both books hold that men are totally free within their situations, *L'Être et le néant* emphasizes man's freedom to define his situation, while *Critique de la raison dialectique* emphasizes the situation in which man exercises his freedom.[2] What Sartre called the 'coefficient of adversity' in *L'Être et le néant*—the extent to which a situation constitutes an obstacle to the fulfilment of a man's project—becomes in the *Critique of Dialectical Reason* the 'field of possibilities'.[3] The tone of *L'Être et le néant* suggests a kind of elasticity in the coefficient of adversity which places the emphasis on man's freedom over his situation, while in *Critique de la raison dialectique* the field of possibilities is, at least for the working man, 'rigorously limited'.[4] While in *L'Être et le néant* man's freedom is 'conditioned' by his situation, viewed a-historically, in *Critique de la raison dialectique* the 'crystallized practice of previous generations' is so powerful that 'l'individu trouve en naissant son existence préesquissé' in such fashion as to include his 'fundamental *attitude*';[5] in a capitalist society, the worker has been 'prefabricated'.[6] In fact, Sartre so tightens the ring of situation around the notion of freedom that it may be wondered whether the significance of the notion of freedom is not lost and the word retained only

[1] *Critique de la raison dialectique*, Tome I, p. 291.

[2] Speaking of the difference between Sartre's play *Les Mouches* and his later play *Le Diable et le bon Dieu*, Simone de Beauvoir writes that in 1944 Sartre 'thought that every situation could be transcended by a subjective movement; he knew in 51 that the circumstances sometimes steal our transcendence; against them there is then no individual salvation possible, but only a collective struggle'. *La Force des choses*, p. 261.

[3] The earlier expression reappears at the end of the volume, however. *Critique de la raison dialectique*, Tome I, p. 749.

[4] Ibid., p. 289.   [5] Ibid.   [6] Ibid., pp. 291–2.

for the sake of terminological consistency: 'For constraint',
says Sartre, 'does not suppress liberty (except by liquidating the
oppressed); it makes liberty its accomplice by leaving it no
other course than obedience.'[1]

The existentialist concept of conflict remains, but while this
was treated essentially in interpersonal terms in *L'Être et le
néant*, it is broadened to include groups and classes in *Critique
de la raison dialectique*. In the former work, interpersonal conflict
was rooted in the very structure of being; in the later work
Sartre adds the material basis of scarcity. Sartre still holds that
one cannot avoid treating another person except as a means,
but he adds that 'the struggle has for its origin in each case a
concrete antagonism which has scarcity, in a definite form, as its
material condition . . .'.[2]

Commentators on Sartre's *Critique de la raison dialectique*
have remarked that the book is not the work on moral theory
which Sartre long ago promised to produce.[3] In the literal sense,
this is correct. Sartre does not argue in this book that men
should do thus and so for this or that reason, nor does he enter
into any discussion of how one might justify choices in general.
In another sense, however, *Critique de la raison dialectique* may
be the closest thing to a moral theory that Sartre can produce.[4]
It may be an attempt to do as Hegel did and to argue as Hegel
argued: to try to understand the historical process with such
profundity and accuracy that this process, properly understood,
carries with it its own justification. If it is, it is doomed to fail,

---

[1] *Critique de la raison dialectique*, Tome I, p. 690.

[2] Ibid., p. 192.

[3] For example, see Hazel Barnes' Introduction to her translation of Sartre's
Search for a Method, p. xxv.

[4] According to Simone de Beauvoir, Sartre had planned for a long time to
write a book on ethics, and in 1948 'he continued to cover with a miniscule hand-
writing the notebooks in which he was developing his moral theory'. About a year
later he abandoned it, because 'the moral attitude appears when technological and
social conditions render positive conduct impossible. Morality is a collection of
idealistic gimmicks to help you live the life that the scarcity of resources and the
inadequacy of technology impose on you'. Still later, near the time of his confrontation with Camus in 1952, he returned to 'the project that he had always
pursued: to build an ideology which while enlightening man on his situation
proposed a practice to him'. *La Force des choses*, pp. 165, 179, 218, and 275.
   In her account of her interview with Sartre, Jacqueline Piatier reports that while
Sartre wanted to produce a moral theory around the time he was writing *La
Nausée*, he no longer thinks about doing so. The liberation of man must come
first. *Le Monde*, 25 April 1964.

for such an effort—even if successful in *really* understanding history—could do no more than equate necessity with goodness. It could result only in asserting that what *really* is ought to be, for the simple reason that it can be no other.[1] Another way of putting it would be to assert that might makes right. Historical understanding can succeed only in explaining why what has happened happened and why what will happen will happen. But unless what happened or what will happen is demonstrated to be good—something that requires a principle of evaluation —Camus' argument that the service of history means only to serve the interest of the strongest holds.

VIII   Conclusion

Existentialism is a descriptive theory of highly questionable validity and limited usefulness; Marxism is a political philosophy whose promise has been belied by experience; Sartre's combination of the theory and the philosophy result in a political dogmatism, if not in a logical contradiction. It should not be necessary to add that this does not mean that everything that Sartre has written relevant to politics is not worthy of attention. His concern with how society looks to its least-favoured group is at least as good a departure for a moral theory as any and probably better than most, and it is an excellent guide for establishing priorities for social action. His view that no man will be wholly free until all men are free probably expresses a moral truth, although it requires no excursion down the laborious path of 'totalization' to appreciate the workings of the moral conscience. And the future-oriented quality of his thinking turns attention to the important question of the extent to which there is capacity for change in different kinds of political systems.

But the argument that the only hope for achieving justice and liberty for all men lies with the communist movement is not credible. Sartre makes no claims that communist régimes have come closer to achieving justice and liberty than have the

[1] For a similar interpretation, see Edouard Morot-Sir, 'Sartre's Critique of Dialectical Reason', *Journal of the History of Ideas* (Ephrata, Pennsylvania, and New York), XXII (October–December, 1961), p. 581. My interpretation of Hegel relies on George H. Sabine, *A History of Political Theory*, N.Y., 1950, p. 627.

western democracies. His preference is not based on a comparison of the current performance of régimes; it is based on an estimate of future performance. And even this estimate of the future is unrelated to those conditions which can give men reason to trust that they can have a better future and participate in shaping it.

Sartre has written that 'rien ne peut remplacer, à l'Est pas plus qu'à l'Ouest, ces approximations successives, ces contestations, ces dialogues qui permettent—lentement, progressivement—de dégager le Vrai'.[1] But questioning and dialogue are characteristic of the western democracies, not of the communist régimes. The democracies permit freedom of expression and organization. They also have institutions, in the form of competing political parties and the suffrage, which sensitize the political leadership to the need for reforms. These institutions work more or less well, depending upon a number of conditions, but they have been and continue to be instruments of social reform. The communist régimes do not permit such freedoms and they have no such institutions. Reforms have taken place in the Soviet Union and other communist régimes. Perhaps the Soviet Union will evolve further and become a liberal society. It has not done so and it may be that it will not do so. Its political leaders are not habituated to the ways of political freedom, and the combination of a single-party system and a wholly state-owned economy gives those leaders powerful instruments with which to enforce close limits to such liberalization as they allow.

No one can say what the future will bring to the western democracies or the communist states, and in this sense no one can demonstrate that Sartre's confidence in the latter has been misplaced. But neither is there anything in the experience of the Soviet Union to demonstrate that communism provides a firmer foundation for the enlargement of human freedom than democracy does. Sartre's argument does not rest on evidence; it rests on hope.

[1] 'Le Fantôme de Staline', p. 677.

7

Bertrand de Jouvenel:
Dux, Rex, and the Common Good

I Introduction

THE post-war political writings of Bertrand de Jouvenel cover a wide range of subjects, including large historical themes like the growth and development of political power, philosophical problems like the nature of the political good, and operational problems like the process of political decision-making. In a limited sense, it may even be said that the evolution of his writings since the Second World War is characteristic of the development that has taken place in the approach to political theory generally in recent decades, most markedly perhaps in United States academic circles, but elsewhere as well. While his main early post-war books, *Power*[1] and *Sovereignty*,[2] were deeply marked by normative concerns—what ought and ought not to be done politically—a more recent work, *The Pure Theory of Politics*,[3] quite deliberately departs from many of the concepts central to the earlier works, and confines itself (in the main) to specific questions of political behaviour.[4] This is not to say that de Jouvenel has given himself

[1] *Du Pouvoir, histoire naturelle de sa croissance*, Édition revue et augmentée, Geneva, 1947. Eng. tr. by J. F. Huntington, *On Power, Its Nature and the History of its Growth*, New York, 1949. All references are to the 1947 edition; the translations are my own.

[2] *De la Souveraineté, à la recherche du bien politique*, Paris, 1955. Eng. tr. by J. F. Huntington, *Sovereignty, An Inquiry into the Political Good*, Chicago, 1957. All references are to the 1955 edition, the translations being my own, except where otherwise noted, in which case they are to the 1957 translation.

[3] Cambridge (England), 1963. French translation by Gabrielle Rolin, Guy Berger, Jean-Claude Casanova, Claude Fouquet, Pierre Hassner, François Hetman, and Maurice Roy, *De la Politique pure*, Paris, 1963. All references are to the English version.

[4] 'This is a basic chapter of a treatise on Politics. I deem it important to stress that no mention has been made of the State, of sovereignty, of the constitution or

over to what C. Wright Mills called 'abstracted empiricism'.[1] De Jouvenel's approach to political behaviour does not resemble the kind of data-gathering, divorced from large social problems, which Mills had in mind.[2] On the contrary, all de Jouvenel's political writings are inspired by one overriding consideration: that politics is dangerous, because if it is not rightly conducted it can produce disastrous consequences for the citizens (or subjects).[3] Whether de Jouvenel writes historically, speculatively, or analytically, this notion is fundamental to his thinking. In this respect, there is a clear thread of continuity running through all his main post-war writings, regardless of the differences there are in the approaches he takes to politics in each of them. It is not an accident that most of his major post-war works terminate with an image of disaster.[4]

There is a clear trend in de Jouvenel's post-war writings from the historical and the philosophical to the behavioural and the operational, but this is not to say that there is a linear development from one distinct type of analysis to a different type. De Jouvenel's work is not so easily schematized. He does get from one pole to the other, but not without some twistings

functions of public authority, of political obligation, etc.' *The Pure Theory of Politics*, pp. 81–82. An even more recent work is devoted to an analysis of the problem of prediction in social and political affairs: see Bertrand de Jouvenel, *L'Art de la conjecture*, Futuribles, Monaco, 1964.

[1] *The Sociological Imagination*, New York, 1959, Ch. 3.

[2] Ibid., p. 73.

[3] 'Political activity is dangerous', *The Pure Theory of Politics*, p. 29.

[4] 'Savons-nous si les sociétés ne sont pas régies dans leur marche par des lois inconnues? S'il leur appartient d'éviter les fautes dont elles meurent? Si elles n'y sont point acheminées par l'élan même qui les porta à leur maturité? Si leur floraison et leur fructification ne s'accomplissent pas au prix d'un éclatement des formes où s'était accumulée leur vigueur? Feu d'artifice qui ne laisserait après lui qu'une masse amorphe, promise au despotisme ou à l'anarchie. . . .' Thus ends *Du Pouvoir*, p. 455.

'Il nous suffit, quant à nous, d'avoir fait voir que la confiance montrée dans la sélection naturelle du juste et du vrai tient étroitement à l'idée de lumière naturelle, à l'idée d'une participation humaine à l'essence divine. Laquelle n'étant plus crue, tout l'édifice s'écroule.' Thus ends *De la Souveraineté*, p. 371. (The English version, however, contains an additional chapter.)

'A specific settlement may contribute to the strengthening or weakening of the public order wherein it occurs; this order or "settled state" is itself not incapable of unsettlement, a thought which should haunt us, to make us more effective guardians of civility.

'That this is no easy task, an image attests: the head and hands of the great guardian Cicero, nailed to the rostrum.' Thus ends, except for a one-paragraph conclusion, *The Pure Theory of Politics*, p. 212.

and turnings back. For this reason, it cannot be said categoric-
ally that one book represents one position and a second one
another, or even that there is a distinct relationship between
one book and another. It can be said, however, that as de
Jouvenel's thought evolves, it pays increasing attention to the
peculiar problems and conditions of modern societies and
displays a growing sense of political discrimination. The latter
development will be remarked on more fully in the second
section of this chapter. The former is apparent from the closing
pages of *Power*, where de Jouvenel tentatively sketches out a
social theory which he pursues along different lines in *Sovereignty*,[1] and which is designed to take into account the highly
differentiated character and dynamism of modern societies. All
of de Jouvenel's political writings rely heavily on historical
example, but a social theory like the one which he presents in
Sovereignty, which not only views society as a kind of galaxy
of initiatives but also places great value upon a continuing
stream of social initiatives, is bound to reduce if not eliminate
the utility for contemporary reform of examples drawn from
very different kinds of past society. In this respect, de Jouvenel's
comment in *The Pure Theory of Politics* that just as the concept of
health was not a productive central concept for medical
science, so the concept of a healthy body politic is not likely to
be a productive central concept for political science, as it may
lead us to seek to turn back 'to some past moment of "health"
with great chances of substituting our fancy for the true past',[2]
appears as a kind of corrective of the impression created by the
idealized versions of past régimes which appear in the historical
account in *Power*.

II Power and Democracy

De Jouvenel's first major post-war work, *Power*, has two
central themes. On the one hand, it is an effort to describe and

---

[1] The link between the final pages of *Power* and the argument in *Sovereignty*
was pointed out in an unpublished paper by Leslie W. Dunbar entitled 'A Non-
Representational Theory of Executive Power', prepared for presentation at the
thirty-first Annual Meeting of the Southern Political Science Association at
Gatlinburg, Tennessee, 5–7 November 1959. I have adopted several elements of
the interpretation of de Jouvenel's work presented in this paper.

[2] *The Pure Theory of Politics*, p. 40.

account for the historic trend in the growth of the power of the central political authorities of the western nations. De Jouvenel had already remarked on the existence of such a trend before the Second World War,[1] and the war itself only strengthened his conviction about its existence, which he believed to be measurable in terms of 'the dimensions of the army, the burden of taxes, the number of civil servants'.[2]

On the other hand, *Power* severely criticizes democratic political systems. According to the view set forth in it, democratic political systems are not immune to the secular trend in the growth of central governmental power; in fact, de Jouvenel argues, they provide the broadest highway to tyranny that has ever existed. *Power* was the first post-war work to speak of 'totalitarian democracy',[3] an expression which de Jouvenel may have originated, and de Jouvenel concluded the book with the sombre comment that everywhere there was a visible trend towards the establishment of a 'social protectorate'— a society in which government provides for the complete security of the citizens, who therefore become merely subjects of a totalitarian régime, because total governmental power is required if the government is to carry out such a large task.

Despite Raymond Aron's comment that *Power* 'is perhaps the finest political book written in twenty years',[4] its didactic tone, its strong air of nostalgia for long-gone régimes, and its indiscriminate discussion of democratic political systems greatly detract from the credit the work deserves for its analysis of the way in which the power of central governments has grown and can grow and for its warnings about the dangers to which democratic systems may fall prey. De Jouvenel's harsh estimate not only of the character of democratic leadership[5] but also of the citizenry generally[6] was hardly likely to provoke much sympathy precisely among those people whose co-operation would be necessary to avoid the potential disasters on which he focused his readers' attention.

---

[1] See *Le Réveil de l'Europe*, Paris, 1938, p. 214.

[2] *Du Pouvoir*, p. 159.   [3] The title of Chapter XIV.

[4] *Espoir et peur du siècle*, Paris, 1957, p. 16, n. 1.

[5] The development of political machines has resulted in 'a prodigious decline in the parliamentary and governmental level'. *Du Pouvoir*, p. 334. Also see p. 430.

[6] 'I do not know where one gets the idea that men have a horror of despotism. I believe, on the contrary, that they love it.' Ibid., p. 439.

De Jouvenel's discussion of the mechanics of democratic politics resembles caricature rather than portraiture, and constitutes a catalogue of all the ills that can befall democratic régimes. The leaders of a party can wield uncontrolled power through a disciplined parliamentary majority;[1] the government can be so paralysed by the competing factions represented in it that it fails to fulfil its essential functions, and the tired, frustrated citizens will seek to end the disorder by turning to a despot;[2] there can be alternating victories by factions which will wield their power in such a way that there will be extreme oscillations in policy, again with the result that a disenchanted citizenry will turn to a despotic solution;[3] the power-holders can destroy each of the major social groups which might oppose them by forming successively different majorities composed of other social groups and picking off the troublesome groups one by one.[4] Throughout the analysis, possibilities are presented as though they were certainties, and the democracies are treated collectively, virtually without regard to the institutional and contextual differences among real democratic systems.

Moreover, the critical discussion of democracy in *Power* has little to do with the assertion that there is everywhere a trend towards the establishment of a 'social protectorate'.[5] De Jouvenel's conception of the social protectorate appears to be modelled on the kind of diffusely oppressive régime which de Tocqueville conceived as one possible result of the development of democracy (and for which he could find no adequate name),[6] but the kinds of breakdown in democratic government which de Jouvenel discusses would be far less likely to result in that sort of beneficent despotism than in the kinds of hardly beneficent tyrannies which emerged in Europe between the two World Wars. Yet in the conclusion of *Power*, de Jouvenel states that the 'revolutions and coups d'état which mark our era are only insignificant episodes accompanying the advent of the social Protectorate'.[7] The result of this kind of analysis, which

[1] Ibid., p. 337.
[2] Ibid., pp. 341–2.
[3] Ibid.
[4] Ibid., p. 323.   [5] Ibid., p. 433.
[6] *Democracy in America*, Phillips Bradley edition, New York, 1946, 2 vols., vol. II, p. 318.
[7] *Du Pouvoir*, p. 433.

treats power as a homogeneous phenomenon and which both finds and extrapolates a unilinear form of political development, is that real and significant differences between political systems are dissolved.

Perhaps all this was due to the wartime situation in which *Power* was written. Whatever the reason for its weaknesses, when de Jouvenel returned almost twenty years later to the same theme of the vulnerability of democratic systems—in his study 'On the Evolution of Forms of Government'[1]—he treated it in markedly more measured tones. There is no longer any mention of a coming social protectorate. Political power is no longer treated as a homogeneous phenomenon, measurable in extent, but rather is differentiated as to both type and quality. In 'On the Evolution of Forms of Government', de Jouvenel no longer speaks generally of democracies turning into despotisms, but rather distinguishes between tyranny and Caesarism, which are similar in that neither brooks any control over its authority, but which are different in that tyranny verges towards totalitarianism while Caesarism permits the existence of a private realm in which the citizen may make his own choices.[2] Even more importantly, while *Power* resounds with the general affirmation that the law has lost its soul, 'On the Evolution of Forms of Government' distinguishes carefully between régimes where the growth in the power of the central authorities has been accompanied by what de Jouvenel calls a 'moral mutation' and régimes where it has not.[3] The false analogy drawn in *Power* between the New Deal in the United States and the nazi régime in Germany[4] reappears in the later study, but

---

[1] In Bertrand de Jouvenel, Editor, *Futuribles, Studies in Conjecture*, I, Geneva, 1963, pp. 65–119.

[2] Ibid., pp. 74–75.

[3] Ibid., p. 115.

[4] 'Eh bien, si l'on garde présent à l'esprit le contraste complet des deux nations et des deux dirigeants, n'est-il pas saisissant d'observer que le rôle de Sauveur assumé par le Pouvoir a justifié, aux États-Unis comme en Allemagne, une prodigieuse avance de l'État, se traduisant par le même prolifération bureaucratique, le même triomphe de l'autorité centrale sur les autorités régionales, la même subordination des commandements économiques au commandement politique.

*   *   *

'Ainsi deux États, pris aussi dissemblables qu'on peut le souhaiter, se sont simultanément avancés à l'omnipotence ou vers l'omnipotence, portés par les mêmes aspirations sécuritaires.' *Du Pouvoir*, p. 427.

this time the moral distinction between the two régimes is emphasized.[1]

Other manifestations of a desire to make finer distinctions also appear in the later work. While in *Power* the discussion of the potentialities for failure of democratic régimes is based on a uniform image of democracy, in 'On the Evolution of Forms of Government', de Jouvenel writes that it would 'be unwise to embark here upon a description of constitutional liberal democracy', because such an attempt would result either in a blurred 'composite image from the features of different countries' or a 'clear archetypal image' which would be 'too simple and probably very subjective'.[2] While de Jouvenel fails almost completely to distinguish between different democratic systems in *Power* and treats them all as subject to the same trends, in 'On the Evolution of Forms of Government' he explicitly rejects the notion that the breakdown of democratic government can be inscribed in an evolutionary model and recognizes that while some countries have succumbed to tyranny, others have not.[3] The assertion in *Power* that in democratic systems the central government can successively crush each major social group by relying on all the others is treated more gingerly in the later study, where the difficulties that stand in the way of such an effort in particular countries are duly noted.[4] And while in *Power* de Jouvenel writes that every advance in central state power seems immediately to reduce the liberty of each citizen, in 'On the Evolution of Forms of Government' he distinguishes between the kind of freedom which such an increase in governmental power will abridge and the kind of freedom which it will enlarge.[5]

Along with the more balanced view of both recent political history and political mechanisms which appears in 'On the

---

[1] '. . . the same degree of unemployment in the United States as in Germany does bring such a concentration [of government] in the hands of Franklin Roosevelt as well as in those of Hitler: but in the case of the U.S. you do not see a change in the manners of government, you do not see a substantial change in the participants of politics: in my view this "moral mutation" is the really awful phenomenon we should understand.' 'On the Evolution of Forms of Government', p. 115.

De Jouvenel returns to the same analogy again in *L'Art de la conjecture*. This time he says: 'Pour frappant que soit le parallélisme, on m'accordera que le contraste est plus important.' P. 138 ; also see pp. 298–301.

[2] 'On the Evolution of Forms of Government', pp. 75–76.

[3] Ibid., pp. 115–16.   [4] Ibid., p. 109.   [5] Ibid., pp. 106–7.

Evolution of Forms of Government' as compared with *Power*, there is also a shift in the focal point of the analysis and therefore in the nature of the problem which is posed for the political theorist. In *Power*, which was written during the Second World War, the problem with which de Jouvenel seems to be grappling is essentially how to limit the exercise of central governmental power, both in order to avoid the advent of the 'social protectorate' and because de Jouvenel saw in the limitation of the power of governments the only means of limiting the destructiveness of war between nations. In 'On the Evolution of Forms of Government', the problem which is posed is how to prevent the 'moral mutation' which takes place when a militant party drives out of power the moderate forces and proceeds to wield power arbitrarily and without regard to moral standards.[1] Closely related to this problem is still another one which de Jouvenel raises: how to get good political decisions in the conditions of modern society. This is the problem which he examines in *Sovereignty*.

III   The Common Good

Sovereignty is the work in which de Jouvenel deals most directly and fully with the problem of what the functions of government should be. Intended to be a direct sequel to *Power*, in which he had described the historic growth of political power, *Sovereignty* is the product of de Jouvenel's concern with what he calls 'the moral emancipation of the public authorities', by which he means the exercise of political power without regard to a closely defined purpose.[2] He contends that there has been excessive concern on the part of normative political theorists with the problem of the legitimacy of political decisions in terms of their source as opposed to the problem of what it is right and proper for the political authorities to do. There is, he argues, a proper distinction to be made between the legitimate source of political power and the legitimate use of political power. De Jouvenel's intention in *Sovereignty* is to direct attention away from the question of who should make decisions and (re)turn it to the question of what kinds of decisions should be made. He is evidently unaware of the

---

[1] 'On the Evolution of Forms of Government', p. 116.   [2] *De la Souveraineté*, p. 8.

existence of a significant body of contemporary literature on precisely the point which he considers to have been neglected.[1]

De Jouvenel's point of departure in treating the problem of what it is proper for governments to do is to seek the meaning of the common good, which is so generally regarded as the end towards which political activity should be directed. He makes a conspicuous effort to treat this problem systematically, but his treatment is obscured because it is difficult to tell from his analysis when he has accepted and when he has rejected various hypotheses concerning the common good which he examines. The main point, however, emerges clearly enough: he separates sharply what it is proper for the political authorities to concern themselves with from what it is proper to leave to the private activities of individuals and social groups.[2] In this respect, his discussion of the common good rests on a distinction between the state and society which is common to most contemporary liberal theory concerning the proper role of the state.

De Jouvenel's analysis of this distinction between state and society holds that, on the one hand, there is what he variously calls (political) power, the sovereign or the government. On the other hand, there is what he refers to as 'a ceaseless sparkling of appealing initiatives',[3] which he sometimes discusses in terms of the groups in which they are embodied, but which he more often discusses in terms of the men who promote the initiatives, to whom he variously refers as notables, social powers, social authorities, leaders, *seniores*, promoters, innovators, master-builders, and the like.[4] This distinction between state and society does not consist of a radical pluralism designating a situation in which political authority is taken as simply one authority among others with no special claim to pre-eminence. De Jouvenel does believe that the authority exercised by the innovator is of a higher order than that exercised by the government, in that those who follow the innovator do so

[1] See A. D. Lindsay, *The Modern Democratic State*, Volume One, New York, 1947, Chs. X and XI; R. M. MacIver, *The Web of Government*, New York, 1947, Chs. XI and XIII; Ernest Barker, *Principles of Social and Political Theory*, London, 1951, Books IV and VI.

[2] *De la Souveraineté*, p. 170.

[3] Ibid., p. 10; also p. 23.

[4] Not only in *De la Souveraineté*; also in *Du Pouvoir*, p. 453; in 'On the Evolution of Forms of Government', pp. 108–9; and in *The Pure Theory of Politics*, Part IV, Chs. 1 and 3.

entirely voluntarily, while governmental authority rests on habits of obedience and instruments of intimidation.[1] He is also concerned lest the political authorities make excessive claims to pre-eminence and either crush the social innovators or sub-stitute themselves for them. He does, however, recognize the need for a final place of command in order to prevent un-acceptably disruptive social behaviour. To put it in the kind of technical language he employs in *The Pure Theory of Politics*, it is necessary to prevent the occurrence of conflicting signals whose incompatibility would prevent the people receiving them from functioning as a community.[2]

According to de Jouvenel's argument, mutual trust, social friendship, and strong social ties are all essential social goods, but they cannot be the direct product of governmental activity. If they were regarded as susceptible of being directly created by governmental power, there would be a constant danger either that they would be weakened by reformers who would impose the changes they believe would promote them or that social life would be ossified by conservatives who would prevent the changes from taking place which they believe would disturb them. The notion that there is some particular form of social organization which can be equated with the common good necessarily leads to tyranny, whether the form of organization envisaged be the perpetuation of the existing one or a concep-tion of some society not yet born. In the former case, the tyranny is conservative, and means domination by the dead hand of tradition. In the latter case, the tyranny is utopian, but no less stifling. Quite apart from the fact that it is, in de Jouvenel's view, impossible to formulate the concrete con-ditions of a utopian society, any governmental effort directly to control behaviours throughout an entire society would require extensive police and propaganda activities which would eliminate whatever utopian qualities the régime might seek. The natural characteristic of modern societies is mobility, resulting from multiple sources of independent initiatives; it is on 'the incessant sparkling of dispersed initiatives' that social enrichment depends;[3] for governments to seek directly to promote mutual trust or social friendship would stifle this

[1] *De la Souveraineté*, pp. 97–99.   [2] Op. cit., pp. 111–13.
[3] *De la Souveraineté*, p. 23.

essential flow of initiatives. Mutual trust, social friendship, and the strength of social ties are not produced by governments; they must develop by themselves through men's regular social relations.[1]

It follows from this kind of analysis that the major function of the state is to foster the conditions under which the free play of initiatives can flourish. In so far as de Jouvenel sums up the essential function of the government in simple terms, it is to ensure the reliability of the environment in which men act.[2] It is not wholly clear whether he identifies the reliability of the environment with the common good, but this appears to be so. De Jouvenel draws a distinction between the common good and what he calls the 'collective social interest'. The former is something for which the 'magistrates' are responsible. The latter, however, is the product of society itself as it contributes towards the development of the contentment and perfection of succeeding generations. Government cannot produce the latter, but it can provide its conditions.[3]

De Jouvenel appears to envisage the reliability of the environment under two headings. On the one hand, he writes that 'all that men can legitimately propose is to discover some basic conditions necessary to the maintenance of society as such and propitious for the development of the well-being of its members'.[4] The most obvious of these, according to him, are avoidance of destruction by an enemy, attrition through the exhaustion of material resources, and disintegration through the dissolution of the bonds of affection. These, he holds, are the least indeterminate aspects of the general welfare, give the clearest direction to the officials as to their duty, and provoke the least dissension in political discussion. But even though these interests are fundamental, they should not always dominate over other social interests; their priority should be asserted only when they are threatened.[5] On the other hand, de Jouvenel speaks frequently, in connexion with preserving the reliability

[1] The argument summarized in this paragraph appears in *De la Souveraineté*, Part Two, Ch. III (Chapter 8 of the English version).

[2] 'I regard it as the essential function of the sovereign to ensure the reliability of the individual's environment.' *Sovereignty* (English version), p. 300. This sentence appears in a conclusion written expressly for the English version and does not appear in the French original.

[3] *De la Souveraineté*, pp. 153 and 169–74.   [4] Ibid., p. 171.   [5] Ibid.

of the environment, of the necessity for the government to engage in a continual process of adjustment.[1] It is on this process of adjustment that he concentrates much of his attention, because the preservation of stability amidst change is, in his view, the principal function of political leadership.

IV   Political and Social Leadership

De Jouvenel distinguishes between two types of political leadership, which he symbolizes directly or indirectly by several sets of paired terms: *dux* and *rex, militiae* and *domi*, the attentive statesman and the intending politic.[2] *Dux* is Napoleon at the Bridge of Arcola, *rex* is Saint Louis under the Oak of Vincennes. Militance means social mobilization in the pursuit of a clearly defined goal, domesticity is the diversity and privacy of freedom. The attending statesman listens and arbitrates in the light of reason, the intending politic is the political man of the project, who moves single-mindedly towards his goal. *Dux* is the political promoter, who leads armies or founds states. *Rex* is the stabilizer, the peace-maker, the enforcer of contracts, the arbiter of disputes, the adjuster of differences. De Jouvenel suggests that political *reges* and *duces* tend to alternate, with *rex* normally at the head of society, *dux* at its head only intermittently. There may be times when leadership by *dux* is essential, but societies cannot support that kind of leadership for very long, as the projects it conceives and the efforts it demands to implement them place too many strains on the social fabric. *Rex* is the image which de Jouvenel presents of political leadership in a well-ordered society.[3]

It is not entirely clear whether de Jouvenel conceives of this distinction between *dux* and *rex* exclusively as an analytical device for distinguishing leadership functions or also as a general system for the classification of actual leaders. In *Power*, where he refers to the distinction only briefly, he refers to it as explaining 'the double character of historic royal Power, a

---

[1] *De la Souveraineté*, Part One, Ch. III (Chapter 3 of the English version) and p. 174; also *Sovereignty* (English version), p. 300.

[2] See *Du Pouvoir*, pp. 111–12; *The Pure Theory of Politics*, Part VI, Ch. 1; and especially *De la Souveraineté*, pp. 50–51 and Part One, Chs. III and IV (p. 34 and Chapters 3 and 4 of the English version).

[3] *De la Souveraineté*, pp. 72; 75–76; *The Pure Theory of Politics*, p. 174.

duality transmitted by it to all its successor powers. It is the symbol of the community, its mystical core, its cohesive force, its supporting virtue. But it is also ambition for itself, exploitation of society, will for power, utilization of natural resources for prestige and adventure.'[1] In *Sovereignty*, however, de Jouvenel writes of *dux* and *rex* as of two types of men, and the alternation between *dux* and *rex* to which he alludes seems to involve changes in leadership and not only in leadership function.

As an analytical device for distinguishing between functions, the *dux-rex* pair is very useful. As a system of classification for leaders, however, it would be too sharply categorical. De Jouvenel cites Napoleon as an illustration of *dux*, and it is unlikely that anyone will disagree as long as the Napoleon in mind is the general rallying his troops at the Bridge of Arcola. But how about the Napoleon who stabilized the forces set into motion by the French Revolution, reached an accommodation with the Church, and promulgated the Civil Code? Perhaps men can agree that, in their separate ways, Winston Churchill and Clement Attlee were *duces*; how should one classify President Franklin D. Roosevelt? Did he innovate more than conserve, promote more than adjust, mobilize more than stabilize? Did he inaugurate a new pattern for the United States of governmental intervention in the economy in order to accomplish preconceived social purposes, or did he act to preserve the kind of social order which makes a continual flow of independent social initiatives possible? The difficulty of fitting so important a political leader into one or the other of the categories of *dux* and *rex* is not simply of academic interest. It does suggest that these categories are of limited utility for descriptive purposes, but it also suggests that some degree of performance of the *dux* function may be necessary in order to achieve satisfactory performance of the *rex* function. Nevertheless, de Jouvenel suggests that the type of political leadership appropriate to a liberal society is the type symbolized by *rex*.

De Jouvenel applies his theory of leadership to social groups as well as to political systems. Just as there are political *duces* and *reges*, so are there social *duces* and *reges*. 'Society offers in fact an intricate texture of *duces* and *reges*,' he writes in the

[1] *Du Pouvoir*. p. 113.

conclusion of *Sovereignty*.[1] Actually, de Jouvenel hardly discusses social *reges* at all in *Sovereignty*; he discusses only social *duces*. He obviously has in mind intermediate bodies of various sorts, such as business groups and trade unions, but he does not indicate which ones belong in the *dux* category and which ones belong in the *rex* category.

De Jouvenel is primarily interested in the social *dux*—the promoter or the innovator—for two reasons. In the first place, he regards the process by which the promoter builds a group to further his project as the very essence of political activity. In the second place, the promoter is the source of social initiatives, and de Jouvenel believes that social enrichment depends upon 'the incessant sparkling of dispersed initiatives'.[2] Consequently, while he tells us that there are social *duces* and social *reges*, he discusses only the former and not the latter, and while he sketches out a simple scheme of classification for social groups, he devotes more than cursory attention only to what he calls the action group (or the work group), which is the kind of group that is formed by the social *dux*. The incompleteness of this treatment of social leadership is important for, as will be pointed out shortly, de Jouvenel assigns an important role in the government of society to the social *reges* whom he does not identify.

Whatever the uncertainties surrounding de Jouvenel's treatment of social leadership types, the political *rex* is the image he presents of proper political leadership. *Rex* is essentially a stabilizing and conserving agent. Men's lives, particularly in modern societies, depend upon the routine performance of uncountable tasks, and it is the special role of *rex* to promote the conditions which will foster the smooth operation of this complex social process. The social process, however, at least in a liberal society—which de Jouvenel defines as one in which the political authorities neither stifle social initiatives nor seek to substitute themselves for social innovators—is constantly being disturbed by the activities of social *duces*, who introduce novelties which disturb old routines and which, if ignored, might weaken or destroy men's confidence in the behaviour of others. It is necessary, therefore, for the political authorities 'to repair the damage' which men's social activities constantly

[1] *Sovereignty* (English version), p. 300.   [2] *De la Souveraineté*, p. 23.

threaten to do to society's 'moral cohesion'.[1] The term which de Jouvenel uses to describe the proper political process in an active society is *filtrage*, 'filtering'. Men's social initiatives must be filtered, 'so that injurious acts are hindered as much as possible'.[2] New practices must be admitted, 'for initiatives are not born everywhere and innovators are not numerous', and it would be harmful to immobilize a society. But 'the essence of the task [of the political authorities] remains conservative. In any society the share of change should be small and that of regularities very large.'[3]

What criteria should the political authorities follow in the filtering process? Which initiatives are harmful, which should be rejected, which admitted? The meaning of filtering, adjustment, regulation, and the like is not self-evident. De Jouvenel generally uses these terms to refer to admitting change, but softening its impact; to creating an atmosphere hospitable to disturbers of routines, but moderating the disturbances they create; to maintaining those conditions of freedom out of which conflicts will inevitably arise, but reducing the intensity of the conflicts which do arise. But most importantly, throughout this process of what might be called trying to control social change, but not directly to produce it, the political authorities must lend their support to the innovators as opposed to the conservatives.

De Jouvenel's discussion of social authorities, or social groups, distinguishes between those which are on the way up and those which are on the way down. In every society, according to the argument,[4] there are some groups whose credit is on the rise and others whose credit is on the decline. The rising groups are the socially dynamic forces, representative of the coming men, the innovators who render social services and create social progress. The groups on the way down are those whose creative and productive phase has passed. These are the groups which represent the vested interests which seek to perpetuate the privileges which they may have won in the past by performing social services, but which in the present can only constitute obstacles to the continuing process of social change.

---

[1] Ibid., p. 170.   [2] Ibid., p. 174.   [3] Ibid., p. 75.
[4] Ibid., pp. 108–10, 113; 'On the Evolution of Forms of Government' pp. 108–10.

It makes a great deal of difference, de Jouvenel argues, whether the political authorities align themselves with the declining or the rising social forces. At great moments of historical uncertainty, when the balance can be thrown either way, such as the years preceding the French Revolution, the direction which the political authorities choose to take can be decisive for the whole future course of a nation's political development. It is logical and proper for the government to help clear the way for the rising groups by 'dismantling the defences which established interests are forever putting up'.[1] It is wise for the government 'to blow its wind upon the old and shine its sun upon the new'.[2] To favour the old privileged groups which have outlived their social utility—as the French king did—is to invite revolution.

How is it possible to tell which groups are on the rise and which are on the decline, which are conducive to progress and which are obstacles to progress, which render social services and which are socially parasitic? De Jouvenel does not treat these questions directly. The implication is strong, however, that one of the main components of the social enrichment on which he places a high value is material enrichment, and that one main criterion for distinguishing between groups on the rise and those on the decline is their contribution to economic development.[3] The prominence of a productive ethic in *Sovereignty*, if only by implication, is something for which the reader of *Power*, in which medieval and aristocratic nostalgia is so evident, is not well prepared. Actually, de Jouvenel has never ignored the importance of productive economic enterprise;[4] it simply tends to be submerged beneath other central themes which he emphasizes.

De Jouvenel's argument that the political authorities must make their presence felt by acting in support of the progressive and productive social groups is an interesting contribution to

[1] *Sovereignty* (English version), p. 81. I cite the English version here as it slightly expands the original.

[2] 'On the Evolution of Forms of Government', p. 110.

[3] *De la Souveraineté*, pp. 204–11.

[4] One reason for de Jouvenel's highly critical view of the French bourgeoisie and his aristocratic sympathies may be that he finds that the aristocracy played a larger role in promoting French industry than the bourgeoisie did. See his *Napoléon et l'économie dirigée, le blocus continental*, Brussels and Paris, 1942, pp. 39–44.

contemporary political thought. The argument is ingenious and provides a middle ground between government planning and laissez-faire which goes beyond simple terms like regulation and adjustment. The government should be an arbiter, but it should not be neutral. It should lend its support, however gently, to those social groups which appear to be the harbingers of social progress. It must act to adjust social conflicts, but in doing so it must make decisive, if discreet, choices as to social direction. The government, in effect, steers the society, but it does not define the route along which the society is to be steered. The definition of alternate routes is the work of social groups; the government's role is limited to selecting among the alternatives which society itself offers.

The argument assumes the existence of a society in which there is a sufficiently vigorous group life to provide the productive and progressive initiatives which the political authorities can and should support. It is less clear from de Jouvenel's analysis what the role of government should be in a society in which such productive activity is lacking or inadequate to serve manifest needs, and it has already been pointed out that he may understate the extent to which some performance of the *dux* function may be essential to the successful performance of the *rex* function.[1] But de Jouvenel is distrustful of the political *dux* because of the concentration of political power with which he associates him and the social mobilization which his projects may require.

In fact, de Jouvenel does not reserve to the political authorities exclusively the performance of the *rex* function. 'It is a good economy of [political] authority to use it only for lack of any other or to redress the vices of another,' he writes in *Sovereignty*,[2] and in the conclusion of the book he indicates that there are many purely social processes by which the adjustment and regulation of social conflicts may be performed.

In the course of this book it has been amply noted that, while this task of adjustment and stabilisation is the essential duty of the

[1] De Jouvenel does say that a concentration of government may be necessary in the new states, although not the kind of political control which produces the moral mutation which he wishes to avoid. 'On the Evolution of Forms of Government', p. 115.

[2] *De la Souveraineté*, p. 108.

sovereign, there are many factors and processes in society which contribute to the adjustment and stabilisation and so take a large part of the load off the sovereign's shoulders. Society offers in fact an intricate texture of *duces* and *reges*. It is the sovereign's business to see that the *reges* operate to repair the insecurity caused by the initiatives, not to preclude them; and it is his duty to intervene to the extent necessary for the adequate fulfilment of the function of *rex*.[1]

It has already been pointed out, however, that de Jouvenel does not examine social *reges* in *Sovereignty*. In his discussion of social leadership, he focuses on the social *duces*. The only type of *rex* he discusses is the political *rex*.

The only place where de Jouvenel discusses what may be called social *reges* is in the final pages of *Power*, which he explicitly says are tentative and subject to revision.[2] Here he speaks of the necessity for the various *potentes* and *seniores* throughout society to formulate concrete ethical standards applicable to their particular social roles and of the need for the spiritual authorities to remind them constantly of this necessity.[3] But in *Power* his lament was precisely that these social leaders were not in fact doing what he thought they should. The social types to which he ascribed the function of *rex*, without so labelling it at this point, were not, in his view at the time, behaving like *reges*. Yet in *Sovereignty* he again ascribes an important role to them, without identifying them or showing whether they are conducting themselves more responsibly than he found them to be when he wrote *Power*.

Moreover, in *Power*, the kind of leadership function which he labels *rex* is attributed to social types whom he labels *duces* in *Sovereignty*.

It is precisely up to those people who create the new conditions, to the innovating élites, sufficiently guided by the spiritual authorities, to create the code of conduct, the images of behaviour which should harmonize the newly invented function with the social order.

These innovating élites, at the same time, must think of the personnel whom they attract, and prepare the moral framework as well as the material framework into which they are received.

In a word, to each function corresponds its law of chivalry and its duty of patronage. Now, in the social movement of our time, the

[1] *Sovereignty*, p. 300. This section appears in a conclusion written expressly for the English version and does not appear in the French original.

[2] *Du Pouvoir*, p. 443.   [3] Ibid., pp. 448–53.

innovators have neither elaborated these laws nor become conscious of these duties.[1]

The discussion of social *duces* in *Sovereignty*, however, implies that, by definition, the social *dux* cannot be expected to do what de Jouvenel asks him to do in *Power*. The *dux* is a master-builder, obsessed by his project, possessed of 'a naïve vigour of desires or convictions', someone to whom an authoritarian approach comes naturally, a disturber of routines and not a stabilizer.[2] The concluding pages of *Power*, therefore, are of little help in identifying the social *reges* to whom de Jouvenel attributes such an important role in *Sovereignty*.

Although de Jouvenel presents a theory of leadership in terms of both *dux* and *rex*, and holds that it is applicable to both political and social life, he applies his theory unevenly. When he deals with political leadership, he emphasizes the *rex* function.[3] When he deals with social leadership, he emphasizes the *dux* function. The reason for this is evident enough: de Jouvenel views government essentially as the stabilizing agency of a society which is constantly being disturbed by social innovators. But just as his preoccupation with the political leader as *rex* leads him to understate the need for some kind of continuing performance by a political *dux*, his preoccupation with social *duces* leads him to neglect the social *reges* to whom he assigns an important political role.

There is some similarity between this aspect of de Jouvenel's thought and the political ideas of Alain. De Jouvenel is more alert to the needs of an industrial society than Alain was and his notion that the political authorities must lend their support to the forces making for social progress contrasts with Alain's view that political decisions automatically reflect prevailing social forces. There is, however, a basis for comparison of the two political thinkers. Like Alain, de Jouvenel fears political power and would prefer to rely on social processes rather than on political commands to secure the adjustment of social conflicts. And for de Jouvenel, as for Alain, the limitations of the

[1] Ibid., p. 449.   [2] *De la Souveraineté*, pp. 86–93.
[3] In *Sovereignty*, but not in *The Pure Theory of Politics*. Here he is also concerned with the rising political *dux*, whom he calls the intending politic, and he says that it is on him that the study of political dynamics must focus. In part this is because he is trying to discover the conditions in which a political *dux* drives out a *rex*, thereby creating the risk of a moral mutation. Op. cit., pp. 173–5.

prescription appear when it is applied to a society in which such social processes are inadequate or lacking. It was argued in Chapter 1 that these social processes were breaking down in France even as Alain wrote. Perhaps they have been restored in France, or exist elsewhere, in which cases de Jouvenel's prescription could be followed. He has not, however, specified what these processes are.

V   Institutions and Attitudes

Governments must regulate the social activities of men to prevent harmful acts from being committed; make continual adjustments so that the disturbances, conflicts, and changes which social activities generate will not destroy the moral cohesion of the community; 'foster the conditions under which initiative will flower'.[1] The task is essentially conservative, in that the social environment should not be too sharply upset, but de Jouvenel argues also that the political authorities must incline in favour of the innovators as opposed to the established elements in society both in order to encourage social progress and to prevent revolution. How is all this to be done? The term which de Jouvenel employs which comes closest to describing the nature of all these activities is *filtrage*.[2] Who does the filtering? By what means?

These questions lead into the general problem of what kind of political institutions are required if the proper functions of government, and only those functions, are to be performed properly. Once the problem of political institutions is raised, a curious situation becomes apparent. De Jouvenel is probably more explicitly concerned with the question of what institutions are good institutions than any of the other political thinkers discussed in this book, yet for all that his discussion of them is quite elusive. In part, this is because the problems with which he deals in his various works change in subtle but significant ways. In *Power* the problem posed is how to limit the exercise of political power, without regard to distinctions between good and bad uses of power. In 'On the Evolution of Forms of Government', the problem posed is how to prevent the arbitrary exercise of political power, interpreted as the brutal form of

---

[1] *Sovereignty*, p. 301.   [2] *De la Souveraineté*, pp. 77 and 174.

rule, without regard to civilized moral values, such as modern single-party tyrannies have exercised. In *Sovereignty*, the problem posed is more specific, as it involves how to carry out a carefully designated set of governmental functions. It is perfectly understandable that if one asks different questions, however much they may bear a family resemblance, the answers proposed may vary, and the total impression they create may be less than coherent.

Still, that is not the only source of the inconclusiveness of de Jouvenel's discussion of institutions. At different times, he has expressed divergent attitudes towards the institutional problem. He has written as though the conception and construction of good institutions were a relatively simple matter,[1] as though the task might be beyond men's capacities to accomplish,[2] and as though the task is exceedingly difficult but still one which men should not admit to be impossible.[3] He has stated that institutional barriers to arbitrary government are more reliable than dislike of it,[4] but in his specific discussion of how to limit governmental power he relies as heavily on attitudes as restraining forces as he does on institutional arrangements. His habit of reducing complicated phenomena to schematic categories, no doubt in order to heighten the relief of his analysis, sometimes contributes to obscuring it.[5] And in the particular case of the problem with which we are concerned here, that of who

[1] 'On peut, par des institutions sagement combinées, assurer la garantie effective de chaque personne contre le Pouvoir. Mais il n'y a point d'institutions qui permettent de faire concourir chaque personne à l'exercice du Pouvoir. . . .' *Du Pouvoir*, p. 315. Also see p. 149.

[2] Referring to the problem of whether a proper balance between political power and social power can be arranged and maintained by 'clairvoyant legislators', or whether such a situation occurs only at certain moments of historical development, de Jouvenel says: 'Nous n'aborderons pas ici ce problème qui implique celui de l'autonomie et de l'efficacité de la volonté humaine, et pour mieux dire, des limites de l'homme.' Ibid., p. 366.

[3] 'It seems therefore that . . . we do not have any clear recipe of free institutions, such as our ancestors felt possessed of. . . . It may of course be said that there exists no such recipe. . . . But I come increasingly to think that no intellectual with a sense of social responsibility should allow himself to take such a position, because it must leave you without any principles you can advocate and champion against arbitrary government.' 'On the Evolution of Forms of Government', p. 119.

[4] Ibid.

[5] As in the case of his frequent references in *Sovereignty* to 'the sovereign'. For the periods when there were sovereigns, there is no difficulty. But de Jouvenel also refers to the sovereign for the contemporary period. Who or what is the sovereign in a modern constitutional system?

does the filtering and how, de Jouvenel makes no institutional recommendations. He makes no reference to specific institutions, but rather relies exclusively on the existence of proper attitudes to bring about the desired results.

The few institutional recommendations which de Jouvenel makes in *Power* are not relevant to the question of how to organize a government so that it will best perform its proper functions as these are defined in *Sovereignty*. The main conclusion with respect to institutions which seems to emerge from *Power* is that only strongly entrenched social interests can effectively limit the exercise of power by central executive authorities.[1] De Jouvenel returns to a similar point momentarily in *Sovereignty*, where he argues that the sovereign should not be unlimited in power, but rather that 'the arrangement of tangible obstacles is the condition of the good operation and conservation of any organism'.[2] The difficulty with this formula is that it does not contain any provision for the prevention of social ossification. It appears to be based on Montesquieu's appreciation of intermediate powers in the form of social and territorial estates, but unless the prescription be refined, it is more suitable to a static society than to the kind of dynamic society which de Jouvenel envisages. It is clear that the stronger and more entrenched social interests are, the greater will be their capacity to raise obstacles to the exercise of executive power, but the obstacles in the way of the development of new social forces will also be strengthened and the capacity of the executive to lean in favour of those new social forces will be reduced.

De Jouvenel does not, therefore, describe a system in detail, although he does have in mind a clear conception of how good government operates. The image which repeatedly appears in his work, whether he is thinking of medieval or contemporary France, is that of an executive which is dependent upon, in

---

[1] 'Cette limitation [of political power] exige des intérêts fractionnaires suffisamment formés, conscients, et armés pour arrêter le Pouvoir lorsqu'il avance sur leur propre terrain, et un Droit suffisamment indépendant pour être l'arbitre des conflits et non l'instrument de la Centralité.' *Du Pouvoir*, p. 366.

Also, 'Si d'une part les intérêts etaient garantis, dotés de moyens d'expression et d'action, on pourrait ensuite constituer le Pouvoir par la seule concurrence des opinions et n'y admettre que les opinions éclairées.' Ibid., p. 330.

[2] *De la Souveraineté*, pp. 271–2.

harmony with, and supported by a parliament consisting of the leaders of progressive and productive social groups who, in turn, have the respect and confidence of their particular followers. In such a situation, the parliamentary leaders can check the executive when his policies appear to them to be unwise, the executive can count on the parliamentary leaders to bring popular support to his policies when they appear to them to be wise, and society prospers in this arrangement which ensures progress and blocks tyranny.[1]

Other much less favourable situations, he points out, can also arise. One such situation is where the executive supports and is supported only by the leaders of social groups who have lost the confidence of the people because they do not perform useful social functions. Another is when the executive is effectively unchecked because the representatives in parliament do not consist of men who are authoritative social leaders in their own right and therefore cannot command independent popular support.[2] These images are all clear enough. The problem is to devise a system which will operate continuously to approximate to the favourable image and to avoid approximating to the unfavourable ones.

When sure institutional formulas are not available, it is only natural to turn towards attitudinal formulas, and this is what de Jouvenel does. He had already written in *Power* that the cohesion of the community cannot be secured by governmental power alone. There must be 'a profound community of sentiments rooted in a common faith, translated into an unquestioned morality and sustaining an inviolable Law', all of which must be beyond the reach of government.[3] It is not clear, however, to what precise range of matters the community of faith, morality, and law should apply.[4] De Jouvenel speaks favourably in *Power* of the social consequences of belief in divine law,[5] but when discussing the problem of the needs of

---

[1] Ibid., pp. 222–5; 'On the Evolution of Forms of Government', pp. 108–13.

[2] 'On the Evolution of Forms of Government', pp. 110–12.

[3] *Du Pouvoir*, p. 376.

[4] Robert A. Dahl raises the questions, in connexion with *Sovereignty*, of whether unity of beliefs is necessary to a society and, if so, over what matters. 'Political Theory: Truth and Consequences', *World Politics* (Princeton, N.J.), XI (October 1958), pp. 98–99.

[5] *Du Pouvoir*, pp. 250–1; 384–5.

modern society, he acknowledges that general moral precepts are inadequate to govern specific behaviours. While holding that spiritual authorities have a guiding role to play, he also recognizes that casuistry—the application of general principles to specific cases—is a highly difficult art 'to which few minds are inclined'.[1] In *The Pure Theory of Politics*, de Jouvenel is still impressed with the importance of what contemporary political scientists generally call a consensus. He refers to the 'fundamental orthodoxy which underlies all political differences' in Great Britain and the United States, although he does not tell us in what this orthodoxy consists.[2]

De Jouvenel also refers to the necessity for a system of common beliefs in *Sovereignty*,[3] but this seems to refer more to a kind of underlying structure of feelings within the framework of which particular governmental decisions are made than it does to any particular attitude which people should bring to bear on a specific political problem. When he discusses the actual conduct of government, however, de Jouvenel still relies on attitudinal rather than institutional prescriptions, and this time he specifies the outlook which he believes the participants in the political process should have.

This outlook is essentially an application of the fundamental idea of Rousseau's *Social Contract*: that the citizens should shed their particular interests and direct their attention to the good of the whole body. But while Rousseau required the application of this method only to problems involving the general will, i.e., the laws and periodic judgements rendered on the quality and personnel of the administration, de Jouvenel extends it to all governmental decisions.

What de Jouvenel presents as 'quite a simple argument' on this basis is not, however, simple at all.[4] The argument appears to be that in a society characterized by numerous initiatives, the government will have many difficult problems to solve. There will, however, only be a given range of feasible solutions to these problems, and if the citizens demand something which lies outside of this range of solutions, or

---

[1] *Du Pouvoir*, p. 448.
[2] *The Pure Theory of Politics*, p. 35, n. 1.   [3] *Sovereignty*, p. 298.
[4] The argument appears in *Sovereignty*, pp. 302–3. It appears in the conclusion written expressly for the English version and not in the French original.

which conflicts with them, the government will not be able properly to fulfil its function. Accordingly, the citizen must give primary consideration to the problem facing the political authorities.

Whether the law of the land grants to all, to many or to a few the right to participate in the exercise of sovereignty, the attending obligation is ever the same; the obligation incurred by the participant is to address himself to the problem arising for the sovereign. He is entitled to manifest his own preference, but within the bounds set by the problem itself. Whether this participant is a peer of an oligarchy or the party-liner of a democracy, he equally disqualifies himself when he expresses his particular will without regard to the problem which the sovereign, as such, has to solve.[1]

It would have helped if de Jouvenel had furnished an illustration of this principle in operation, as that would have reduced the risk of misinterpretation of his thought, particularly as the argument presented involves a conceptual difficulty which he later seems to recognize. The difficulty lies in the distinction he makes between what he calls the problem facing the sovereign and the demands which men may make on the sovereign. In practice, there are many problems which the political authorities discover only because they are called to their attention by some popular demand, or at least there are many problems which the political authorities will try to do something about only after they are called upon to do so by some popular demand. Governments normally adjust, regulate, and prohibit only after solicitation to do so by some interested group which believes itself harmed by the activities of another group. When one group makes a demand, it may uncover a problem, but when another group makes a counter-demand, is it possible to distinguish between the problem uncovered and the problem constituted by the conflicting demands? Do not the problems which face the political authorities consist as much in conflicting demands as they do in the situations out of which those demands arise?

De Jouvenel appears to have come to believe so later, for when he returns to the subject of political problems in *The Pure Theory of Politics*, this is the position which he takes:

[1] Ibid., p. 302.

Nor is it worthwhile to say that but for the passions of the parties concerned, the problem would be easily solvable, because these passions are the very data of politics. It is all too easy for an outside observer to say that there exists a solution which people would accept if they but knew their true interests: what the outside observer then means is that the people concerned would all accept what seems to him desirable if they all agreed with him as to what is desirable: which is true enough, but trivial and irrelevant. Of course the outside observer, who deserves no attention if he passes an armchair judgement by merely overlooking what constitutes the problem, merits more consideration if he turns himself into an inside operator seeking to win the people concerned to his view: but then he himself and his followers become an element of the problem.[1]

Moreover, in this later work, de Jouvenel rejects the very notion that there is such a thing as a solution to a political problem. He takes the view that what creates a political problem is the fact that it involves a conflict of claims which cannot be fully satisfied by any decision. In this view, political problems are not solved; they are settled, by compromise if possible, or by either the application of a principle or the dictate of an authority (or both together), which may satisfy some but cannot satisfy all of the claims involved.[2]

De Jouvenel does not refer back to what he had written earlier in *Sovereignty*, so it is not possible to tell whether he would amend his earlier statement in the light of the more recent one. It is possible, however, to put a reasonable construction on the earlier statement, even in the light of his later remarks, although there is, of course, no certainty that this is the original intention of the argument.

The argument might be reconstructed as follows. Rousseau held that when men are called upon to participate in sovereignty they must think not of their own interests but of the good of the whole body. This, in so far as it is legitimate for the political authorities to pursue it directly, consists in maintaining the reliability of the environment. Therefore, when men participate in the political process, at any stage from the launching of a demand to the making of a final decision, they must not demand or decide in favour of what they prefer except in so far as it represents a feasible way of maintaining the reliability of the environment.

[1] *The Pure Theory of Politics*, p. 207.   [2] Ibid., pp. 207–8.

So far, the reconstruction of the argument has been linked to de Jouvenel's conception of that element of the common good which it is the proper function of the political authorities to pursue. It may also be linked to what de Jouvenel rejects as constituting the common good. In the discussion of the common good in *Sovereignty*, de Jouvenel rejects the notion that it consists of the subjectively perceived good of individuals. He does so because he believes that to assert that the government is the servant of interests will 'stimulate them to assert themselves shrilly and to encumber the forum with their clamouring', while he can find no satisfactory criterion by means of which competing claims for personal satisfaction can be measured.[1] De Jouvenel, therefore, wants to keep the pursuit of private interests out of politics as much as possible and to leave it to the private sphere, which must, however, be adjusted and stabilized by the political authorities.

De Jouvenel knows, however, that demands cannot be kept out of the political forum completely and, in order to avoid the deleterious consequences he foresees if these demands become only the expression of group interests, he suggests a formula to which they should adhere. The formula is to limit them to the range of feasible solutions to the social problem to which they are relevant. The social problem consists of the existence of some kind of disturbance to the reliability of the environment. It is by no means clear just what this means,[2] but it does seem clear that feasible solutions to the problem would consist of any course of action which would not produce an equally bad or a worse situation.

If this construction be correct, the argument reduces to the requirement that the people who make demands on the political authorities show that the course of action they propose is likely to produce a better situation than the existing one. This is reasonable. It does raise two further questions, however.

[1] *De la Souveraineté*, p. 146.

[2] De Jouvenel's conception of the reliability of the environment would have emerged more clearly if he had provided illustrations of reliable and unreliable environments not based on extreme cases. He illustrates an unreliable environment with the fanciful case of a change in Parisian street names every week (ibid., p. 75), and it is possible to think of other extreme cases (rampant inflation, widespread violence, etc.). An examination of marginal cases, however, would have left a clearer impression of what de Jouvenel thinks is the proper function of government.

One is institutional. The possibility of enforcing the recommendation would depend upon a well-devised set of institutions and procedures. De Jouvenel says that his argument is not against democracy but against irresponsibility,[1] and efforts to avoid irresponsibility in politics have usually involved trying to create political institutions through which responsibility can be enforced. He does not, however, have much to say about institutions in *Sovereignty*. He does say that 'one can say that the régime which presents the greatest chances of good decisions is the one which provides for the most preliminary discussion, the enlargement of the "council" ', but that is not very specific, and he adds immediately: 'still, that all depends on the moral attitude and the enlightenment which are displayed in the council, whether it be small or large, private or public'.[2] In the immediate context of the argument itself, he treats the performance of government as a function of the public spirit, not the public spirit as a function of the institutional structure.

The second question involves the manner in which one can actually make the sort of demonstration that is suggested. How does one go about showing that a course of action is likely to produce a better situation than the existing one? This, it will be remembered, was a problem with which Simone Weil grappled. De Jouvenel outlines in *Sovereignty* what he believes to be the components of the common good, but these are expressed in very general terms. When faced with a specific problem, how does one go about trying to decide which course of action will actually be a good one? De Jouvenel raises this question early in *Sovereignty*,[3] but his discussion of it is brief and he does not return to it later in the book. In *The Pure Theory of Politics*, however, he takes up the question of the position of the decision-maker.

VI   Conclusion

The Pure Theory of Politics is as different from *Sovereignty* as *Sovereignty* is from *Power*. *Power* analysed political power, traced its development historically, and presented a severe criticism of modern democracy. *Sovereignty* is more diffuse in

---

[1] *Sovereignty*, p. 302.   [2] *De la Souveraineté*, p. 123.   [3] Ibid., pp. 20–22.

subject matter, but it represents an effort to analyse a dynamic society and to determine what the proper functions of government in a liberal society should be. *The Pure Theory of Politics* is an effort to analyse how men actually behave politically. De Jouvenel makes no effort in this book to conceal his convictions as to what is good or bad. He makes it clear that he distrusts the person whom he calls the intending politic[1]— the emergent political *dux* who seeks control of the state—and he deplores the use of violence,[2] but the book is intended as a descriptive and not a prescriptive work.[3]

Describing and prescribing may be, as de Jouvenel says, distinct tasks,[4] but description and prescription are not unrelated. Any description is bound to identify conditions or practices which seem to the observer appropriate candidates for abolition or improvement, and any prescription, if it is to be acted on successfully, must take into account how men behave. Recommendations concerning what men ought to do must bear some discernible relationship to what men can be expected to do. Otherwise, political prescriptions become either futile exhortations or invitations to establish by coercion patterns of behaviour which men would not normally follow because they are too distant from the behavioural patterns to which they have become accustomed.

It is important, of course, not to view this relationship so strictly that it becomes circular. Every prescription which is not a recommendation on behalf of the *status quo* is a call for a change of some kind, and therefore calls for something which does not exist. But the relationship between the existing situation and the potential situation may be more or less close, depending upon the extent of change that is called for and the congruence between the potential situation and the predispositions, habits, and expectations which are the causes and consequences of the existing situation. It is on this relationship that the likelihood of the acceptance of political prescriptions depends.

The Pure Theory of Politics is an important book in this respect. By directing his attention to how men behave politically, and by focusing in particular on what he calls 'strong political

---

[1] *The Pure Theory of Politics*, p. 174.   [2] Ibid., p. 184.
[3] Ibid., p. xi.   [4] Ibid.

behaviour'—what happens when passions mount—as compared with what he calls ' "weak" political behaviour'—such as voting[1]—de Jouvenel high-lights the difficulties that confront the normative approach. We have already seen that while in *Sovereignty*, when making a behavioural prescription, he distinguishes between the problem facing the political authorities and the demands made on the political authorities, in *The Pure Theory of Politics*, which is a descriptive work, he treats the demands as elements of the political problem itself and even concludes that political problems are not amenable to solution, properly so called.

Political description can be relevant to political prescription in other ways also. In *The Pure Theory of Politics*, de Jouvenel describes the situation of the political decision-maker. He tells us that the decision-maker is essentially forward-looking, that he is concerned with the outcome of his decision, that he cannot view his decision simply as the application of a principle, that one may wonder whether there are any principles which honest men will abide by at all times and in all circumstances, that the decision-maker must take into account the probable reactions to the decision that he makes, that these reactions will be part of the outcome of the decision and these reactions may actually determine what the outcome of the decision will in fact be.[2]

De Jouvenel does not say that he approves of all this; he simply says that this is what happens. But if this is what happens there are important implications here for the quality of a good decision. In so far as the decision rests on a principle, the principle must be appropriate to the circumstances. In so far as men's reactions to the decision are a determinant of the outcome, those reactions must be properly anticipated to make sure that the end result is not something other than what is intended. And as men's reactions are so important to the outcome, their needs, wants, and beliefs must be taken into account.

By suggesting through his description of the situation of the decision-maker that principles must share attention with circumstances, that the inspiration of decisions must share attention with their probable outcome, and that their probable outcome is a function both of circumstances and men's reactions to the decisions themselves, de Jouvenel introduces considerations which are among the central notions of the political thought of Raymond Aron.

8

Raymond Aron: The Sociology of Politics

I   Aron and Weil

RAYMOND ARON is one of the most prolific and versatile political thinkers of the twentieth century. His works range over the fields of sociological theory, the philosophy of history, ideological criticism, international relations, nuclear strategy, and domestic French politics. No effort will be made here to encompass all these facets of his thought. The effort will be made, however, to extract from the broad range of Aron's writings the central principles and assumptions which he applies to the analysis of political systems and on which he relies in reaching decisions about both political systems and specific policies.

Aron has been both a participant in and a critic of his generation's debates about the proper organization of society. In fact, it is his critical approach which constitutes his major contribution to these debates. His scientific preoccupations and his concern for political pedagogy have been rightly pointed out,[1] and in these respects, as in others, Aron's work is more directly comparable with the early writings of Simone Weil than with the writings of any other political thinker treated in this book. Simone Weil's early writings never reached as wide an audience during her lifetime as do the works of Raymond Aron, and they probably do not even now, but there are strong similarities in the approaches of the two thinkers to the political arguments of their respective times.

The central element of Aron's political thought is precisely the same as that which appears in the early writings of Simone

[1] Alfred Grosser, ' "Espoir et peur du siècle": La Passion de l'explication sans passion', in *Revue Française de Science Politique*, VII (July–September 1957), p. 669.

Weil: that the extent to which men can be successful in translating their values into social or political realities depends upon the conditions of existence. If men are to be successful in the pursuit of their goals, both the goals themselves and the kinds of action undertaken to achieve them must not be incompatible with the conditions of existence. It follows from this that if men are to pursue their objectives reasonably, they require an understanding of those conditions which are likely to set limits to what they can achieve. The fundamental notion of both Simone Weil and Raymond Aron points directly to the need for a political science.

Just as Simone Weil was sharply critical of the French political disputants of the nineteen thirties, Raymond Aron has been critical of many of the participants in the French political debates of the nineteen forties and nineteen fifties, and for precisely the same reasons. Simone Weil earlier, like Aron today, believed that political debate had reached a dangerously high pitch because men were arguing on the basis of expectations that were excessive and fears that were unnecessary because of their inadequate knowledge of either the social structure or social processes. Simone Weil developed her sociological theory in order to discover what scope the social structure allowed for the implementation of certain ideals. The scope of Simone Weil's sociological theory was narrow. Its basis was functional, but she did not adequately explore the extent to which identical or similar functions might be performed in various ways. She concentrated her attention largely on economic and military functions and gave only cursory consideration to political functions, partly because of her special preoccupation with working-class conditions and probably also because she was greatly interested in probing into what she regarded as a critical weakness of Marxism: its omission of any consideration of the impact of war on social and political organization.[1] The result was that her projection of the future envisaged a convergence of political forms. In her view, the impact of industrial and international competition on all

[1] For Simone Weil's criticism of Marx and the Marxists for their failure to consider war, see her 'Sur les Contradictions du marxisme', in *Oppression et liberté*, Paris, 1955, pp. 199–200, and her fragment written in London in 1943, ibid., p. 213.

modern states would fashion them in the image of the bureau-
cratically organized totalitarian régime of the Soviet Union
of the early nineteen thirties.

Aron's sociological method is more complex than Simone
Weil's, and his conclusions are different. He looks much more
closely into alternate forms of political organization than
Simone Weil did, and he believes in the primacy of political
organization over other social phenomena.[1] This is not, of
course, to be interpreted to mean that Aron adheres to a single-
factor deterministic theory, which takes politics as the exclusive
determinant of social characteristics and which would permit
one to deduce every characteristic of a society from knowledge
of its political system. It is to be interpreted as meaning that
societies which have certain identical or similar social or
economic characteristics may be governed by very different
kinds of political system, and that the latter, in turn, may be
more decisive in determining the style of interpersonal and
intergroup relations in each society than the social or economic
characteristics which they share.

In this respect, Aron follows in a sociological tradition which
he has himself identified as 'the French school of political
sociology' and 'of which the founder is Montesquieu and the
second great man Tocqueville'. This is a 'school of sociologists
who are not dogmatic, who are essentially preoccupied with
politics, who do not overlook the importance of the social
infrastructure, but who recognize the autonomy of the political
order and who are liberals'.[2] Montesquieu and de Tocqueville
analysed societies in terms of both their social and political
characteristics, and in terms of the relationship of each of these
characteristics to each other. By establishing a relationship
between the form of government, the manner of rule, and the
style of interpersonal relations, Montesquieu implied that the

---

[1] 'Le régime politique commande, pour une large part, le style de la collectivité.
A l'âge de la société industrielle, c'est lui qui est constitutif de la différence
spécifique entre collectivités appartenant à un même type.' Raymond Aron,
'Les Sociologues et les institutions représentatives', in *Archives Européennes de
Sociologie*, I (1960), 156–57. See also his *Démocratie et totalitarisme*, Paris, 1965,
pp. 24–35.

[2] Raymond Aron, *Les Grandes Doctrines de sociologie historique* (Cours de Sorbonne,
Paris, C.D.U.), 1960, pp. 222–3. 'Probably I am a latter-day descendant of this
school,' he adds. Eng. tr. by Richard Howard and Helen Weaver, *Main Currents of
Sociological Thought*, Vol. 1, New York, 1965.

character of social life varies with the manner of rule.[1] De Tocqueville, of course, held that all modern societies were developing the conditions of equality but that the form of government they would have might be either despotic or liberal. Aron, too, sees the political system as decisive for the social system, and envisages the possibility of more than one form of government for societies that are similar in other important characteristics.

Aron, therefore, not only pays close attention to the political structures and processes which Simone Weil neglected, but he also envisages a developmental divergence of the political systems of those modern nations for which Simone Weil envisaged a unilinear type of political development. Such a developmental conception is bound to be more complicated sociologically than Simone Weil's, because it requires an analysis of the essential structural and procedural characteristics of more than one type of political system. Despite these differences in outlook, however, the intellectual approach that Raymond Aron and Simone Weil take to the problems of political behaviour is the same. Ideals, and actions based upon them, must be related to the conditions of existence, both in order to moderate the passions which the conflict of ideals can generate and to ensure the probability of success in realizing the ideals through the actions pursued.

In her attack on abstractions, with which Camus was so sympathetic, Simone Weil criticized the 'words beginning with capital letters' and the 'words ending with ism'. She wrote that 'our political universe is exclusively peopled with myths and monsters; we know only entities, only absolutes. All the words of the political and social vocabulary could serve as examples. Nation, security, capitalism, communism, fascism, order, authority, property, democracy, one could take them all one after the other.' If words like these could be reduced to the realities to which they refer, she argued, they would lose their capacity to incite to violence, and she both illustrated her point and indicated the form such analysis should take with reference to the way in which the word capitalism had become for one social group the symbol for human suffering and for an opposing group the symbol for social order, while neither of the

---

[1] *Les Grandes Doctrines de sociologie historique*, pp. 25 and 54.

opposing groups had taken the trouble to examine carefully the extent to which the concrete institutions and practices of capitalism could reasonably be identified either with suffering or with social order.[1] Emmanuel Mounier touched briefly on a similar consideration when he distinguished between eternal values and the diverse forms in which they can appear historically, but he never pursued the distinctions in a systematic fashion himself.[2] Raymond Aron has undertaken central aspects of the dual task suggested by Simone Weil and Emmanuel Mounier. He has taken what the linguistic analyst calls emotive words and subjected them to critical examination in the light of current social and political conditions. In *The Opium of the Intellectuals*[3] he dissected what he calls the myths of the 'left', the 'revolution', and the 'proletariat'. Continuing 'the confrontation of ideologies with reality', he then wrote an essay on the 'myths of the right' in *Espoir et peur du siècle*.[4] Here he brings under examination such concepts as equality and inequality, hierarchy, property, materialism, tradition, reason, authority, power, and grandeur. His effort throughout is to analyse their meaning, to suggest the concrete attitudes and policies with which they are compatible in contemporary France, and to find the ways in which specific applications of the concepts might provide a basis for harmony, rather than conflict, among the groups which conflict over them in the political struggle.

Aron is less explicit about his method of analysis than Simone Weil was, but the method he employs is essentially similar to hers, although it is broader in application. The meaning of a doctrinal preference and the probable outcome of following policies inspired by it are affected by the conditions of industrialization and international competition and by the ideals and aspirations to which the community is already attached. For Aron, therefore, the socialist cannot expect to alter the exigencies of the work process simply by transferring ownership from capitalists to the state;[5] a doctrinal commit-

---

[1] Simone Weil, 'Ne Recommençons pas la guerre de Troie (Pouvoir des mots),' in *Écrits historiques et politiques*, Paris, 1960, pp. 265, 258–9, and 266–8.

[2] See Chapter 3, pp. 85–86.

[3] *L'Opium des intellectuels*, Paris, 1955.

[4] *Espoir et peur du siècle, Essais non partisans*, Paris, 1957, p. 9.

[5] *L'Opium des intellectuels*, p. 169.

ment to communism cannot be made without reference to the real institutions of the Soviet Union;[1] a single-party system with the most benign of objectives cannot be established except by methods which would quickly lose benign qualities;[2] obsolete means of production cannot, in the long run, survive in a materialistic society.[3]

The concern with sociological analysis which Aron shares with the early Simone Weil, and which he develops more fully and broadly than she, distinguishes both of them from the other political thinkers treated in this book. Emmanuel Mounier, Albert Camus, and Jean-Paul Sartre are all fundamentally preoccupied with moral problems rather than sociological ones. Mounier understood clearly the need for a sociology but he did not develop one. Camus was exclusively a moralist. The sociological concepts that appear in the works of Sartre are mainly borrowed from Marx; Sartre has only recently begun to develop certain such concepts of his own, in his *Critique de la raison dialectique*. Bertrand de Jouvenel obviously has sociological interests, but his *dux-rex* duality is not fully elaborated, and his *Sovereignty* is primarily a study in moral and political philosophy.

This is not to say that Aron is indifferent to moral problems. He takes them for granted. Camus and Sartre treat the absence of ultimate justifications for human behaviour with Cartesian self-consciousness and make it a central object of reflection. Aron is not concerned with a presumed loss of, or impossibility of, moral certainties. He does not seek moral certainties, but structural certainties. He is not uninterested in the sources of morality or values,[4] but his main effort lies in trying to discover the scope of their applicability to specific situations. In Aron's view, sociology does not found values, nor can it ever tell men which values they must hold, but it is an indispensable aid to men as they make specific choices in pursuit of the values which they do hold.

[1] Ibid., pp. 68–69.   [2] *Espoir et peur du siècle*, p. 109.   [3] Ibid., p. 78.
[4] See especially Raymond Aron, *Introduction à la philosophie de l'histoire, Essai sur les limites de l'objectivité historique*, Paris, 1948, pp. 293–308. Eng. tr. by G. J. Irwin, *Introduction to the Philosophy of History*, New York, 1961.

11   The Nature of Political Thought

Aron has nowhere set forth a systematic political theory. The elements of one appear in his writings, particularly his works of ideological criticism and his lectures on the sociology of industrial societies, but one cannot extract from his writings a neat structure of goals, conditions, and prescriptions for the general governance of societies. For Aron, the creation of such a logical structure would be to approach politics ideologically, and Aron—along with Simone Weil and Albert Camus—is a vigorous opponent of approaching politics ideologically. In fact, Aron is no doubt the best known in this context of the three political thinkers.

This is not to say that Aron holds no values, is unconcerned with the study of societies, and makes no prescriptions. There can be no doubt that he is philosophically committed personally to the revolutionary and liberal values of liberty, equality, and fraternity. As a sociologist, he is professionally committed to the study of societies, and he is tireless in his exhortations that political disputants should examine what is real. He continually commits himself to specific courses of action, whether related to the choice of a policy or to the choice of a régime. What he does not do, however, is commit himself to a general theory in which goals, conditions, and prescriptions are crystallized in permanent form. Goals are multiple and he accepts no fixed hierarchy among them; conditions change; prescriptions depend upon goals and conditions. Aron is the most explicitly relativistic political thinker treated in this book, more so even than Camus, whose thought is very similar to Aron's in this respect.

Aron briefly formulates what might be the starting-point for a political theory. He reduces the 'political problem', for analytical purposes, to how to reconcile 'the equality of men as men with the inequality of their functions in the community', and he describes the task more specifically as how to 'obtain from the subordinate recognition of his superiors without causing him to suffer constraint or to lose his dignity'.[1] Elsewhere in the same work he writes that 'man is . . . a moral being

[1] *L'Opium des intellectuels*, pp. 163–4. See also Raymond Aron, *Dix-Huit Leçons sur la société industrielle*, Paris, 1963, pp. 86–87.

and the community is human only on the condition that it offers a participatory role to everyone'.[1] There is, therefore, a constant problem of politics: that of maintaining a community in which equality and hierarchy are reconciled, and Aron seems to view such a reconciliation in terms of the participation of everyone in the community.

Aron does not, however, use this statement of the political problem as the point of departure for the construction of a general political theory. He does not speculate about the kind of institutions, or even about the general conditions, that might be expected optimally to produce a reconciliation of equality and hierarchy. Nor does he pursue closely the concept of participation in the community. He speaks of participation in a society's culture, which is made possible by the increase and general distribution of a society's wealth. He also speaks of participation in the political life of the community, but on this point he is ambiguous. At one point, he refers to participation in a way which would make it applicable to any role, however passive or ineffective, which people might play in the total organization of society.[2] At another, he seems to have in mind such a Rousseauian notion of participation that he refers to democratic elections as being 'perhaps only a degraded form of this universal participation of the citizens in the State', although they are at the same time its symbol, 'which may become a reality'.[3] He also suggests the possibility of conceiving a kind of continuum of participation, extending towards the caste system in one direction and, in the other, towards the political equality of men in a system which seeks to promote social and economic equality.[4] But however he may conceive of the notion of participation in the community, Aron does not set out to define the ways in which it, or any other goal or group of goals, might be fully achieved.

Aron's statement of the solution of the political problem in terms of the participation of everyone in the community is to be regarded as a Kantian end rather than as a concrete goal. Aron regards the 'radical solution' to the political problem as

---

[1] *L'Opium des intellectuels*, p. 110.
[2] *Dix-Huit Leçons sur la société industrielle*, p. 87.
[3] *Démocratie et totalitarisme*, p. 352.
[4] *Dix-Huit Leçons sur la société industrielle*, p. 87.

conceivable, but he also holds that it cannot be identified with any concrete set of institutions or known society. This is the core of his anti-ideological attitude. Aron has defined ideology in a variety of ways,[1] but the way he uses the term most frequently indicates that what he means by ideological political thinking is the attribution of absolute value to a given set of institutions or practices. In this interpretation, the liberal who exalts parliamentary institutions is as ideological as the communist who attributes absolute value to the conquest of power by his party.[2] It is both legitimate and necessary to envisage a perfect society, in which all conflicts would be reconciled, 'in which the sage would be satisfied, in which men would live according to reason'. Such a vision is necessary to provide the criterion against which to measure the imperfections of real societies and to serve as a guide in the task of making real societies less imperfect. But it is a grave error, in Aron's view, to identify any real society with the ideal society, both because we cannot know concretely what the ideal society would be and because to do so would be to glorify excessively a set of prosaic human institutions.[3]

In this argument, Aron is much closer to Camus than he is to Simone Weil, whose thought is so similar to his own in other fundamental ways. Simone Weil is much more specific in her definition of the ideal than Aron is in his image of perfection. Like Aron, she held the ideal to be essentially a criterion and not a goal, but she believed it should be more concretely conceived than Aron does. In this respect she is a spiritual descendant of the classical Greek political philosophers.[4] Aron deliberately makes the image of perfection formal. By doing so he preserves it as a criterion for the evaluation of existing societies, accepts the legitimacy of debate over how society can be improved, and leaves open the question of whether the end is actually attainable. Camus is close to Aron

---

[1] In *Introduction à la philosophie de l'histoire*, p. 329; *Démocratie et totalitarisme*, p. 92; 'Thucydide et le récit historique', in *Dimensions de la conscience historique*, Paris, 1961, p. 127; and *L'Opium des intellectuels*, pp. 286 and 317.

[2] *L'Opium des intellectuels*, pp. 325–6.

[3] The quotation is from 'La Notion du sens de l'histoire', in *Dimensions de la conscience historique*, p. 46. See also 'Histoire et politique', in *Polémiques*, Paris, 1955, pp. 178–84 and 195.

[4] See Chapter 4, pp. 94; 102–4.

on this point. Camus believed that the formal principles of the French Revolution—justice, reason, truth—could legitimately be used as guides in the constant effort to solve the problems of politics, but that they should not be regarded as goals, for then they would fall into what Camus believed to be the contradictory category of values to come.[1] For Aron, as for Camus, justice lies only in its pursuit.

What Aron offers, therefore, is not a political theory but a way of thinking about politics with a view to making specific decisions in given circumstances. He is more explicitly concerned with the meaning and function of political thought than any of the political thinkers discussed in this book.

For Aron, the function of political thought is to determine what goals one can reasonably pursue in a given situation and what means can be employed to attain them. Every situation leaves some margin for choice, but it does not permit an unlimited number of choices which have a reasonable chance of coming to fruition. The function of political thought is to determine both the margin of choice that exists in the circumstances and the content of the choice itself. The political thinker must analyse the existing situation, define goals which are capable of being attained, and suggest means which have some reasonable probability of attaining the goals.[2] The goals, of course, are inspired by values, but the situation includes structural necessities. The role of political thought, then, is to reconcile moral claims with structural necessities, a generalization of which the 'political problem' is both a specific and ultimate formulation.

III   Equality, Hierarchy, and Industrialization

The distinction between the construction of a political theory and Aron's conception of the nature of political thought, as well as the value and the limitations of the latter, can be illustrated by his treatment of the meaning of equality and hierarchy in contemporary society. Aron's discussion of equality and hierarchy appears in the context of a critique of traditional conservative political principles and takes the form of an examination of the conflicting claims of the

[1] See Chapter 5, pp. 138–40.   [2] 'Histoire et politique', pp. 174–6.

hierarchical-minded traditionalist and the equalitarian radical. It does not take the form of a development of a solution to the 'political problem'. Aron does not seek ways, institutional or otherwise, of reconciling hierarchy with equality in the conditions of industrial society. Instead, he seeks to determine the extent to which it is reasonable to hold equality or hierarchy as values in the conditions of industrial society. The kind of reconciliation which Aron tries to establish is not between equality and hierarchy, but rather between equalitarians and partisans of hierarchy.

By examining the meaning of equality and hierarchy in the conditions of industrial society, Aron is being faithful to his principle of relating values to existing conditions. Aron not only takes industrial society as the central social fact from which any analysis of modern societies must depart; he is also among the first apostles of industrialization (understood as the application of science and technology to the productive process) for post-war France.[1] One reason why he has been an advocate of industrialization is precisely because he sees a relation between its economic fruits and the satisfaction of the urge for equality. Equality is related to industrialization in that only an industrial society can remove poverty and reduce inequalities among men. Industrialization is not an end in itself: 'To make an ultimate goal of it is to fall into the idolatry of power.'[2] It does not automatically produce moral or spiritual progress.[3] All its consequences may not be desirable. Only an industrial society, however, can eventually provide the conditions of a decent life for everyone. Industrialization raises the level of wealth and relieves misery. It appeases the class struggle and makes possible the establishment of tolerable limits to the inevitable clashes over the distribution of income.[4] No society has ever experienced economic equality, social equality, or equality of opportunity, but industrialization is a necessary condition of the reduction of economic and social inequalities and the enlargement of equality of opportunity.[5]

Because Aron places such a high value on industrialization,

[1] Raymond Aron, *L'Âge des empires et l'avenir de la France*, Paris, 1945, esp. Introduction and Part I.
[2] *Espoir et peur du siècle*, pp. 91–92.   [3] *Le Grand Schisme*, Paris, 1948, p. 342.
[4] *L'Opium des intellectuels*, p. 162; *Espoir et peur du siècle*, pp. 362–3.
[5] *Le Grand Schisme*, p. 313.

not for its own sake but because of the social benefits which can
flow from it, his discussion of industrialization and equality
does not imply a distinction between equality as exclusively a
moral claim and industrialization as exclusively a social
necessity, in the sense of a set of social conditions which must
be taken into account as a kind of obstruction around which
men must navigate in the pursuit of their values. There is no
sharp dichotomy generally in Aron's thought between moral
claims and social necessities, between facts and values. His
treatment of equality and industrial society suggests that he
views them as fact and value simultaneously. Some degree of
equality is necessary before there can be the human communication that is essential to the very existence of a community;[1] industrialization contributes towards establishing
such equal conditions. Equality, therefore, may be interpreted
as a value, but some measure of equality is also a condition
embedded in the very definition of a community. Industrialization creates conditions which limit men's choices, but it also
produces goods which serve men's values.

Industrialization is not related only to equality, however.
It reduces material inequalities, but it also produces functional
hierarchies, which imply inequalities of power, prestige, and
status. Aron does not provide, as Simone Weil did, any statement of why these hierarchies are necessary; he simply takes
them as facts of organizational life.[2] Depending on their places
in the hierarchy, people expect to be differentially rewarded
for their services, although Aron is not sure that unequal
rewards are essential to a productive industrial society.[3]
He does, however, regard inequalities of prestige and power as
inevitable, although he does not tell us why. Presumably inequalities of power are inseparable from the need for decisions

---

[1] *Dix-Huit Leçons sur la société industrielle*, p. 50.

[2] Raymond Aron, 'Science et conscience de la société', in *Archives Européennes
de Sociologie*, I (1960), pp. 8 and 14.

[3] In *L'Opium des intellectuels*, pp. 34–35, he holds that some degree of inequality
'is inseparable from the very principle of competition' and that 'to compensate
the most active, the best endowed, is . . . probably necessary to the growth of
production', although 'neither enormous incomes nor great fortunes are indispensable in our era'. In *Espoir et peur du siècle*, p. 69, he writes that he does not think
it impossible to demonstrate that the equalization of incomes would not operate
against the production of increased wealth. 'Perhaps', he adds, 'certain inequalities
are unnecessary and others indispensable.'

and inequalities of prestige from the structure of human psychology.

Aron's view is that the conditions and consequences of industrial society facilitate, although they do not inevitably produce, a reconciliation between radicals and conservatives. His argument is not comforting to the traditionalists who identify hierarchy with a pre-industrial social structure, as his general position is that only those inequalities which perform a social function are tenable. But industrialization replaces old hierarchies with new ones and therefore is compatible with the general principle of hierarchy, if not with the traditionalist's particular principle of hierarchy. At the same time, industrial society requires and helps to create equality of opportunity, as it both depends on an increasing supply of technical and intellectual skills and produces sufficient wealth so that educational opportunities for the young and poor can be enlarged without sacrifice to other social groups. The basis for the reconciliation of equalitarians and the hierarchical-minded, Aron holds, lies in the requirements and consequences of industrial society itself.[1]

This reconciliation cannot come about automatically. It can come about only if the partisans of equality and of hierarchy abandon unconditional ideological attachment to these values and exercise 'reasonable co-operation'.[2] The policies that Aron treats as reasonable are the reduction of inherited privilege and the enlargement of social mobility on the one hand, and the requirement that the privileged should justify themselves by contributing to economic progress on the other. In effect, what he is saying is that the traditionalist should exchange the baronial manor for the executive suite and, once there, earn whatever privileges it may entail; that the equalitarian should forego doctrinaire redistributive measures and concentrate on those directly related to the productive process, such as building schools and providing scholarships.

The analysis is sound, but its limitations are evident. It grounds in social utility, understood as the enlargement of society's wealth, the partial satisfaction of equalitarians and the hierarchically-minded, but it does not reconcile hierarchy with equality. Aron's purpose in entering the debate between

---

[1] *Espoir et peur du siècle*, pp. 87–88.   [2] Ibid.

conservatives and radicals is to show that industrial society is hospitable to the hierarchical and equalitarian principles they respectively espouse, provided that they are not pushed to their extremes, which represent opposing concepts of the good life and are ultimately incompatible. Aron seeks to show each of the opposing groups the kind of goal which it can propose with a reasonable probability of attaining it. The main thrust of his argument is in support of enlarging equality of opportunity and, in a sense, its achievement could be interpreted as contributing towards reconciling equality with hierarchy. But equality of opportunity would only broaden the base from which power-holders are drawn; it would leave intact the problem of ensuring control over the power-holders, as well as the problem of creating the means by which people can obey in dignity. If Aron is right when he says that 'the increase in resources and the reduction of inequalities leave men and societies the same as they have been, the former unstable, the latter hierarchical',[1] the effort to reconcile hierarchy with equality requires institutional arrangements for the control of political and economic power. This takes us from the realm of governmental policies into that of political systems.

IV   Political Relativism

Raymond Aron is an anti-utopian political thinker. He does not believe in the possibility or the desirability of definitive political solutions and he does not want to glorify any concrete set of political institutions. All the solutions for the political problem that men have so far produced have been imperfect, and Aron holds a sufficiently Machiavellian view of human nature and is sufficiently convinced that all societies must be hierarchical to reject the possibility of any millennial solution to the political problem.

This outlook is not to be confused with pessimism or cynicism. There may be no perfect society, but there are degrees of imperfection and improvement is possible.[2] The process of improvement, however, is characterized by difficult choices,

---

[1] *L'Opium des intellectuels*, p. 165.
[2] Raymond Aron, *La Lutte de classes, Nouvelles leçons sur les sociétés industrielles*, Paris, 1964, p. 55.

uncertainty, and error. All political choices are relative in that the alternatives facing the decision-maker are always imperfect, and there is no way of determining absolutely which choice is best.

This is not to say that Aron believes that all choices are equally good (or bad). One can quite legitimately argue that some decisions are better than others without attributing absolute goodness to the decisions that one makes. 'Between the unverifiable, the unknowable, and the arbitrary, there remains a legitimate distinction.'[1] And insistence upon the relativity of political choice is not incompatible with holding ultimate values. Aron's statement of the political problem and his formal conception of its solution obviously rest on an ultimate conviction concerning the proper human condition. At one point, Aron even grounds in an absolute an argument in favour of popular participation in the discussion of the affairs of the community, although I think that he does so contrary to his intention. Like John Stuart Mill, he meets the argument that popular participation in the affairs of the community risks permitting people of limited knowledge to make crucial decisions by replying that it is only through such participation that people can improve their knowledge and increase their capacity for making responsible decisions. But after having said that his political sociology is not linked to any ultimate view of human nature which would presuppose that one can determine the best political system as a function of the 'imminent vocation of man', he states that everyone who wants to should be able to participate in the discussion of how best to organize the community and of what the community ought to do, both because it is 'in conformity with the essence of our societies' and because it is in conformity with 'the human vocation'.[2] A good system is not only conceivable; it can be justified by human destiny. But there is nothing incompatible between grounding the desirability of popular participation in government in the fulfilment of man's destiny and emphasizing the uncertainties, difficulties, and disappointments which confront men as they seek to fulfil that destiny. Aron's

---

[1] *Introduction à la philosophie de l'histoire*, p. 318.
[2] *Démocratie et totalitarisme*, pp. 50 and 352–3. Also see *Espoir et peur du siècle*, pp. 216–17.

argument neither implies a rejection of natural law concepts (whether or not religious in origin) nor denies the operative power of ultimate moral imperatives.[1] The argument simply holds that the kind of choices which men must make politically (or economically) are limited, specific, and 'irreducible to the abstract laws of ethics'.[2]

According to Aron, 'relativism is the authentic experience of politics' because there is a multiplicity of values and because of what he calls the 'ingrate laws of social existence'.[3] No specific decision of the kind that men must make in political or economic affairs can be regarded as absolutely or totally good because its consequences can legitimately be judged by a variety of criteria which will not be satisfied simultaneously. 'A certain degree of individual liberty implies a certain degree of economic inequality.'[4] It is legitimate to admire the independent farmer or shopkeeper as a social type; it is legitimate also to demand economic efficiency.[5] Both of the values implied are unlikely to be served by a single decision. What is true of specific decisions is also true of whole political systems. These too correspond differentially to the diverse values by which they can be and are judged. Social existence requires constraints on human behaviour, and each political and social system has its particular forms of constraint and patterns of organization.[6] Some systems may be preferable to others, but they are all imperfect, not simply because constraints themselves violate the vision of life according to reason, but also because each system has both advantages and disadvantages depending upon the values by which it is weighed. It follows that when men choose a political system, they must be prepared to accept both the good and the bad of the system. Each political system is a whole which expresses certain values and which necessarily involves certain institutions, prejudices, and traditions which are both integral parts of the system and inseparable from the values which the system expresses. 'Passage from one régime to another does not bring about improvement of the existing order, but the substitution of one order for

---

[1] *L'Opium des intellectuels*, pp. 168–9.
[2] *Introduction à la philosophie de l'histoire*, p. 326.
[3] 'Histoire et politique', p. 195; *L'Opium des intellectuels*, p. 169.
[4] 'Histoire et politique', pp. 193–4.   [5] *Espoir et peur du siècle*, pp. 77–78.
[6] *L'Opium des intellectuels*, p. 169.

another.'[1] In real life, men must choose wholes, with all the grandeur and servitudes attached to those they choose.[2]

V   Social Wholes

The notion of what we may call 'social wholes'—situations which are defined by the logic of the fundamental choices on which they rest and by the necessary relations of their constituent elements—is Aron's basic tool of sociological analysis, and Aron relies on it regularly to demonstrate why some choices are more or less reasonable than others. One cannot accept capitalism and destroy capitalists;[3] one cannot accept dictatorial political controls and expect liberty;[4] one cannot reject technological progress and expect to remove poverty;[5] one cannot accept de Gaulle and expect government by assembly.[6] The concept of social wholes is the bridge between Aron's sociology and his polemics with the 'left-bank intellectual Marxists' who, he believes, are 'the partisans of a régime, never yet seen, which would be both as organized as that of the East and as liberal as that of the West',[7] just as it links his sociology with his criticism of the traditionalist who dreams of establishing in an industrial society, where materialism and popular sovereignty are deeply rooted, some benignly authoritarian régime 'in which quarrels would be stilled, in which authority, unquestioned and wise, would come from on high . . .'.[8] Aron's criticism of both positions rests on the same logic: political systems are wholes whose parts are indissociable. The left-bank Marxist makes the mistake of thinking that one can construct 'an ideal society with fragments borrowed from the most diverse régimes . . .', while 'no doctrine, in fact, is more dangerously utopian . . .'.[9] The

[1] 'Histoire et politique', p. 194.

[2] *L'Âge des empires et l'avenir de la France*, p. 15; *Introduction à la philosophie de l'histoire*, p. 279.

[3] 'Réflexions sur les problèmes économiques français', *Revue de Métaphysique et de Morale*, 44 (1937), p. 809.

[4] *L'Opium des intellectuels*, p. 169.   [5] *Le Grand Schisme*, p. 342.

[6] 'Propos d'un conservateur', in *Le Monde*, 22 August 1958.

[7] 'Science et conscience de la société', p. 27. See also *Les Grandes Doctrines de sociologie historique*, p. 160.

[8] *Espoir et peur du siècle*, p. 108.

[9] *Introduction à la philosophie de l'histoire*, p. 279. Also see *L'Âge des empires et l'avenir de la France*, p. 15.

right-wing traditionalist makes the mistake of thinking that a political system congruent with one kind of social system and set of popular beliefs can be superimposed on an entirely different social and belief system. Both positions, in other words, disassociate mentally what is indissociable in fact.

The concept of social wholes, with its emphasis on the solidarity of the component elements of any given social and political system, naturally leads to the construction of a typology of systems, as we need to know the kinds of social wholes with which we are confronted. The construction of such a typology requires, in turn, a method of sociological analysis, as we need an instrument with which to isolate the basic types and identify the essential elements of each type. The concept of social wholes is a variant of the concept of the ideal-type, with which Max Weber is associated, although Aron is probably closer to Montesquieu and de Tocqueville than he is to Weber in the particular way he constructs his ideal-types and discriminates among different systems. Aron is unreserved in his respect and admiration for Max Weber, whom he believes to be the greatest of sociologists,[1] but he believes that Weber was excessively relativistic in his interpretation of the significance of the relationship between reality and the ideal-type which the scientist creates in order to render reality intelligible. Weber believed that the scientist always superimposes his conception of reality upon the event or the phenomenon he investigates. Without subscribing to the contrary view, Aron believes that there is a coherence inscribed in reality which can be reproduced by the concepts which the scientist employs. The scientist is partial, in that he selects for analysis only some of the many orders which exist, and there is more than one way to interpret the orders which the scientist uncovers, but it is possible to uncover partial orders which exist within the social object. There is no single true sociological theory which explains the social order in its entirety, according to Aron, but he rejects a radical sociological relativism at the same time as he rejects a total sociological dogmatism.[2]

[1] *Les Grandes Doctrines de sociologie historique*, II (Cours de Sorbonne, Paris, C.D.U.), 1963, p. 242.
[2] *Dix-Huit Leçons sur la société industrielle*, pp. 26–28.

Accordingly, Aron's analysis of political systems assumes that they are intelligible, that they are not accidental structures, and that they have some 'minimum of unity' which can be extracted from observation of their structural and operational characteristics.[1] His analytical method is to try to discover the critical determinants of each system. The critical determinants of the system are what is essential to it: those characteristics without which the whole system would be something other than it is, as opposed to those characteristics which may vary without affecting in any fundamental way the nature of the system. This is an economical way of making political systems intelligible, as well as of furnishing a guide to the margins of choice open to people who are committed to the essential elements of the system. Aron tries to make political systems intelligible by uncovering 'the major characteristics on the basis of which the internal logic of each system can be understood'.[2] By isolating what is essential to each system and tracing the implications of the essential elements, Aron tries to show which characteristics of the system are necessary if it is to remain the same system and which characteristics may be varied without affecting the coherence of the system.

VI The Comparative Method

The construction of ideal-types is essential to Aron's sociological analysis, but it does not exhaust it. Aron also employs the comparative method. He does this because he regards sociological analysis not only as a means of understanding political systems, and as a means of discovering the margins of institutional and behavioural variation within each type of political system, but also as a guide to choice between political systems. Ideal-types represent the kinds of social wholes among which men must choose; the comparative method aids the choice between them. If sociological analysis is to serve this purpose also, it follows that the types of political system to be considered must be compatible with the social characteristics of the society which may have to choose between them. Aron's concept of social wholes is applicable to any system of any time

---

[1] *Démocratie et totalitarisme*, pp. 54–55.   [2] Ibid., p. 73.

or place, but however useful the construction of a variety of types might be for understanding the ways in which radically diverse political systems have operated or do operate, types modelled on Athens or Sparta, for example, would not be particularly useful for Frenchmen who want to decide on the best kind of political system for France. In this context, as in every other, Aron is interested primarily in discovering what is possible. His sociological analysis deals principally with industrial societies, and it is the political alternatives available for industrial societies which he seeks to analyse. Experience and logic show that a single-party system and a plural-party system are both compatible with industrial society. Accordingly, his comparison focuses on these two types of political system, of which the Soviet Union and the western democracies are real-life applications.

Aron thus compares the political system of the Soviet Union with that of the western democracies within the framework of a theory of political systems which consists essentially of the establishment of two ideal-types compatible with industrial society. The essential variable by means of which he distinguishes between the two basic types is the party system.[1] Where one party has a legal monopoly of the exercise of power there is what he calls the monopolistic-party system. Where two or more parties are legally permitted to compete for the exercise of power there is what he calls the constitutional-pluralist system. The Soviet Union is in the first category; the western democracies are in the second.

The structural solidarities and behavioural possibilities of each type of system consist of the implications which flow from the decisive fact of the kind of party system which characterizes each type. The advantages and disadvantages of each system emerge from a consideration of their structural and behavioural probabilities. The constitutional-pluralist system legitimizes political debate and gives more protection to the governed than does the monopolistic-party system.[2] It also carries with it political conflict and the risk of corruption, in the sense in which the classical political philosophers used the word.[3] The monopolistic-party system implies the bureaucratic solidarity of the rulers and the establishment of ideological

[1] Ibid., Ch. IV. [2] Ibid., pp. 137–8. [3] Ibid., Ch. IX.

conformity. It carries with it the risk of totalitarianism.[1] At the same time, 'it is not absurd to prefer the authority of a single party to the slowness of parliamentary deliberations . . .'.[2] It is possible, therefore, by means of comparative analysis, to discover both the logical necessities (or probabilities) attaching to each type of system and the advantages and disadvantages of adopting one system or the other.

Aron also compares the same two types of political system on the basis of the extent to which they realize the values which their respective proponents profess. On this dimension of comparison, he sees a sharp distinction between the monopolistic-party system and the constitutional-pluralist system. The imperfections of the latter consist of the possibilities of oligarchical excesses, demagogic excesses, and limited efficacy in solving domestic and foreign problems. These imperfections are what Aron calls 'imperfections of fact'.[3] They are, in other words, shortcomings in the implementation of the system which are not intrinsic to the system itself. The imperfection of the monopolistic-party system, in Aron's view, is of a different nature. This system holds that a single orthodoxy is logical because society is homogeneous and free of conflict over essential matters. It also claims to be democratic in pronouncing that the monopolistic party acts in the name of the people. Yet, by enforcing an orthodoxy, the monopolistic-party system implicitly admits that society is not homogeneous and that there are conflicts over essential matters which would find expression if the conditions of free expression were established. In Aron's view, this form of imperfection is fundamental in that it is linked to the essential element of the system—the monopolistic party itself.[4] Like Camus, who drew a distinction between the failure of bourgeois democracy, which he believed had not practised what it preached, and the failure of the communist system, which he believed had practised what it preached, but which had practised what he believed to be wrong,[5] Aron also distinguishes between an extrinsic and an intrinsic imperfection of the same two systems.

There is a difference, however, in the nature of the com-

[1] Ibid., pp. 80–85, 289.   [2] *L'Opium des intellectuels*, p. 169.
[3] *Démocratie et totalitarisme*, p. 346.   [4] Ibid., pp. 347, 350, and 357–8.
[5] See Chapter 5, p. 143.

parative imperfections which the two thinkers uncover, and there is a difference in the direct conclusions which the two men draw from them. On the imperfections of bourgeois democracy, the two men are close. The régime in practice falls short of the ideal, and it is not stretching Camus' interpretation too far to say that it can be included in Aron's category of excessive oligarchy. On the imperfections of the communist system, however, there is a difference between the two analyses. Camus sees a harmony between communist practice and communist theory; Aron sees a contradiction between the two. Camus objects to the practice because of the justification; Aron objects to the justification because of the practice. Camus renders a philosophical judgement which is final. Aron makes a sociological declaration which implies no final judgement. He makes a distinction between imperfections, but draws no conclusion from it about what one must do. '. . . it is possible that, in certain circumstances, this essentially imperfect régime may be preferable to the effectively imperfect régime.'[1]

Aron does not claim that comparative analysis can tell men what choices they should make. He does claim, however, that it can lead them into a situation in which their choices will be reasonable. A reasonable choice in this perspective is one which is made only after considering the probable consequences of the possible alternatives in the light of the goals one wants to achieve. It is not reasonable to fail to consider alternatives; to fail to do so would be either to decide arbitrarily or to act ideologically. Equitable critical analysis uncovers the implications of what is essential to each alternative; these implications constitute the probable consequences of each choice. The choice is made reasonable, in other words, when the chooser has reflected on the relationships between the probable consequences and his own goals. A man does not, therefore, act unreasonably by choosing an intrinsically imperfect régime if this imperfection is irrelevant to his goals. He does act unreasonably if he chooses it because of a goal which it proclaims but which it is intrinsically unable to achieve.

[1] *Démocratie et totalitarisme*, p. 358.

VII   Political Science and Political Choice

Aron's greatest contribution to contemporary political thought is his effort to link science to choice, political sociology to political decisions. His concept of social wholes and his comparative political analysis are not only analytical devices for the purpose of making political systems intelligible; they are also designed to bring science to bear on political choices. Aron willingly accepts the proposition that science cannot tell men what they must do, but he will not go as far as Max Weber in distinguishing the realm of science from the realm of politics. In between the impossible notion of scientifically demonstrated choice and what Aron regards as the repugnant notion of arbitrary choice, there is the domain of reasonable choices.[1] Some choices are more reasonable than others, even though they are never of the same nature as a scientific truth, and, in Aron's view, science (in the form of comparative political analysis) aids in demonstrating which choices are reasonable.

It is perhaps excessive to claim, as Aron does, that 'the results of scientific comparison flow spontaneously into counsels of wisdom',[2] but the importance of his effort to bring science closely to bear on political choices can hardly be overestimated. His intention is to reduce to the minimum the ingredients of political argument which are not susceptible of empirical determination or which bring into confrontation radically distinct and, hence, incomparable claims. To put it another way, and in a vocabulary with which Aron is closely associated, his effort is to direct political debate away from ideological arguments, at least to the extent that ideological arguments tend to attribute all advantages to one set of institutions and all disadvantages to a different set of institutions. Each political system has its advantages and its disadvantages, but these do not derive from its ideological foundations; they can be determined only by the analysis of its institutions and from the confrontation of its claims with its consequences. The choice between systems, accordingly, requires equitable examination of alternative systems, and while the choice itself may not be

---

[1] 'Science et conscience de la société', pp. 23–24. Also see *Les Grandes Doctrines de sociologie historique*, II, p. 243.

[2] 'Science et conscience de la société', p. 23.

scientific, the comparative analysis must be, and it is this analysis which points to the issues on which the choice turns. This form of reasoning does not imply that the ultimate choices which men make politically will not be based squarely on their value preferences. We will see shortly that Aron's own choice is precisely of this kind. It does mean, however, that the values on the basis of which one makes one's choice should be demonstrably related to the system which one chooses.

It follows from this line of argument that political systems are the more amenable to scientific comparison as the values which they claim to express converge.[1] If two political systems proclaim or express quite different values, the choice between them can hardly be aided by an effort at scientific comparison, except in so far as that comparison is designed only to identify the values which the respective régimes express. The choice between them must be entirely ideological or philosophical. Aron argues that the kind of choice presented by the conflict between the ideals of the Old Régime and the revolutionary ideals of the Rights of Man could appear to those confronted with it to be a philosophical choice of this kind. (Although, he goes on to say, the English found a way to avoid a decisive rupture between the two sets of ideals and their proponents.)[2] Even here, however, Aron may make a greater concession to the moral element, at the expense of the scientific, than is required by his argument. It is perhaps true that what de Tocqueville called democracy and aristocracy demand a radical ideological or philosophical choice, but his own *Democracy in America*, which Aron so greatly admires and which so clearly serves as a source of inspiration for his own work,[3] is an intuitive, if not scientific, effort to demonstrate the implications which flow from making one choice or the other.

Whatever role political science might have been able to play in guiding the actors during the conflict between the Old Régime and the revolutionary forces, it is clear that Aron believes it to be greater in providing a basis for choice between a Soviet-type system and a democratic-type system in the contemporary world. He repeatedly asserts that both régimes

[1] Ibid.   [2] *Espoir et peur du siècle*, pp. 102–3.
[3] See especially Raymond Aron, 'Idées politiques et vision historique de Tocqueville', in *Revue Française de Science Politique*, X (September 1960), pp. 509–26.

proclaim similar values and mutually reproach each other for failing to realize values which they each profess. 'Let us not forget that Soviets and Westerners, representatives of the two versions of industrial society, lay claim to the same values, they both have as goals the exploitation of natural resources, the elevation of the standard of living, the reign of abundance. Politically, they compete with each other in declaring themselves to be democrats, partisans of the liberation of peoples and of the sovereignty of the common man.'[1] Or again, 'most of the régimes of our century (the Hitler régime excepted, of course) lay claim to the same values: development of productive forces with a view to guaranteeing to all men the conditions of an honourable existence, rejection of inequalities of birth, consecration of the legal and moral equality of the citizens'.[2] The two régimes not only proclaim common values, they in fact share certain common values: 'Economic growth and universal citizenship characterize the régimes called popular democracies and the régimes called western democracies alike.'[3] Accordingly, the comparison of the two kinds of system in terms of their fidelity to the values they claim to express is not simply an empirical task, nor is the choice that one finally makes a kind of abstract moral decision. The comparison itself involves a weighing of advantages and disadvantages, and the final choice is closely linked to the scientific consciousness as well as to the moral consciousness.[4]

Aron, therefore, arrives at a middle ground between the radical Weberian distinction between moral choice and scientific demonstration on the one hand and the scientific demonstration of moral choice on the other. He hesitates to follow Weber all the way because Weber's position rested in part on the assumption of the existence of an anarchical system of incompatible values.[5] He cannot completely unite science and choice, however, because *all* the values proclaimed by rival industrialized régimes are not identical and, even if they were,

[1] Raymond Aron, *La Société industrielle et la guerre, suivi d'un tableau de la diplomatie mondiale en 1958*, Paris, 1959, p. 63.
[2] Raymond Aron, 'La Responsabilité sociale du philosophe', in *Dimensions de la conscience historique*, p. 306.
[3] Ibid., pp. 306–7.
[4] 'Science et conscience de la société', p. 23.
[5] Ibid., p. 24.

values are not equivalent. People may share the same values and even agree on the extent to which they are expressed by different régimes, but they may still not place those values in identical hierarchies. If they do not, science can narrow the issues, but the final choice will rest on the hierarchy of values one has established.

In this respect, it may be doubted whether the kind of choice represented by the alternatives of the Soviet-style régime and the western democratic-style régime is less radical than that represented earlier by the alternatives of 'the Old Régime, monarchical, Catholic, stable, and the new world, egalitarian, oriented towards the future and the development of the planet'.[1] For all the similarity which Aron sees in the value systems of the Soviets and the democrats—a similarity which is rooted in their common rejection of traditionalism and their common acceptance of industrialization—he also emphasizes the profound differences in the values which are expressed by their respective modes of political organization. 'The antithesis between the single party and parliamentary institutions, between the imposed orthodoxy and intellectual pluralism concerns the primordial values of the community.'[2] The notion that some values are primordial suggests the existence of a hierarchy of values. What are the primordial values to which Aron refers?

The western democrat objects to a Soviet-type régime, Aron writes, because it 'has brought with it, until the present moment, a State ideology and the monopoly of the party; it eliminates freedom of thought, individual security, partisan rivalry, and guarantees of constitutional authority'.[3] He has not attempted to establish any hierarchy among the values expressed in this statement, but of those that are implied, the one which he clings to most firmly is freedom of thought. Aron discusses various concepts of liberty, but he attributes primary importance to one concept of liberty in particular which he regards as the matrix of western civilization. This is what we may call freedom of criticism, the absence of constraints upon the pursuit of the truth through reason and research.

[1] *Espoir et peur du siècle*, p. 103.
[2] 'Nations et Empires', in *Dimensions de la conscience historique*, p. 207.
[3] *La Société industrielle et la guerre*, pp. 65–66.

The essence of western culture, the principle of its triumphs, the
source of its radiance, is liberty. Not universal suffrage, a late and
debatable institution of the political order, not the parliamentary
jousting, a procedure, among others, of government by opinion,
but the liberty of research and of criticism, progressively conquered,
of which the historical conditions have been the duality of temporal
power and spiritual power, the limitation of state authority, the
autonomy of the universities.[1]

Viewed in this way, liberty is a condition that is architectonic
in character. It not only reflects a culture but also contributes
to defining that culture. As any culture is a combination of
institutions and values, liberty is both a creator of institutions
and a source of values. It leads not only to new ways of doing
things but to new reasons why we want to do things. Liberty,
as Aron defines it, plays the role that Charles Frankel ascribes
to theory:[2] it liberates men from custom and opens up prospects
of new practices. It is liberty which gives to our views of what is
right and wrong that amount of independence of tradition and
social forces which they have.[3]

Aron refuses to treat any value, including liberty, as an
absolute, and he once indicated that there might be circumstances in which he would be tempted to accept the abandonment of liberty, for a time, although he does not discuss how one
emerges from a state of temporary abandonment of liberty.[4]
The implication of a more recent comment on liberty, however,
is that it is liberty alone which gives moral significance to a
society, that liberty is the only purity of our civilization. 'The
authentic westerner is he who accepts totally from our civilization only the liberty that it leaves for criticizing it and the
chance that it offers to improve it. . . .'[5] Liberty, therefore, is

---

[1] *L'Opium des intellectuels*, p. 269.

[2] *The Case for Modern Man*, New York, 1955, 1956, Ch. VIII.

[3] *Introduction à la philosophie de l'histoire*, pp. 305-8.

[4] 'It may be that liberty is in the first rank of political values but, for whoever
thinks historically, it cannot be absolute. In decadent Athens, it safeguarded the
comforts of life, it did not arrest, in certain respects it facilitated the corruption of
the city. If we thought that an authoritarian régime were capable, and alone
capable, of reversing the demographic trend, of equipping industry, of moderniz-
ing agriculture, in spite of our intimate preferences, we would be tempted to
accept, for a time, the purgatory of despotism. But our conviction is quite different.
Whether we like it or not, France is launched on the adventure of liberty.' *L'Âge
des empires et l'avenir de la France*, pp. 14-15.

[5] *L'Opium des intellectuels*, p. 69.

not the only value and it is not the single criterion for evaluating political systems. It is, however, a primary value, and it is the fundamental basis for Aron's own political choice between the constitutional-pluralist and monopolistic-party régimes.

Aron argues that, in terms of political leadership, the choice presented by these two types of political system is between rule by the elected and rule by dialecticians—'a degenerate transposition of the Athenian philosophers'.[1] The reason he gives for his own preference for the elected is that industrial societies are heterogeneous, and while society is heterogeneous, 'the human truth of this society is communication, agreement, rivalry, or conflict. For heterogeneous societies to accept the dialogue . . . it is necessary, if not that no group should pretend to possess the ultimate truth, at least that none should have sufficient power to impose by force obedience to the truth that it takes to be ultimate.'[2]

The implications of the monopolistic-party system include the probability of an ideology being presented as the truth and the probability that the bearers of the ideology will be sufficiently strong to maintain that orthodoxy. The implications of the constitutional-pluralist system are that rivalry and dialogue are legitimized and that because each view is legally susceptible of challenge no one of them will be imposed by force. Although Aron takes the party system as the essential variable for the differentiation of régimes, the party system itself is of symbolic, secondary importance.[3] The distinction between the monopolistic-party system and the constitutional-pluralist system is reduced to the contrast between the absence and the presence of critical freedom. The party system reflects the posture of the régime towards critical freedom, and it is this which is both primary and real. Aron's comparative analysis demonstrates

[1] *La Lutte de classes*, p. 365.

[2] Ibid., p. 366.

[3] 'The least important plurality, although it is cited most readily, is that of parties. This plurality has its inconveniences, it maintains a quarrelsome atmosphere in the city, it disturbs the sense of common necessities, it compromises the friendship of citizens. It is tolerated in spite of all this as a means, as a symbol of irreplaceable values, a means of limiting the arbitrariness of Power and of guaranteeing a legal expression of discontent, a symbol of the secularism of the State and of the autonomy of the spirit which creates, questions, or prays.' *L'Opium des intellectuels*, p. 332.

the values at stake in the choice; the choice itself rests on one's appreciation of the values, and this, in turn, rests on a philosophy.

The question whether the difference between a philosophy which prizes critical freedom and one which does not is more or less great than the difference between the philosophy of the Old Régime and that of the Rights of Man is less important for an evaluation of Aron's position than the question whether his comparative analysis of political systems conflicts with the anti-ideological attitude for which he is so renowned. The core of his anti-ideological position is that ends must be kept formal, that the political practitioner should stay within the limits of what science shows to be possible, that institutions should not be idealized. In his treatment of the alternatives facing industrial societies, however, and in his examination of the values expressed by the institutional patterns of each alternative, Aron comes very close to producing a scientific justification for an ideology.

Aron's application of his scientific method to the problem of determining what is possible politically for industrialized societies narrows the fundamental choices to two: the constitutional-pluralist system and the monopolistic-party system. He displays some uncertainty as to whether other options are also possible, but his view of intermediate forms is that they are hard to define and difficult to operate for very long in the conditions of industrial society. In industrial societies, he argues, there are forces at work which tug in one direction or the other in a way that demands a conclusion. Industrial society requires social co-operation and, in order to secure it, it is necessary either for a leadership group armed with an ideology to enforce social discipline or for co-operation to be allowed to emerge from a process of discussion and institutionalized competition.[1] Aron, in effect, poses the same types of alternative that were posed by de Tocqueville more than a century ago. De Tocqueville believed that two political options were open to what he called democracies: despotism and liberalism. Aron believes that two options are open to what he calls industrialized societies: the constitutional-pluralist system,

[1] Raymond Aron, George Kennan, Robert Oppenheimer, et al., *Colloques de Rheinfelden*, Paris, 1960, pp. 315–16.

which permits dialogue among parties, and the monopolistic-party system, which, 'in the name of an absolute ideological truth, pretends to model society in its image'.[1]

After narrowing the alternatives to two, Aron then proceeds to show that only one of these alternatives is compatible with liberty. But if it is only those institutions implied by the constitutional-pluralist system which sustain liberty (in the conditions of industrial society), is not the liberal justified in attributing as much value to those institutions as he does to liberty? Is he not, in other words, justified in behaving ideologically, if not by proclaiming an eternal identity of liberty and the institutions which fall within the range of implications of the constitutional-pluralist system, at least by refusing to disassociate those institutions from the value which they express in the conditions of industrial society? Aron argues in another context that science unmasks ideologies.[2] His application of his sociological method to the problem of determining the range and meaning of the political choices open to industrial societies suggests that science, by confirming the claims of an ideology, can also justify it.

It is a measure of the rigorously honest and open-minded quality of Aron's search for a political science that there are few criticisms of his efforts which he has not produced himself. Summarizing and concluding a conference on the subject of the political and philosophical implications of industrial society,[3] he referred to what he regarded as the generally disturbed quality of the discussion that had taken place about the question of the relevance of western democratic political institutions to the countries of the underdeveloped world. The discussion was disturbed, he said, because the westerner hesitates to urge western political institutions on the underdeveloped world, both because he is aware of their shortcomings and because he is sensitive to being charged with committing a kind of ideological imperialism, while at the same time he cannot logically be a partisan of those institutions at home and not recommend them to others without falling into the racist

[1] Ibid., p. 315.
[2] 'Classe sociale, classe politique, classe dirigeante', in *Archives Européennes de Sociologie*, I (1960), p. 281.
[3] *Colloques de Rheinfelden*, pp. 313–16.

position of holding that what is good for his country is not good for other countries as well.

The escape from this dilemma which was found in the discussion, Aron continued, consisted in distinguishing between 'concrete political institutions: parties, elections, Parliament, whose historical particularity we acknowledge, and the inspirational ideas: liberalism, opening up of dialogue, respect for the wishes of the governed by the governors, which seem to us to have universal validity eventually'.[1] In other words, a way out of the dilemma was sought by applying the non-ideological or anti-ideological approach which is so central to Aron's political thought: the ends were formalized and the concrete institutions left undetermined. But while Aron naturally accepted this distinction as fundamental, he was not happy with it, precisely because he believes that the con-stitutional-pluralist system, with the institutions it implies, is the only system which will actually express those formal values once traditionalism is overwhelmed by the forces of industrial-ization. The non-ideological viewpoint did not, in this case, produce a solution: 'it is a point of departure rather than a point of arrival . . .'.[2] In *L'Opium des intellectuels*, Aron had written that 'the Westerners . . . would be wrong to attribute universal significance to the ideologies which glorify these [parliamentary] institutions'.[3] Five years later, after developing his theory of political systems, he was coming closer to attribut-ing universal significance to those institutions, thereby coming closer to justifying the ideologies which glorify them.

VIII Conclusion

Aron has been criticized for not taking adequately into account in his various analyses the moral imperatives under the impulsion of which men act. The burden of this argument is that men will follow certain courses of action if they are moved by strong moral impulses even if their activity is not consistent with existing social circumstances and not, therefore, likely to produce the results intended.[4] The criticism is perhaps

---

[1] *Colloques de Rheinfelden*, p. 314.   [2] Ibid., pp. 314–15.   [3] Op. cit., p. 325.
[4] Alfred Grosser, ' "Espoir et peur du siècle": La Passion de l'explication sans passion', p. 673. Also see David Thomson, 'The Three Worlds of Raymond Aron' *International Affairs* (London), 39 (January 1963), pp. 49–58.

valid for those cases in which Aron is simply trying to analyse the forces present in a given situation, but it should be recalled that Aron's principal aim is precisely to try to persuade men not to act against probabilities and not to cherish values in forms which appear doomed to failure in the light of existing conditions. While it is possible that he may misread the intensity of certain motivations based on moral certitudes, his purpose is to reduce the terrain over which political conflicts take place to an area in which there is some probability of successfully realizing the values in the name of which the conflicts take place.

A more generally valid criticism of Aron's political thought is that it does not confront the problem of the extent to which and the circumstances under which people may be persuaded to change their minds. He clearly must believe that it is possible to persuade people to change their minds; that is why he writes. But in analysing what Simone Weil called the conditions of existence and what he calls the 'ingrate laws of social existence', Aron takes into account not only existing structures and processes but also what he regards as the prevailing values of the society. To urge adaptation to the world in this context can produce troublesome dilemmas. If one incorporates the value preferences of others into the image of the social structure within which one must operate, and with which one's actions must be reasonably congruent, one runs the risk of attributing greater importance to the values of others than to one's own. This is not to say that Aron's method of analysis is wrong. It has already been pointed out, in connexion with the political ideas of Bertrand de Jouvenel, that political prescriptions must not be too far removed from what men may reasonably be expected to accept, and this view is essentially the same as that on which Aron bases his criticism of the conservative traditionalist. But it is important to point out that Aron's political thought, like Simone Weil's, raises the problem of how to distinguish between those conditions of existence which are obstacles to action and those which are susceptible of modification.[1]

Aron himself recognizes the dangers of attributing greater importance to the world than to oneself, to use the language of Sartre, although he does so in a different context. After

[1] See Chapter 4, pp. 105–6.

criticizing the interpretation of history which synthesizes determinism and Providence (history is inevitably moving towards a
happy end), Aron goes on to indicate what *'usage régulatif'* can
be made of the notion of determinism.

There are, in fact, at each epoch, forces to which one must adapt
because one cannot conquer them, there are movements that one
must channel and orient because one would try in vain to stop them.
Certainly, this kind of reasoning is dangerous, because it often
serves as an excuse for cowardice or as justification for accepting
defeat. It is not for the philosopher but for the historian to say when
the argument is well-founded. The philosopher can and must mark
the error of principle committed when one applies the argument to
all of history, while it is at most acceptable in limited domains.[1]

Aron's (and Simone Weil's) method of establishing the margins
of choice for political actors requires the identification of those
forces to which one must adapt and which one must channel;
the problem is to rest within the limited domains to which the
method applies.

There is a kind of dampening quality to Aron's writings,
which is perhaps the inevitable result of sustained ideological
criticism. Science does unmask ideologies, and unmasking is
bound to lead to some disappointments and restrained en-
thusiasms. In a certain sense also, the thrust of much of Aron's
writings is conservative. Some of his works of ideological
criticism in particular reflect the defence of a fortress be-
leaguered by attackers from two sides; his criticisms of the
myths of the left and of the right operate against the Marxists
and the traditionalists who are discontented with the contemporary French social and political order, with the result that
his own position almost automatically appears to be conservative.

Aron's analytical method, however, is not intrinsically
conservative. The search for what is possible can have positive
as well as negative implications for action. The formal structure
of Aron's thought is progressive in so far as it seeks to determine
the conditions of the achievement of formal ends. He will not
go as far as the view which he attributes to Max Weber—
that 'if politics is the art of the possible, one must try the

[1] 'La Notion du sens de l'histoire', p. 45.

impossible often in order to attain the possible'[1]—but for all his forceful polemics against millennial political thought, he acknowledges that 'in tranquil and happy epochs . . . millennialism teaches us never to be satisfied with the results so far obtained . . .'.[2] The promise may be all but destroyed by the condition of tranquillity which Aron attaches to it, but it represents a concession to millennialism which even Albert Camus, the philosopher of revolt, was not willing to make.

Surprisingly, perhaps, there is a great deal of common ground between Camus the moralist and Aron the sociologist. Camus elevated rebellion into a philosophic principle, while Aron has spent much effort combating revolutionaries of our time, but both men seek, in their different ways, to map the terrain that lies between abstract moralism and historic necessity. To be sure, there are major differences in tone and emphasis in the works of the two men. Although Camus is generally identified with stoicism, the tone of some of his work is promethean by comparison with that of Aron. Aron calculates probabilities and seeks to make our history intelligible, while Camus wants periodically to interrupt history, thereby throwing off the calculations on which probabilities must be based. What the rebel does is, for Aron, an accident of history; for Camus, it is history's only essential and creative work. But in a fundamental sense, Aron's problem is also Camus' problem. For Camus did not say that rebellion in itself advanced history; 'it is those who know how to rebel, *at the appropriate moment*, against history who really advance its interests'.[3] As Aron tells us, only the historian, looking backward, can tell us what the appropriate moments really were. But this does not prevent Aron, the sociologist, from seeking to discover the conditions of those moments in the present, just as it does not prevent Camus, the moralist, from seeking to keep alive the predisposition to act in them.

[1] *La Sociologie allemande contemporaine*, Paris, 1950, p. 131. Eng. tr. by Mary and Thomas Bottomore, *German Sociology*, Glencoe, Illinois, 1957.

[2] 'Histoire et politique', p. 194.

[3] *The Rebel*, p. 302. Italics mine.

9

Patterns of Contemporary French Political Thought

I Questions and Answers

IT is inevitable, at the conclusion of a study of this sort, which attempts to identify and analyse leading political ideas which have emerged over a period of several decades, that one should be left with an impression of diversity. It could hardly be otherwise when the mode of analysis has been to look for what is distinctive in the works of half a dozen political thinkers, some of whom have engaged in polemics with one another, as in the cases of Camus, Aron, and Sartre. The questions which these people ask themselves are not the same, and the answers they give to them naturally represent a variety of conclusions—or new points of departure—which it would be foolish to try to assimilate into a limited number of coherent currents of political thought.

Emmanuel Mounier asked himself why a community of Christians was not a fraternal community, and how it could be made one, and in the process of trying to find the answers, he concluded first that it was necessary to infuse Christians with revolutionary ideas and later that it was necessary to infuse revolutionaries with Christian ideas. Simone Weil asked why there was oppression and sought the conditions of an ideal society—conceived in terms of the total power of self-determination of each individual—and in the course of working out the answers she developed a functional sociology which, combined with her Hobbesian view of human psychology, all but destroyed any hopes for social improvement. Later, she turned to religious concerns, but while ruminating on ways to revitalize liberated France, she produced a design for the art of government which included the requirements that the motives invoked on behalf of any action and the mode of action itself be consonant with the goals intended.

Camus set out first in quest of the absolute and ended up by proclaiming the necessity for 'an active consent to the relative'.[1] After a futile (and youthful) search for a principle which would explain and justify the universe, he turned his attention to the search for a principle which would operate to prevent men from killing one another in the name of principles. His answer was that principles must be guides to action, but not absolute values to be pursued at any cost. Where the consequences of action can reasonably be expected to promote violence, the emphasis must be placed on doubt over certainty, on moderation over excess. Men should act on their principles but realize that they may be wrong; their action may be uncompromising but it must be limited.

It is less simple to deduce the questions which Sartre asks than it is to understand, or at least interpret, his affirmations. Perhaps the most accurate way to state it would be to say that while Camus was transferring the locus of his search for principles from the cosmos to man, Sartre was transferring the locus of his search for principles from man to history. In *Being and Nothingness* Sartre ruthlessly destroys all *a priori* principles and leaves man alone and unaided as the irreducible source of all that falls within the range of his consciousness. In *Critique de la raison dialectique* he seeks nothing less than a method of understanding the totality of the historical process, a principle which would make, not the universe, but history intelligible. The political applicability of either approach is difficult to discern. The first approach leads to frustration and paralysis; the second (if successful) could do no more than provide a surrogate for a theory of action which Sartre has so far failed to produce and which alone might give guidance to men who seek some reasonable way to confront the exigencies of political choice.

Bertrand de Jouvenel's questions have all been inspired by the single consideration that the exercise of political power can be dangerous and, with this as his touchstone, he has successively asked how power can be limited, how it should be exercised, and how, in fact, men actually exercise it. These

---

[1] *The Rebel*, p. 290.

related yet different questions have yielded a variety of answers, of varying contemporary relevance. De Jouvenel's most notable conclusion is that the political authorities must support the dynamic and productive groups in society and at the same time maintain enough environmental certainty so that the static and unproductive groups are neither ruthlessly destroyed nor driven to revolt.

For Aron, the questions are different. In a sense, his reasoning process is as radical as Sartre's, for he starts out by raising the question of what political thought actually is, in order to give coherence to the manner in which he thinks about political questions. Having decided that political thought consists of the determination of objectives which have some reasonable probability of being achieved, as well as of the means by which they can be reasonably expected to be achieved, Aron then applies his method to various problems, of which only two have been examined in any detail in this study: the conflict between the equalitarian and the hierarchical-minded traditionalist and the conflict between the advocate of western democracy and the advocate of the Soviet-type system. Like Simone Weil, Aron becomes deeply involved in sociological analysis because the social structure is a major determinant of what is possible, but unlike Simone Weil, who saw no real possibilities for reasonable choice, Aron sees the possibility of choice, and his effort becomes one of trying to enlarge to its limits the scientific ingredient of a choice which cannot be totally governed by science.

While there is diversity in the questions to which these six thinkers have addressed themselves and variety in the conclusions, provisional or otherwise, which they have reached, it does not follow that one cannot speak of patterns of contemporary French political thought. It is not possible to force the products of six independent, original, and powerful minds into narrow, uniform categories, but there are certain general characteristics which are displayed to a greater or lesser extent in the works of all these people, as well as other more specific patterns of thought which, while expressed by only some of them, are notable because of their intrinsic importance and, in some cases, also because they have been arrived at by separate routes.

II   Distance from the Past

The first and most obvious characteristic which these six thinkers display in common is a distance between their own findings and those represented by the three principal currents of French political thought on the eve of the nineteen thirties— Alain's liberalism, Maurrassian traditionalism, and Marxism.

There is, of course, permanent wisdom in Alain's unremitting concern for the protection of the citizen against the power of the state, which reappears in every variant of liberal political thought, and of the six thinkers treated in this book, only Sartre seems to reject Alain totally, but none is content to leave matters where Alain left them. Simone Weil's preoccupation with oppression may owe something to the philosopher of Radical Socialism who had been her teacher, but she reached far beyond him in her efforts to understand why power is exercised and how it might be diffused. Mounier and Aron are explicitly critical of Alain. De Jouvenel comes closest to being a latter-day bearer of Alain's message; he clearly shares Alain's abiding suspicion of political power and preference for socially induced harmony over politically imposed order. But de Jouvenel has a greater understanding of the problems of an industrial society than Alain had, his conception of the role of the state in relation to society is both more positive and more subtle than Alain's was, and he is more inventive than Alain in devising modes of political analysis.

French traditionalism dies hard; Raymond Aron believed it useful in 1957 to subject some of its claims to close criticism. None of the six writers is a Maurrassian, although de Jouvenel gives sympathetic treatment to the traditionalist theme which was part of the Maurrassian doctrine. He does so, however, not to put the historic past at the service of nationalism, but because his conception of good government is based on the image of the king in parliament and because of his interest in limiting the power of the central state. De Jouvenel's political preferences emerge more or less clearly from his writings, but not the specific kind of régime he might recommend for a modern society. His references in *Power* to the need for a common faith and in *Sovereignty* to the need for common beliefs suggest the desirability of a revival of religious authority which, as de Jouvenel indicates clearly himself, runs counter to the trend of modern thought and practice since the Enlightenment. In *The Pure Theory of Politics* he refers to the favourable consequences of a fundamental orthodoxy without specifying its basis. He has a conception of good institutions but not a design. Such approbation as he gives to traditionalist institutions, when combined with the productive ethic that appears in *Sovereignty*, suggests Orleanism more than the Old Régime.

Every political thinker of the twentieth century has to establish his position with respect to Marxism, and the French men and woman treated in this book are not exceptions: each of them is in some way a student of Marx. Simone Weil and Raymond Aron are among the most knowledgeable and penetrating critics of Marxism to be found anywhere. Albert Camus is less original as a critic of Marxism, but his formulations are no less impressive for bearing the stamp of a master of language. De Jouvenel is less directly concerned with Marxism than any of the others, but it is clear that he finds Marxist prescriptions unacceptable. Mounier was attracted to Marxism, particularly as expressed in Marx's early writings, both because he saw a certain analogy between it and Christianity and because it represented a powerful force which was, like Mounier himself, in opposition to the bourgeois democracy which Mounier believed was doomed to disappear. But Mounier's attitude towards Marxism always displayed the ambivalence which was characteristic of the whole cast of his thought, and he could not be an unqualified Marxist, so strong and pervasive were his religious convictions. Sartre, of course, comes closest to being a Marxist; for him, Marxism is *the* philosophy of our time. But even Sartre will accept it only on his own terms, and it stands in an uncertain relationship to his own existentialist 'ideology'. He is a Marxist of a sort, but his Marxism is not of the kind that inspires either of the two Marxist branches of the French socialist movement.

The distance between each of the six thinkers discussed in this book and the ideas which predominated in France on the eve of the nineteen thirties is uneven, but in every case it is clear that there has been a discernible movement away from the ideas which governed in the past.

III   From Concrete Ideals to Political Action

Contemporary French political thought rejects the analyses and prescriptions of the previous generation, but this rejection is neither its only nor its most important characteristic. There are common patterns to the content and substance of contemporary French political thought as well. The most important of these are the virtually complete abandonment of any effort to describe a good society in concrete terms and the concentration instead on trying to understand the conditions and determine the requirements of political action.

This is not to say that for this generation of French political thinkers ideals are meaningless, principles have no applicability to political affairs, values are empty. Camus believes in the legitimacy of justice, reason, and truth as guides; he also seeks a principle that can perpetuate the possibility of men acting on their principles. Aron believes that the vision of a society free of all conflicts is a legitimate and necessary criterion for the evaluation of existing societies and he searches for the ways in which principles can be applied with some probability of success. Both men place great value on freedom. Simone Weil made an ideal of self-determination; Mounier was inspired by the vision of a fraternal society which he called a personalist community; de Jouvenel conceives a good society as one in which initiatives sparkle without causing any break-down in the mutual trust of the citizens. Even Sartre, who goes the farthest in his destruction of *a priori* principles, acknowledges that men act on behalf of values which they create, and his own ideal appears to be the indefinite enlargement of the human being's freedom of choice.

But while ultimate ideals of this sort are held, and their legitimacy thereby acknowledged, virtually no effort is made to try to describe a society in which they would be presumed to be permanently and definitively achieved. Simone Weil is the only self-confessed utopian in the group, but her Utopia is almost as formal as the notions of truth, justice, and reason which Camus accepts as guides but not goals, or the vision of life according to reason which Aron accepts as a criterion of evaluation for existing societies but which he refuses to identify with any existing society. Simone Weil specifies the conditions, not the institutions, of the ideal society, but with the exception of her allusion to such a society as necessarily being small these conditions are abstract and not concrete. Moreover, she too produces a conception of an ideal society in order to have a criterion, not a goal, and her eventual formulation of the least bad society—'where the common man is most often obliged to think while acting, has the greatest possibilities of control over the whole life of the community, and possesses the most independence'[1]—leaves open the question of what institutions would be most likely to satisfy its several requirements.

The others believe that an attempt to define an ideal society concretely is either impossible, or dangerous, or both. Mounier devoted more attention to specific institutional questions than any of the others, but he shifted his emphasis from a functional and geographical federalism of Proudhonist inspiration to a more centralized type of socialism in order to keep his prescriptions consonant with the nature of the problems he was trying to overcome, thereby implicitly recognizing the relativity of institutions—a relativity to which he was in any case committed, for he believed that perfection was not possible on this earth and that the human condition was characterized by perpetual tension. De Jouvenel believes that it is simply not possible to establish a just social order, because he does not believe that there is any common measure of justice applicable to the great variety of human relations, even though it is possible for men to act in the spirit of justice by seeking and applying that measure of justice which may be applicable in each of the situations in which they must act.[2] Aron and Camus reserve judgement about the eventual possibility of a society in which all contradictions would be resolved,[3] but Aron explicitly and Camus implicitly make it clear that it is impossible to define such a

---

[1] Simone Weil, 'Réflexions sur les causes de la liberté et de l'oppression sociale', in *Oppression et liberté*, p. 136.

[2] Bertrand de Jouvenel, *Sovereignty, An Inquiry into the Political Good* (translated by J. F. Huntington), pp. 160–5.

[3] 'If the [natural or civil] rights are expressed without hesitation it is more than probable that, sooner or later, the justice they postulate will come to the world.' Camus, *The Rebel*, p. 291.

'La fin des contradictions interviendrait le jour où l'homme serait parfait ou résigné à ses imperfections.' Raymond Aron, *Les Guerres en chaîne*, Paris, 1951, p. 484, Eng. tr., *The Century of Total War*, N.Y., 1952.

society in the here and now. Sartre makes no claim that existing socialist societies are ideal—quite the contrary; for Sartre, these are necessary starting-points en route to the fulfilment of the socialist ideal, but he tells us nothing about the concrete structure of this ideal.

De Jouvenel is most explicit in his conviction that the concrete definition of an ideal society is dangerous. '. . . The attraction exercised by pictures of this kind lures men into importing them into reality and leads them on to tyrannical actions to achieve their ideals: there is a tyranny in the womb of every Utopia.'[1] Aron similarly worries about the possibility of a minority trying to impose its conception of 'a social order in conformity with the law of History or of Reason' and sacrificing men to the order which is supposed to serve them.[2] The same concern is at the heart of Camus' opposition to what he calls the contradictory notion of values to come and his objection to treating any historical action as absolutely good.

There is more to this abandonment of the quest for an ideal state than fear, however. The refusal to rigidify social or political forms reflects the common recognition that society is characterized by changing needs and aspirations. The revolt against idealized descriptions, so marked in all the people discussed except Simone Weil, is the result also of the desire to keep society open to the vicissitudes of change. Even Mounier, who comes closest to Weil in seeking to specify the conditions of a good society in more than formal terms, acknowledges that unforeseeableness must somehow be incorporated into political philosophy, and he made it clear that he regarded his own personalist philosophy as in no way obviating the need for research or protecting its practitioners against 'disquiet, trial, and risk'.[3] Camus shares with Sartre the existentialist's appreciation of human dynamism. Camus' rebel is the embodiment of active discontent and simultaneously rejects the existing situation and seeks to transcend it. Sartre's notion of engagement, for all its ambiguities, is surely a social expression of the individual's project, the expression of that autonomous inner impulsion which constantly operates to permit a man to choose what he will, at death, turn out to have been. For all

[1] *Sovereignty*, p. 10. [2] *Les Guerres en chaîne*, p. 484.
[3] Emmanuel Mounier, *Le Personnalisme*, p. 6.

his suspicion of what he calls 'the intending politic'—the political *dux* on the make—de Jouvenel thinks in terms of a dynamic society, places a high value on social innovation, takes it as axiomatic that 'Man is forward-looking', and holds that 'the technology of politics is essentially concerned with dynamics . . . .'[1] For Aron, the only elements of our civilization which are worth accepting totally are the freedom of criticism and the chance of improving it which it allows. Possibly never before has a single generation of political thinkers been so alert to the need to accommodate the forces making for change.

Possibly never before has a generation of political thinkers also predominantly been so self-consciously prudent. With the exception of Sartre, who opts for a Marxist social revolution, these thinkers are notable for the caution with which they approach political decisions. De Jouvenel's preoccupation with limiting the power of the state is evident; all the others are deeply concerned with the implications of political acts for the values which inspire them or the ends they are designed to serve, and even Sartre applies this consideration to the states of what, in 1957, could be called the socialist camp. Mounier and Camus pay close attention to the dilemmas of means and ends, and, for all his talk about revolution, Mounier was essentially a man of peace and his prescription for political behaviour is basically the same as Camus'. Camus distinguished between two types of efficacy—'that of typhoons and that of sap'[2]— and there is no question as to which category Mounier's model of Christian behaviour during the Roman Empire belongs. Simone Weil drew a pretty picture which de Jouvenel may regard as dangerous, but her own caution was monumental, and she was as opposed to conferring absolute value upon prosaic human institutions as Aron or Camus. She was the first of them to object to treating as absolutes the abstract concepts, such as capitalism, socialism, fascism, authority, property, and democracy, which men make of observable institutions, instead of examining those institutions themselves in order to determine with precision the relationship which they actually bear to the values (or evils) attributed to them.

It is precisely in order to try to limit the violence of politics that Aron investigates the meaning of similar concepts in

---

[1] *The Pure Theory of Politics*, pp. 174, 47, and 8.   [2] *The Rebel*, p. 292.

contemporary society. Weil was appalled by what she regarded as the disappearance of 'the essential notions of intelligence, the notions of limit, of measure, of degree, of proportion, of connexion, of relationship, of condition, of necessary connexion, of relationship between means and results'.[1] Camus' philosophy of rebellion is a 'philosophy of limits';[2] the kind of rebellion which Camus has in mind, that which moves a man beyond the possibility of abandoning his cause but permits him to accept approximations and requires him not to murder in its pursuit, 'in itself is moderation'.[3] Aron enlarges upon Simone Weil's method; Camus enlarges upon her mood.

Prudence is a characteristic of the political thought of all of these thinkers except Sartre, but at the same time there is a clear awareness that men and governments must act. Simone Weil, in her discussion of the art of government, places the emphasis on how governments should act; Camus places emphasis on how individuals should act. In the age of democracy, however, the distinction between government and citizen diminishes, as de Jouvenel's *Sovereignty* illustrates. Here he tells us that he is more concerned with the duties of sovereigns than with the rights of the citizens,[4] but in the end he prescribes a form of behaviour, modelled on Rousseau's notion of the general will, which applies as much to the citizens who make demands on the government as it does to the government itself. Similarly, Aron, who shares de Jouvenel's view that the power of the people viewed collectively is essentially fictional, produces a method for considering political action which is appropriate for the citizen as well as for political office-holders.

The notion of complicity which attaches to the Sartrean concept of responsibility and which is shared by Camus and Mounier (and even, in a sense, by Aron)[5] is clearly democratic in its implications, in that it implies no distinctions of birth or place in its attribution of responsibility for what happens politically. Sartrean engagement, Mounier's technique of

---

[1] 'Ne Recommençons pas la guerre de Troie (Pouvoir des mots)', in *Écrits historiques et politiques*, pp. 258–9.

[2] *The Rebel*, p. 289. [3] Ibid., p. 301.

[4] *Sovereignty*, p. 88.

[5] 'L'adhésion à un régime réel, par conséquent imparfait, nous rend solidaires des injustices ou des cruautés dont aucun temps et aucun pays n'ont été exempts.' *L'Opium des intellectuels*, p. 69.

spiritual methods, and the role which Camus casts for the rebel as the interrupter of history are prescriptions for anybody and everybody, and are as relevant to the citizen as they are to the official. In this limited but important sense there is a link between this pattern of political thought and Alain's prescriptions for the behaviour of the citizen. But Alain's precepts to obey while resisting, to act in such a fashion as to control the power-holders, were largely negative. Mounier, Camus, and Sartre have positive intentions: they want to change society. There is, of course, a sense in which these three thinkers share Alain's view of the necessity of the citizen saying 'no' to the government, but in all cases it is joined with the positive aspiration for change which inspires the refusal.

IV   The Conditions of Political Choice

Contemporary French political thought, therefore, focuses directly on problems of political action. In one form or another, each of the participants in the discussion is grappling with the problem of identifying the properties of a good political decision. And in the discussion itself, ends, means, and circumstances are all brought to the fore, separately or in combination, as the crucial elements.

In the case of Sartre, this is true in a limited and peculiar fashion. Sartre has equipped himself with a doctrine which requires the abolition of capitalism under Marxist auspices in the bourgeois democracies, but in the socialist states it requires policies which will sustain confidence in the socialist movement. The former is sheer dogma, but the latter involves a relationship between means and ends: in the eyes of participants in the socialist movement the means employed should be consistent with the pursuit of justice for all men. But Sartre's commitment to the liquidation of capitalism rests on a philosophical choice and does not depend upon the experience of socialist states. The latter may arouse his indignation on occasion, but it has not caused him to change his philosophy.

Camus prescribes a mode of behaviour—one which has been adopted with notable success by the non-violent Negro action groups in the United States—but he does not prescribe the goals in the service of which it should be exercised. These depend upon circumstances. Mounier establishes general goals, but worries incessantly about the proper means of attaining them and shifts the means to fit changing circumstances. He moves from trying to render the spiritual revolutionary to trying to render the revolutionary spiritual; he moves from Proudhonian institutions to centralized socialist institutions. De Jouvenel undertakes an inquiry into the political good and concludes that the business of government is to solve problems which will be the greater as the social initiatives which create them (and which he believes should be encouraged) multiply in number and variety. He calls attention to the need for inventiveness in the face of novel situations;[1] what the problems (and their solutions) will be, in other words, depends upon circumstances. Simone Weil has a clear notion of the conditions of the least bad society, but she worries whether the circumstances will permit the achievement of those conditions. Simone Weil asks the question: 'Do the circumstances permit these goals?' Aron caps the dialogue by adding the question: 'What goals do the circumstances permit?'

If circumstances are such an important factor in the determination of good political decisions, it follows that the better the knowledge of the circumstances the greater the probability will be of arriving at good political decisions. It is this reasoning which leads Simone Weil and Raymond Aron to place so much emphasis on the analysis of what the former calls the conditions of existence, the latter the ingrate laws of social existence. These conditions, these laws are made the object of scientific study so that men may know by more than intuition the ground over which they must move.

The kind of sociological method which Weil and Aron employ is related to Sartrean existentialism's concepts of freedom and the situation. Man, according to Sartre, is always free to choose, although he is not free to choose anything. The range of choice is circumscribed by what he calls the 'coefficient of adversity' in *Being and Nothingness* and 'social and historical reality' in *Critique de la raison dialectique*.[2] For Aron also, 'the freedom of concrete choice is limited by the nature

---

[1] *Sovereignty*, p. 301.

[2] 'Question de méthode', in *Critique de la raison dialectique* (*précédé de Question de méthode*), Tome I, p. 64.

of communities and by historical conditions. But the freedom of the individual remains complete, for he judges history at the same time as he judges in history.'[1] But if there is this similarity between Sartre and Aron, there are also important differences. Sartre has in mind the impossibility of undertaking some action, not whether the action undertaken will succeed or fail. Aron has in mind whether the action will succeed or fail, not whether it can be undertaken. Sartre thinks of the prisoner who cannot choose to walk out of the prison because he is nowhere near the door; Aron thinks of the politician who can choose to try to turn France into a Sparta but who will simply fail. More importantly, however, there is a great difference between the modes of analysis which the two men apply to the social situation in which men must act. Sartre analyses that situation by applying Marxist categories, while Aron has produced his own sociological method and theory of political systems in order to try to determine just what the possible political choices are for the inhabitants of modern industrialized societies.

If this kind of effort fails to reflect 'the urge to construct grand designs for the political future of mankind', it is not, as it has been alleged, because of the dampening impact on men's hopes of theories of historical determinism or of cultural fatalism.[2] It is true that Simone Weil came close to succumbing to a sort of cultural fatalism. Paradoxically, however, she did so precisely because of an excessively narrow application of a sociological method which constitutes a frontal assault on the very notion of determinism.

Simone Weil's transformation of the notion of determinism into the concept of the natural selection of human initiatives, and Raymond Aron's concept of the *usage régulatif* of determinism, which is similar to it, are major contributions to the understanding of history and the conditions of political action. Nothing is determined, but not everything is possible. The conditions of existence 'operate not by imposing a determined direction to each person's efforts, but by condemning to

---

[1] *Introduction à la philosophie de l'histoire, Essai sur les limites de l'objectivité historique*, p. 334.

[2] Judith Shklar, *After Utopia, The Decline of Political Faith*, Princeton, 1957, pp. vi and ix.

inefficaciousness all efforts directed in ways which they prohibit'.[1] This view leads to cultural fatalism only if the conditions of existence bar efforts in all directions but one, which is
essentially what Simone Weil considered to be the case.
Observation of the world around us, however, provides considerable evidence that more than one political way is possible.
Aron's special contribution is to try to show as specifically as
possible what those political ways are, as well as to specify how
much latitude there is for variation within each of the larger
possible choices. This is the significance of his theory of political
systems, with its designation of two basic types, and its analysis
of the probable implications of each type in the conditions of
industrial society. This is neither determinism nor cultural
fatalism. It is quite the opposite; it is an effort to discover 'the
points of application of the human will'.[2]

[1] Simone Weil, 'Réflexions sur les causes de la liberté et de l'oppression sociale',
pp. 83–84.
[2] Raymond Aron, 'Du Pessimisme historique', in *L'Homme contre les tyrans*.
Paris, 1946, p. 249.

Select Bibliography

THE footnotes cite the works on which I have relied for specific matters, but it seemed useful also to provide a select bibliography of the main political writings of the people whose political ideas are discussed in this book as well as of those general works which readers will find useful who wish to pursue the subject further.

I

Emmanuel Mounier's books have conveniently been collected into four volumes of *Oeuvres*, Paris, Éditions du Seuil, 1961–3. Most of Mounier's books consist of selections which he made from his contributions to *Esprit* and other collective works. Volume I of the *Oeuvres* contains the books Mounier published between 1931 and 1939, as well as two essays written in 1937 and 1939 respectively but not published in book form until they appeared in his *Liberté sous conditions*, Paris, Éditions du Seuil, 1946. Volume II contains *Traité du caractère*, which was first published in Paris by Éditions du Seuil in 1946; the posthumous volume includes Mounier's notes and additions for an enlarged and revised edition. Volume III contains the books published by Mounier between 1944 and his death in 1950. Volume IV contains the books which Mounier planned before his death and which were published posthumously; a revised and enlarged version of *Mounier et sa génération*, which was first published in Paris by Éditions du Seuil in 1956 and contains extracts from Mounier's voluminous correspondence and from his notebooks; and the most complete bibliography of Mounier's writings.

I have relied most heavily on *Révolution personnaliste et communautaire*, Paris, Éditions Montaigne, 1935 (*Oeuvres*, Vol. I, 1961, pp. 127–416); *Carnets de route*, Vol. I, *Feu la Chrétienté*, Paris, Éditions du Seuil, 1950 (*Oeuvres*, Vol. III, 1962, pp. 527–713); *Carnets de route*, Vol. II, *Les Certitudes difficiles*, Paris, Éditions du Seuil, 1951 (*Oeuvres*, Vol. IV, 1963, pp. 7–291); and *Mounier et sa génération*. None of these four works has been translated into English. Two general accounts of personalism by Mounier have been translated. *Qu'est-ce que le Personnalisme*, Paris, Éditions du Seuil, 1946 (*Oeuvres*, Vol. III, 1962, pp. 177–245), along with *La Petite Peur du XXe siècle*, Paris, Éditions du Seuil, 1948, and Neuchâtel, Éditions de la Baconnière, 1948 (*Oeuvres*, Vol. III, 1962, pp. 339–425), appears in *Be Not Afraid; a Denunciation of Despair* (tr. by Cynthia Rowland, Foreword by Leslie Paul), London, Rockliff, 1951, and New York, Sheed and Ward, 1962. *Le Personnalisme*, Paris, Presses Universitaires de France, 1950 (*Oeuvres*, Vol. III, 1962, pp. 427–525) appears as *Personalism* (tr. by Philip Mairet), London, Routledge and Kegan Paul, 1952.

A main source of biographical information and commentary on Mounier's life and work is *Esprit*, 18 (December 1950), entitled 'Emmanuel Mounier'. The leading study of Mounier's thought is Candide Moix, *La Pensée d'Emmanuel Mounier*, Paris, Éditions du Seuil, 1960. A shorter study is Lucien Guissard, *Emmanuel Mounier*, Paris, Éditions Universitaires, 1962.

The Association des Amis d'Emmanuel Mounier (19 rue Jacob, Paris) publishes a *Bulletin* once or twice a year which contains material of interest to the specialist.

II

Simone Weil's main political and social writings include: *La Condition ouvrière*, Paris, Gallimard, 1951; a small portion of this book appeared as 'Factory Work' (tr. by Felix Giovanelli), in *Politics* (New York), 3 (December 1946), pp. 369–75. *Écrits de Londres et dernières lettres*, Paris, Gallimard, 1957. *Écrits historiques et politiques*, Paris, Gallimard, 1960. *L'Enracinement; Prélude à une déclaration des devoirs envers l'être humain*, Paris, Gallimard, 1949; English tr., *The Need for Roots, Prelude to a Declaration of Duties toward Mankind* (by Arthur Wills, with a Preface by T. S. Eliot), New York, G. P. Putnam's Sons, 1952, and London, Routledge and Kegan Paul, 1952. *Oppression et liberté*, Paris, Gallimard, 1955; English tr., *Oppression and Liberty* (by Arthur Wills and John Petrie), London, Routledge and Kegan Paul, 1958.

English translations of several of the essays in *Écrits de Londres et dernières lettres* and in *Écrits historiques et politiques* appear in Simone Weil, *Selected Essays 1934–1943*, Chosen and Translated by Richard Rees, London, Oxford University Press, 1962. Simone Weil's letters in those two works as well as those in *La Condition ouvrière* appear in Simone Weil, *Seventy Letters*, Some hitherto untranslated texts from published and unpublished sources, Translated and Arranged by Richard Rees, London, Oxford University Press, 1965.

Leçons de philosophie de Simone Weil (Roanne 1933–1934), présentées par Anne Reynaud, Paris, Plon, 1959, consists of notes which the author took while she was a student in Simone Weil's class.

The principal biography is Jacques Cabaud, *L'Expérience vécue de Simone Weil*, Paris, Plon, 1957. An enlarged and revised English version is Jacques Cabaud, *Simone Weil, A Fellowship in Love*, New York, Channel Press, 1964, and London, Harvill Press, 1964. This work contains a detailed bibliography. Other useful accounts include E. W. F. Tomlin, *Simone Weil*, New Haven, Yale University Press, 1954, and Cambridge, England, Bowes and Bowes, 1954, and Richard Rees, *Simone Weil, A Sketch for a Portrait*, London, Oxford University Press, 1966.

III

Albert Camus' early Algerian newspaper articles appear in *Alger-Républicain* from October 1938 to October 1939 and in *Le Soir Républicain* from September 1939 to January 1940. Some of his later articles for *Combat* and other political essays appear in Albert Camus, *Actuelles*, 3 vols., Paris, Gallimard, 1950, 1953, and 1958. Some of these articles appear in Albert Camus, *Resistance, Rebellion, and Death*, Translated from the French and with an Introduction by Justin O'Brien, New York, Alfred A. Knopf, 1961, and London, Hamish Hamilton, 1961. An English translation by Dwight Macdonald of Camus' *Combat* articles entitled 'Ni Victimes ni bourreaux' (reprinted in *Actuelles I*) appears as 'Neither Victims Nor Executioners', in *Politics* (New York), 4 (July–August 1947), pp. 141–7.

Le Myth de Sisyphe, Paris, Gallimard, 1942, appears in English in *The Myth of Sisyphus and Other Essays*, Translated from the French by Justin O'Brien, New York, Alfred A. Knopf, 1955, and London, Hamish Hamilton, 1955. *L'Homme révolté*, Paris, Gallimard, 1951, appears in English as *The Rebel*, With a Foreword by Sir Herbert Read, Translated by Anthony Bower, London, Hamish Hamilton, 1953, and New York, Alfred A. Knopf, 1954. A revised and complete translation by Anthony Bower was published in New York, Vintage Books, 1956.

Two volumes of Camus' notebooks have been published: *Carnets mai 1935–février 1942*, Paris, Gallimard, 1962; English tr., *Notebooks 1935–1942*, Translated from the French, and with a Preface and Notes, by Philip Thody, New York, Alfred A. Knopf, 1963, and London, Hamish Hamilton, 1963. *Carnets janvier 1942–mars 1951*, Paris, Gallimard, 1964; English tr., *Notebooks 1942–1951*, Translated from the French by Justin O'Brien, New York, Alfred A. Knopf, 1965.

Camus' plays, adaptations, and novels have conveniently been collected into a single volume, with many useful notes, in Albert Camus, *Théâtre, récits, nouvelles*, Préface par Jean Grenier, Textes

établis et annotés par Roger Quilliot, Paris, Gallimard (Bibliothèque de la Pléiade), 1962.

Works containing biographical, interpretive, and critical accounts
include: Germaine Brée, *Camus*, New Brunswick, New Jersey,
Rutgers University Press, 1961; John Cruickshank, *Albert Camus and
the Literature of Revolt*, New York, Oxford University Press, 1960;
John Cruickshank, editor, *The Novelist as Philosopher*, *Studies in
French Fiction 1935-1960*, London, Oxford University Press, 1962;
Thomas Hanna, *The Thought and Art of Albert Camus*, Chicago,
Henry Regnery, 1958; Georges Hourdin, *Camus le juste*, Paris,
Éditions du Cerf, 1960; Roger Quilliot, *La Mer et les prisons*, *Essai
sur Albert Camus*, Paris, Gallimard, 1956; Philip Thody, *Albert Camus
1913-1960*, New York, The Macmillan Company, London,
Hamish Hamilton, 1961.

IV

Jean-Paul Sartre's main philosophical work is *L'Être et le néant*,
Essai d'ontologie phénoménologique, Paris, Gallimard, 1943; English tr.,
Being and Nothingness, *An Essay on Phenomenological Ontology*, Trans-
lated and with an Introduction by Hazel Barnes, New York,
Philosophical Library, 1956, and London, Methuen, 1957. His
most recent theoretical work is *Critique de la raison dialectique (précédé de
Question de méthode)*, Tome I, 'Théorie des ensembles pratiques',
Paris, Gallimard, 1960. Only the relatively brief 'Question de
méthode' appears in English, as *Search for a Method*, Translated
from the French and with an Introduction by Hazel Barnes, New
York, Alfred A. Knopf, 1963, and London, Methuen, 1963. Wilfred
Desan has undertaken a commentary on the entire *Critique* in his
The Marxism of Jean-Paul Sartre, Garden City, New York, Double-
day & Co., 1965.

All of Sartre's main articles from *Les Temps Modernes*, as well as
essays originally published elsewhere, have been collected in his
Situations, 7 Vols., Paris, Gallimard, 1947-1965. English translations
of articles from Volumes I (1947) and III (1949), including the
important 'Materialism and Revolution', appear in *Literary and
Philosophical Essays* (tr. by Annette Michelson), London and New
York, Rider, 1955. Volume IV (1964) appears in English as
Situations (tr. by Benita Eisler), New York, George Braziller,
London, Hamish Hamilton, 1965. Volume V (1964) is subtitled
'Colonialisme et néo-colonialisme'; Volumes VI (1964) and VII
(1965) are subtitled 'Problèmes du marxisme'. Volume VI includes
'Les Communistes et la paix'; Volume VII includes 'Le Fantôme de
Staline'.

Biographical information appears in Sartre's *Les Mots*, Paris, Gallimard, 1964; English tr., *The Words* (by Bernard Frechtman), New York, George Braziller, London, Hamish Hamilton, 1964. See also the three autobiographical volumes by Simone de Beauvoir: *Mémoires d'une jeune fille rangée*, Paris, Gallimard, 1958; English tr., *Memoirs of a Dutiful Daughter* (by James Kirkup), Cleveland, World Publishing Co., London, André Deutsch and Weidenfeld and Nicolson, 1959. *La Force de l'âge*, Paris, Gallimard, 1960; English tr., *The Prime of Life* (by Peter Green), Cleveland, World Publishing Co., 1962, London, André Deutsch and Weidenfeld and Nicolson, 1963. *La Force des choses*, Paris, Gallimard, 1963; English tr., *Force of Circumstance* (by Richard Howard), New York, G. P. Putnam's Sons, London, André Deutsch and Weidenfeld and Nicolson, 1965.

Works containing biographical, interpretive and critical accounts include: Maurice Cranston, *Sartre*, Edinburgh and London, Oliver and Boyd, New York (as *Jean-Paul Sartre*), Grove Press, 1962; John Cruickshank, editor, *The Novelist as Philosopher*, *Studies in French Fiction 1935–1960*, London, Oxford University Press, 1962; Norman N. Greene, *Jean-Paul Sartre*, *The Existentialist Ethic*, Ann Arbor, Michigan, University of Michigan Press, 1960; Iris Murdoch, *Sartre: Romantic Rationalist*, New Haven, Yale University Press, 1953, and Cambridge, England, Bowes and Bowes, 1953; Philip Thody, *Jean-Paul Sartre: A Literary and Political Study*, New York, Macmillan, 1960, and London, Hamish Hamilton, 1960.

V

Bertrand de Jouvenel is a prolific writer. I have referred in this book principally to the following works: *Le Réveil de l'Europe*, Paris, Gallimard, 1938. *Du Pouvoir, histoire naturelle de sa croissance*, Geneva, Éditions du Cheval Ailé, 1945; revised and enlarged edition, 1947; English tr., *Power, The Natural History of its Growth* (by J. F. Huntington, with a Preface by D. W. Brogan), London and New York, Hutchinson, 1948; also *On Power, Its Nature and the History of its Growth* (by J. F. Huntington, with a Preface by D. W. Brogan), New York, Viking Press, 1948. *De la Souveraineté, à la recherche du bien politique*, Paris, Éditions Marie-Thérèse Génin, 1955; English tr., *Sovereignty, An Inquiry into the Political Good* (by J. F. Huntington), Chicago, University of Chicago Press, 1957, and Cambridge, England, Cambridge University Press, 1957. 'On the Evolution of Forms of Government', in Bertrand de Jouvenel, editor, *Futuribles*, *Studies in Conjecture*, I, Geneva, Droz, 1963, pp. 65–119. *The Pure Theory of Politics*, Cambridge, England, Cambridge University Press, 1963, and New Haven, Yale University Press, 1963, French tr., *De la Politique pure* (by Gabrielle Rolin, Guy Berger, et al.), Paris, Calmann-Lévy, 1963.

Other post-war works by de Jouvenel include: *Du Contrat social de Jean-Jacques Rousseau, Précédé d'un essai sur la politique de Rousseau par Bertrand de Jouvenel*, Geneva, Éditions du Cheval Ailé, 1947. *The Ethics of Redistribution*, Cambridge, England, Cambridge University Press, 1951. *L'Art de la conjecture*, Monaco, Editions du Rocher, 1964.

There are no book-length studies of de Jouvenel's political thought.

VI

Raymond Aron's numerous political writings cover a wide range of subjects. I include here, with one exception, only those works on which I have mainly relied.

Aron's main works on the philosophy of history include: *Introduction à la philosophie de l'histoire, Essai sur les limites de l'objectivité historique*, Paris, Gallimard, 1938; English tr., *Introduction to the Philosophy of History* (by G. J. Irwin), New York, Beacon Press, 1961, and London, Weidenfeld and Nicolson, 1961. *Dimensions de la conscience historique*, Paris, Librairie Plon, 1961. This work contains a detailed bibliography of Aron's writings to date.

Aron's works of ideological criticism include: *L'Homme contre les tyrans*, New York, Éditions de la Maison Française, 1944, and Paris, Gallimard, 1946. *Polémiques*, Paris, Gallimard, 1955. *L'Opium des intellectuels*, Paris, Calmann-Lévy, 1955; English tr., *The Opium of the Intellectuals* (by Terence Kilmartin), New York, Doubleday & Co., 1957, and London, Secker and Warburg, 1957. *Espoir et peur du siècle, Essais non partisans*, Paris, Calmann-Lévy, 1957. *Essai sur les libertés*, Paris, Calmann-Lévy, 1965, appeared too late to be taken into account in this book.

Aron's works of sociology include: *Dix-Huit Leçons sur la société industrielle*, Paris, Gallimard, 1963. *La Lutte de classes; nouvelles leçons sur les sociétés industrielles*, Paris, Gallimard, 1964. *Les Grandes Doctrines de sociologie historique: Montesquieu, Comte, Marx, Tocqueville, les sociologues et la révolution de 1848*, Cours de Sorbonne, Paris, Centre de Documentation Universitaire, 1960; English tr., *Main Currents of Sociological Thought*, Vol. I, *Montesquieu, Comte, Marx, Tocqueville, The Sociologists and the Revolution of 1848* (by Richard Howard and Helen Weaver), New York, Basic Books, 1965. *Les Grandes Doctrines de sociologie historique*, II: *Emile Durckheim, Vilfredo Pareto, Max Weber*, Cours de Sorbonne, Paris, Centre de Documentation Universitaire, 1963. 'Science et conscience de la société', *Archives Européennes de Sociologie*, I (1960), pp. 1–30.

Aron's works on political institutions include: *Démocratie et totalitarisme*, Paris, Gallimard, 1965. (With François Bondy, George Kennan, et al.) *Colloques de Berlin, La Démocratie à l'épreuve du XXe siècle*, Paris, Calmann-Lévy, 1960. (With George Kennan, Robert Oppenheimer, et al.) *Colloques de Rheinfelden*, Paris, Calmann-Lévy, 1960; English tr., *World Technology and Human Destiny* (by Richard Seaver), Ann Arbor, Michigan, University of Michigan Press, 1963.

There are no book-length studies of Raymond Aron's political thought.

Index